W9-BPL-439

GET Slightly FAMOUS

GET Slightly FAMOUS

Become a Celebrity in Your Field and Attract More Business with Less Effort

STEVEN VAN YODER

BAY TREE PUBLISHING

BERKELEY, CALIFORNIA

© 2003 Steven Van Yoder

All rights reserved. Printed in the United States of America. No part of this book may be reproduced or transmitted in any form or by any means, electronic or mechanical, including photocopying, recording, or by any information storage and retrieval systems, without written permission from the publisher. For information, write to: Bay Tree Publishing, 721 Creston Road, Berkeley, CA 94708.

Get Slightly Famous™ is a trademark of Steven Van Yoder, San Francisco, California.

Bay Tree books may be purchased for business or promotional use or for special sales. Please contact: Special Sales Department, Bay Tree Publishing, 721 Creston Road, Berkeley, CA 94708.

Library of Congress Control Number: 2002116535

ISBN: 0-9720021-1-1

Cover design by Bryan Bindloss

Interior design and composition by BookMatters

03 04 05 06 07 5 4 3 2 1

CONTENTS

How to Break Out of the Anonymity Trap

If business seems ever harder and more competitive, that's because it is. Working in a global economy means the number of businesses competing for the same customers, even in a local market, has grown proportionately.

For a small business, it's no longer possible to assume a home turf advantage, and so the challenge of marketing has changed. You can now work with a travel agent, a graphic designer, or an insurance broker across the country as easily as someone across town. You can find the same products on the Internet and the corner store, and often it's more convenient to make your purchase from your desk and take delivery on your porch tomorrow.

Against this backdrop of increased competition, every business must fight to avoid blending into a sea of look-alikes. If you're in business and looking for more customers or clients, you need to ask yourself these questions: Do the right people fully understand what I do? Have I targeted my most likely customers and delivered a message that speaks to their unique needs? Do I struggle to differentiate myself from competitors? When a local paper or trade journal does a story on my area of expertise, do they call me?

If you can't answer these questions with an unequivocal "yes," *Get Slightly Famous* will boost your marketing into a new realm of effectiveness. It is based on proven strategies that can help you get more business with less effort. Even if you're already practicing these general principles, you will find lots of specific techniques that you can add to your ongoing efforts.

This book provides a roadmap to help any small business break out of the anonymity trap and effectively attract clients and customers. It's filled with practical tips and techniques, advice from leading marketing experts, and dozens of real-world success stories from *slightly famous* entrepreneurs.

Get Slightly Famous was written to be read, reread, and put into action. For additional inspiration visit www.getslightlyfamous.com where you will find further resources and small business success stories.

Welcome to marketing in the twenty-first century!

PART I THE CENTER OF YOUR UNIVERSE

CHAPTER 1

Just a Little Fame Will Do

Some business owners seem to attract clients and customers by magic. Their marketing seems effortless. They may not have made a cold call in years, they may not spend a dime on advertising, yet somehow they're regularly featured in newspapers and magazines, and get invited to speak at conferences. Everyone knows their name, and they get all the business they can handle. It's almost as though they were famous.

In fact, they are, but not in the way movie stars and top athletes are famous—they're just *slightly famous*. Just famous enough to make their names come to mind when people are looking for a particular product or service, and let them reap the benefits. They get more business—not only more, but the right kind of business—and they don't have to work so hard to get it.

Want to join them and enjoy this ideal state of affairs, where customers come to you? You can, but it may require a new way of thinking and a new marketing strategy. And though it may seem effortless to the outside observer, it does require work.

The Slightly Famous You

In a crowded marketplace, where your potential clients and customers have lots of choices, you can stand out by being just slightly famous. This is the exact opposite of mass marketing. It's not about being all things to all people, but being a mini-celebrity to the right people. It's about targeting your market and developing a reputation as a great resource—trustworthy, knowledgeable, and close at hand. Your goal is to become the lord of a small, profitable domain of your choosing. Within that domain, you will attract more customers and clients, including those you want most.

Naturally, such results require thoughtful and consistent efforts. These efforts will take many different forms, but underlying and guiding them are just six basic principles:

1. Targeting the best prospects
2. Developing a unique market niche
3. Positioning your business as the best solution
4. Maintaining your visibility
5. Enhancing your credibility
6. Establishing your brand and reputation

Working on these principles is your recipe for getting out of the anonymity trap, creating a slightly famous you, and building a successful business. In the pages that follow, we'll look more closely at what these principles call for in the way of action on your part.

Targeting the Best Prospects

Market research is like sticking your toe into a lake before jumping in. If you know who you want to reach and what their needs are, you avoid wasting time and money in poorly conceived marketing programs. You can alter your products or services to fit the needs of your target market, and you can craft a message that reflects your business and your customer. Moreover, market research needn't involve expensive consultants, surveys, or focus groups—it can be as simple as asking your best customers the right questions.

For example, Larry Klein discovered his target market from the inside. A successful financial advisor, he retired from his primary job and became a marketing guru to other financial professionals. He knew they needed several kinds of marketing help, but as he talked to them and worked with them, he discovered that what they wanted most were ways to reach seniors.

Klein explains, "I'm not 60. So, you don't have to be a member of your ideal marketplace. But if you talk to enough people in that market group, you're going to get it. You have to be awake and aware and be listening for what it is.

"All the information you need to target and succeed in an ideal marketplace is out there waiting to be found," says Klein. "You can take the guesswork out of building a business."

Having talked to enough seniors to understand their needs, Klein refined a series of methods for approaching them with investment opportunities. Now he offers seminars and writes articles about these strategies, and offers himself as a consultant to his former colleagues. You and I may not have heard of him, but within his targeted sector of the financial planning community, Klein is slightly famous.

Developing a Unique Market Niche

Large companies aspire to total market domination. Small businesses with a "slightly famous" strategy flourish by establishing themselves within a carefully selected segment of a market; they target a market niche that they can realistically hope to dominate.

Market niches can be defined by region, by special customer needs, or by demographics, such as a particular ethnic or age group; sometimes a market niche can be generated just by a product that's a

REAL-WORLD SUCCESS STORY

Mari Gottdiener Finds a Market She Didn't Know Was There

Sometimes people find themselves thriving in a niche without planning it. Such was the case with Mari Gottdiener, who refocused her credit and consumer advocacy business from general consumers to the narrowly defined market of professional mortgage brokers.

Mari specializes in getting credit bureaus to address and correct credit-report errors. After struggling to find clients throughout the general population, she discovered that mortgage brokers were ready-made prospects. They had an ongoing need for her services on behalf of their loan applicants. She began networking with brokers at trade association meetings, and gave presentations at several mortgage offices.

"My decision to focus on the mortgage broker sector transformed my business," says Gottdiener. "The more I focused on being the person who fixes credit problems for mortgage brokers, the easier it became to define what I could do for them. Now, my name gets passed around, and I've developed a special reputation within that market that makes getting business easier than ever."

Mari's niche fame really became apparent when the California Association of Mortgage Brokers invited her to talk about credit issues at their luncheon. Since then, she's spoken to broker groups regularly, and has reached out to similar associations in other states.

"Word-of-mouth referrals built my reputation at a local level," she says. "Now I'm expanding to reach a national audience of mortgage brokers by writing articles in national mortgage broker trade publications and even doing online seminars."

variation on an established one. (Interestingly, the word *niche*, which comes from French, means "nest." As a small business you want to build your nest somewhere away from the hawks of big business.)

Positioning Your Business as the Best Solution

In a crowded marketplace, it may not be enough just to carve out a niche. You've narrowed your focus, but you still have competitors. This is the time to distinguish yourself as the pre-eminent source of

Fred Phillips Finds His Special Niche

REAL-WORLD SUCCESS STORY

Fred Phillips, a restaurant industry veteran, landed his first job at a hamburger franchise when he was in his teens. Now, twenty years later, he is president of RestQuip, a supplier of environment-friendly restaurant equipment.

Rather than blend into the woodwork of look-alike restaurant supply houses, Phillips focused on helping restaurants reduce waste. Drawing on his knowledge of industry issues, Phillips observed what he foresaw would be a major industry problem: "a ten-fold decrease in the amount of landfill space available for dumping refuse."

Within this situation he saw the business opportunity. "As a greater emphasis was placed on waste reduction by government agencies, my clientele needed options to deal with this potentially costly problem."

RestQuip developed a number of programs that addressed these issues, and at the same time made sure that their environmental products and services got plenty of attention in the trade press. They have consistently stayed abreast of environmental issues and solutions, and take advantage of this knowledge to market themselves as the experts within their industry.

---

solutions by refining your expertise and conveying it to your target audience. You need to know more about something, or be better at something, than anyone else, and you have to let people know.

When you can honestly convey such a message, potential customers and clients see you as the obvious answer to their problems and challenges, and the logical choice when they're looking for a supplier.

Maintaining Your Visibility

When was the last time your name appeared in print? Yesterday? Last week? A month ago? Even if you remember, that doesn't mean a potential customer will.

One key to succeeding in the marketplace is to have your message out there, if not continuously, then often enough to keep your name alive in customers' minds. This is the meaning of visibility, and if you're not visible to your potential clients, you cease to exist. If you haven't done any marketing in months, you'll miss getting clients because they forget about you, and instead call your competitor, whose name was in this morning's paper.

Visibility is a cornerstone of every *slightly famous* business strategy, and it begins by placing your core marketing message in front of as many of your target customers as possible, as often as possible.

Enhancing Your Credibility

Visibility, of course, is only a means. To produce results, visibility must be combined with credibility. This means that you need to embrace visibility strategies that display your distinction, competence, expertise, authority, and leadership—and this is where the slightly famous strategies in this book go beyond marketing strategies that rely on advertising.

"Exposure plus 95 cents might buy you a decent cup of coffee," says networking expert Bob Burg. "The key is to position yourself in your market as the expert, the resource, the only person your prospect would ever even think of doing business with, or referring to others."

The surest way to make a credible name for yourself is by becoming a "recognized" expert. Who counts as an expert? Experts include authors, speakers, consultants, business owners, managers, and professionals. If you have in-depth knowledge about a specific subject—and that subject can be your business—you qualify, too. The test is how much you know, and if you know a lot about something, you can leverage that knowledge into a halo of authority.

As an authority, you can write articles for trade and special interest publications (if you're too busy to write, or uncertain of your writing skills, it's easy to find help—use the Web or the Yellow Pages to look for "Editing and Writing Services"). You can give talks. And you can become a news resource, providing quotes to the media on issues relating to your industry.

Theresa Iglesias-Solomon started Niños, a Spanish/English bilingual catalog business, out of her home in Michigan several years ago. Realizing that her focus on the Hispanic market made her newsworthy to business writers pursuing stories on niche markets, she regularly notified reporters and editors about new ethnic products and buying trends.

Over time she built a reputation as an expert on the Hispanic market, and this has led to frequent media mentions, including some in the *Wall Street Journal, Entrepreneur, USA Today,* and *Catalog Age.*

In addition to making the news, you can augment your marketing and your business by creating information products—booklets, e-books, classes, audiocassettes—around your area of expertise. These will cement your place as the leader in your market niche.

A business coach herself, C. J. Hayden markets to other professional business coaches, marketing consultants, and sales trainers. While her book, *Get Clients Now!,* helped to establish her credibility in this field, Hayden took the concept one step further. After writing her book, she trademarked the name and developed the "Get Clients Now! Licensee Kit," which includes a 60-page facilitator's guide, audiovisual aids, and tools for marketing the program to students. The result has been a profitable package that helps others reproduce her program.

Hayden has sold more than 200 licenses internationally, and the program has helped her land book deals in the U.S. and China, and publicity in several national magazines. This is a perfect example of visibility and credibility building on each other.

Establishing Your Brand and Reputation

Nothing overcomes consumer skepticism more effectively than a good report from someone who's dealt with you before. When people get a recommendation about you from a friend, they approach you with positive expectations. In essence, they have an insurance policy that reduces the risk of doing business with you. If, on top of hearing about you from someone they know, they also see your name in print, the effect grows synergistically. Marketing guru Marcia Yudkin expresses this idea in an algebraic formula:

Visibility + Credibility + Word-of-Mouth = REPUTATION

None of this is possible, of course, if you don't provide customer satisfaction. There are a number of good books on the subject of customer service, and you should take their advice seriously. Without visibility, you can provide excellent services and still find yourself without enough business. But if you pursue visibility and credibility marketing strategies *and* provide an outstanding product or service, word-of-mouth will take on a life of its own. And although you can't personally be present at every moment your prospects are about to buy, your reputation will function as a surrogate salesperson within your prospect's mind.

Roseann Sullivan, a corporate trainer and owner of San Francisco–based Sullivan Communications, has an excellent local reputation as a public speaking coach. Nevertheless, she credits the articles she has written with providing the lion's share of new clients.

"I've landed work from clients who hear about me through my published articles," says Sullivan, whose work has been featured in numerous professional journals and business publications, including *Apartment Owners News, Southwest Airline's Spirit,* and *The Business Journal.* "And I get calls from prospects who had already heard about me, but were then 'nudged' to call and hire me after reading one of my articles."

Big corporations spend millions to promote a brand identity because it pays. The best-known brands spread with the speed of

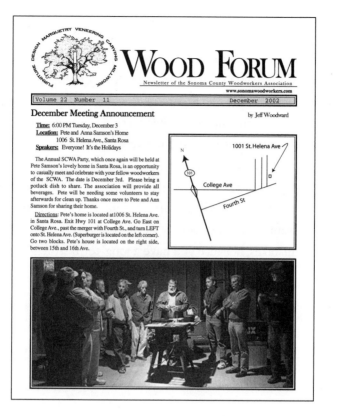

spicy gossip, jumping from prospect to prospect, community to community. While you're probably not in a position to spend your way to success as they do, there are economical ways you can make your business an attractive, distinguished, and distinguishable microbrand that represents your values and expertise.

Your brand will integrate all your marketing around a core idea and vision. It will actually make knowing what to do to successfully market yourself easier. Because you have a unique identity, you will have less to fear from competitors, thereby opening the door for mutually beneficial partnerships with other businesses.

The Sonoma County Woodworkers Association (SCWA) emerged when a handful of independent furniture retailers in Northern California banded together to survive the recession of the early 1990s through cross-promotion and buying strength. Together, the group bought advertising at local radio stations and newspapers, and developed combined events where customers were eligible to win prizes. They even printed a joint brochure that included a map to their locations, along with a headline that read, "People You Can Trust." Because each retailer had a distinctive identity, they were able to work together to survive rough times.

Your *slightly famous* brand identity will become the guiding star of your entire business. It will ensure that all your marketing efforts pull in the same direction. You'll waste less time, and make fewer marketing mistakes, because you have a long-term strategy of investing in your *slightly famous* reputation.

CHAPTER 2 Aim for a Target

Harry Shepherd started his bookkeeping service with the same concerns facing most start-ups. He needed clients right away. But because he was in competition with dozens of other bookkeepers selling essentially the same thing, he knew he needed to find a way to differentiate his company.

After asking around, Harry discovered that many businesses had recently taken to doing their own bookkeeping with accounting software. He also learned they were having a hard time because they lacked basic accounting knowledge—and here Harry saw his opportunity.

He quickly mastered QuickBooks, a popular accounting program, and started marketing himself as a "QuickBooks Software Training Consultant." Immediately, Shepherd went from blending into a sea of look-alike competitors to occupying a unique market niche.

Word spread fast. He introduced himself to accountants as a resource, and they gladly referred him to their clients. In addition, other bookkeepers, who were formerly his competitors, became his clients as he trained them to use accounting software. Harry's new niche meant that his services were in hot demand. He charged higher fees, and he did not have to work as hard to get new clients.

This chapter examines the process Harry pursued in targeting a market and establishing a profitable market niche—the process you will be going through as well. You must first develop a keen understanding of your market by doing research. With this knowledge you can position your business as a slightly famous provider of choice that understands the needs, desires, and challenges of your target market.

To Find a Niche: Focus!

Many entrepreneurs think that selling to the widest possible market is the likeliest path to success. They are afraid to pursue a market niche because they fear they'll lose business by turning away customers. But this "take all comers" approach is not very effective. It's hard to stand out when you market your business without a distinctive set of prospects in mind.

Occupying a niche means you won't be competing with a lot of similar businesses solely on price. And because you will be selling products and services that are customized to the specific needs and predispositions of a select group of people, you can often charge more. Your products and services serve a market that can't easily find alternatives.

To determine if a particular niche is right for you, ask yourself these questions:

- Do I have an identifiable target population with similar interests and needs?
- Is the market large enough to support my business?
- Can I tailor my products, services, and business identity to address that market's particular needs?

- Is my target market currently underserved?
- Can I reach my potential customers in a cost-effective manner?

Your niche will give your marketing efforts a natural, sharp focus. The more you specialize, the more your market will see the value of your services because you speak directly to their unique situation. Assuming your niche is large enough, you can do quite well by becoming a provider of products and services that can't be found anywhere else.

Dan Poynter is a successful self-publisher who started writing books about parachuting and hang-gliding over thirty years ago. Though it might sound as if his audience would be too small to generate significant sales, he knew his market and where to find them. Best of all, he had the market all to himself.

Rather than try to fight for attention in general bookstores, he sold books to skydiving clubs, parachute dealers, and the U.S. Parachute Association. He developed a reputation in skydiving circles, and has enjoyed steady sales of his books for more than three decades. Because Poynter's topic was tailored to a group of people he could easily target, and because he provided useful information where little was to be found, he found greater success than if he had pursued a more general audience.

For small businesses, niches are, above all, manageable. You can get your mind (and pocketbook) around them well enough to design a marketing strategy that speaks in personal terms to real prospects. Conversely, you can avoid wasting time and money broadcasting your message to a general population that isn't particularly interested in what you have to offer.

Tony Roeder learned this when he launched RedWagons.com, a specialized retailer of Red Flyer toy wagons on the Internet. Roeder knew that there was no way he could compete with the likes of Amazon.com and eToys.com, which all carry Red Flyer wagons in their huge toy inventory. Instead, he decided to deal in Red Flyer wagons exclusively, and offer their entire product line. Now, while Roeder's big competitors carry only a few models, he has the entire Red Flyer collection, and is the first resort of any avid Red Flyer wagon enthusiast.

The key is identifying your ideal customers—and the communities they belong to. By targeting the best, most favorably inclined prospects within a niche, you can become your target market's vendor of choice, and sell more with much less effort. Having done this, you've mastered your market—and if that market is large enough, you're a success.

As you identify possible market niches, consider how to specialize your products and services to the unmet needs of the most qualified prospects in them. By developing inside knowledge of this group, and giving them exactly what they want, you will inspire the loyalty that people give those who understand them.

This is what Tom Williams, of WestMark Realtors in Lubbock, Texas, accomplished when he began his career in real estate. Looking for ways to differentiate himself, he soon noticed that the majority of his colleagues gravitated to older, repeat clients who were comfortable with the home-buying process.

Because conventional wisdom says that first-time homebuyers are too much trouble and not worth the small commissions, Williams realized he could have this potentially lucrative market to himself. He threw himself into his newly discovered niche with great success, and his clients found his dedication, advice, and upbeat attitude refreshing.

Niche by Design

Although many discover their niches by accident, the most rewarding market niches are usually identified through deliberate effort. Choosing a market niche is a strategic process that matches your

Dean of Beans
Reaches Coffee Shops Worldwide

REAL-WORLD SUCCESS STORY

Although you've probably never heard of Alex Fisenko, in the world of coffee he's known as "the Dean of Beans." The 60-something coffee expert started his first espresso shop in Berkeley, California, in the 1960s. Since then he's owned 16 coffee shops and now sells his expertise on launching a successful coffee business to aspiring entrepreneurs.

"Espresso is my life," says Fisenko. "I started this business back when there were only a few coffee houses across the country, and they served mainly as 'beatnik' hangouts and coffee was incidental to the whole setting. And it's my personal expertise that makes my niche so successful."

Alex is a coffee guru who conducts coffee shop seminars and also sells a training course called "Espresso Business Success." He brought his niche onto the Internet. His Web site, www.espressobusiness.com, generates thousands of dollars a month in product sales and consulting engagements in the United States, Thailand, South Korea, Belgium, Saudi Arabia, and Barbados.

While Alex's target market of aspiring coffee shop owners is narrow, his business of selling them how-to information is so focused that he easily stands out and finds all the business he can handle.

"My Web site gets close to 18,000 visits a month because my niche is so narrowly defined," says Fisenko. "By narrowing my market niche to aspiring coffee shop owners, I now make more money through book sales and consultations than when I ran coffee shops."

desires and resources to opportunities in the outside world. You can define your niche to include all existing customers, just a subset of them, or a wholly new population. First identify those customers you most want to serve within market niches large enough to sustain you, but not dominated by competitors. Then, steer your research in that direction.

Identify your niche category or the overall industry or consumer segment you wish to serve, and try to find what members of your prospective niche have in common. Additional factors may include:

Your Niche: A Special Region Your niche might comprise prospects in a particular neighborhood, city, county, or state. You might work with veterinarians in Chicago, restaurants in San Francisco, or lobster fishermen in Cape Cod. Or you could consider ethnic and linguistic boundaries, or a particular age cohort of those that reside in your community.

First-time author Amit Gilboa, author of *Off the Rails in Phnom Penh*, stumbled across his market niche during a visit to Cambodia in 1995, just as the country was opening its doors to outside travelers. The result was a best-selling book, based on his travels in Cambodia, that caused a stir in Southeast Asia.

Gilboa's success is due to the fact that he essentially had the Cambodian travel niche all to himself, and his book continues to sell well throughout Asia. "I'm world famous in Southeast Asia" is the way Gilboa puts it. "My publisher is too small to cram the book down the throat of Barnes & Noble, but I still do very well, even though for every person on this planet who has read or even heard of my book, there are millions who haven't."

Your Niche: Meeting Unmet Needs Are there groups with needs you can serve that are not currently being met by other businesses? If so, you have the basis for a successful niche.

Your Niche: Offering Industry-specific Specialties A business can easily focus on a particular industry niche. A chiropractor, instead of seeking as patients "everyone with a back," could target trucking companies, offering treatment and safety seminars to their employees.

Your Niche: How and When You Work Do you specialize in fast turnaround? Are you open seven days a week, twenty-four hours a day? If so, you may be able to capitalize on your schedule to develop your niche.

Your Niche: The Group You Serve Sometimes, if you are the only business that specializes in working with narrow categories of customers, such as seniors, children, or Hispanic-owned small businesses, you can use your knowledge of that special population as the basis for building an identity.

Next, narrow down your chosen category to a more focused subgroup. If your category is health care, for example, your subgroup might be nursing, gynecology, hospital administration, or surgical suppliers. Consider other attributes of your niche that will help you focus as specifically as possible on groups of people with common needs.

The more you narrow your focus, the more likely you are to find a profitable niche market. Terry McVey realized this when he started a medical insurance seminar business. Terry teaches doctors' offices how to collect fees from insurance carriers. Because he targets specific medical specialists, such as orthopedic surgeons, his seminars have a higher perceived value than his generalist competitors.

Knowledge Is Power

Once you have a working idea of the market you'd like to serve, you need to dig deeper to test your assumptions. The process starts with market research: analyze your best potential customers, your competitors, your market's predisposition toward your products and services, and your ability to serve these people so well as to make you their vendor of choice.

Market research can provide relevant information for establishing a solid foundation under any business. Even if you have been in business for years, it's a good idea to stay up-to-date with market research that might help you understand where your market niche is going.

Market research can, among other things, help you understand your potential customers, the likelihood that they'll buy your products and services, why they'll buy them, and how much they'll pay.

Market research can also help you evaluate your competitors' strengths and weaknesses, thereby providing one of the keys to dominating your niche.

There is no rule to tell you where exactly you will find the information you need to qualify your market niche, or just how much market research is necessary, but you can assume that your research will involve analyzing the market, the market's response to your product or service, and how you will effectively market to your niche audience

You begin by looking at primary data. This is data that you generate from direct personal experience or from within your own business. It can come from customers, clients, vendors, existing contacts, or business associations to which you belong. You can gather primary data by talking to people, performing surveys, holding focus groups, or bouncing ideas off prospects on the Internet.

At a more abstract level, secondary data is information and research that has been compiled by others. This can include census reports, articles in trade and consumer publications, and surveys by business associations. All secondary data comes from sources outside your business, and can contain valuable insight into your potential market niche and those already involved with it.

Effective market search combines primary and secondary research to arrive at an adequate understanding of your market niche. By exploring as many secondary sources as possible, combined with a commitment to "get out there" and connect with people who can help you better understand your target market, you'll find the information you need to make intelligent, informed decisions about the viability of your market niche.

A trip to the library can be worthwhile, too. You can look at business directories (several are listed in the appendix) that can provide specific information about your target group, search periodical databases for articles related to your business, and research industry associations and professional organizations (many of which publish their own reports).

Librarians can help you locate a huge amount of free material, including listings for:

- local, state, and national chambers of commerce
- industry associations
- trade journals
- periodicals
- vendors and suppliers
- government agencies and departments

The Internet is another great market research tool. You can do a tremendous amount—from reading articles about your niche and visiting trade and business organization Web sites, to actually chatting with potential prospects in online chat rooms—all from the comfort of your office or study.

Finally, of course, it's important to get out and talk to people. Visit local offices of trade and business associations. Find people on the inside willing to help, and invite them to lunch for a brainstorming session. Approach industry insiders, and tap their knowledge. They are the ones who can best help you refine your niche marketing strategy, because they understand your market better than anyone else. These are people who can point you to specific information about your prospects, and tell you whether your products and services are in demand.

Competitive Intelligence

Before you expand your business, you better know what you're up against. You'll need to thoroughly investigate your competitors to understand their products and services, and how they are being received by your prospects.

Approach competitive businesses as though you were a customer. Visit their business sites if possible. At a competitor's location, watch the customers and their interactions with the employees. Do they seem happy? Are they buying anything? Do you see things that could be improved? This is a time when being critical and nosy is essential.

Request your competitors' marketing materials. Make frequent searches to see if they are appearing in the news. Study their Web sites. Talk to their vendors and past customers. Do everything you can to understand your competitors and how they are received.

Consider both direct competitors and indirect competitors. Determine how many competitors you have and their size. If your intended market niche lies in a specific geographic location, start your search with the phone book. There are a few good online telephone search directories, such as Switchboard.com, that allow you to search by industry category and zip code.

Study competitors through the North American Industry Classification System (NAICS) codes. The Census Bureau uses these codes to report on businesses, including such information as payroll size. You can access the census data yourself at the U.S. Census Bureau Web site. Most public libraries also carry business directories that can help you determine business classifications.

Trade shows are great places to get information, not only about the market, but also about your competition. At a trade show you can get copies of your competitors' literature and samples of their products, see demonstrations, experience their sales pitches, listen to what their prospects are asking them, and even interview attendees. With a little detective work, you can come away from a trade show with a gold mine of market research.

Getting Close

As you refine your market niche, you need to develop an insider's understanding of your prospects. This means personally experiencing the world your clients and customers live and work in, so that you really understand their daily concerns.

You need to know how your customers live, work, and spend their time, both on and off the job. You need to know the key players within the niche, and understand the structure and dynamics of your market. This requires that you get personally involved enough to see through the eyes of your prospects.

Identify points of entry, such as associations, related businesses, and the people who contribute to the world of your niche market. Your list should include:

- Organizations they belong to
- Places they network
- Conferences or workshops they attend
- Competitors and other businesses already serving them
- Magazines or publications they read
- Web sites they frequent
- People they use as guides or mentors

Read every magazine that targets your niche, and contact editors at these publications. Subscribe to news clipping services, or do periodical Web searches on key words related to your niche. Visit trade associations representing your niche audience, and learn everything you can from their Web sites and newsletters, or call and ask to speak with a representative.

Talk to members of your niche and tell them about your business. Talk to businesses that already serve your niche. They can often help you understand not just where your niche is today, but also where it's been and where it may be going.

Develop a questionnaire about your prospective products and services and distribute it to several prospective customers. You'll find that most people are willing to help. Their answers will help you fine-tune your offerings, and tailor your services and marketing messages.

What's Your Position?

Positioning communicates, in no uncertain terms, the benefits your brand delivers to your target market. It is a statement of value. Defining your market position is about articulating the clear customer benefits you offer relative to competitors who serve the same market niche.

You do this for two reasons. First, it helps you develop a clear public image for your own business, so that potential customers know why they should do business with you rather than with someone else. And second, by defining for yourself precisely who your customers are, you can choose appropriate sales and marketing techniques and messages.

A deliberate positioning strategy addresses the fact that people no longer respond to one-size-fits-all marketing. It does this by clearly expressing the Ultimate Benefit of your business, answering the question "What's in it for me?" while cutting through the clutter and confusion of the marketplace.

Positioning emphasizes your strengths, and differentiates you from competitors. In turn, prospects cultivate a mental image of your company that lives and thrives in their minds.

Big companies know this well, and work hard to identify some key attribute of their company and its product, something that focuses customers' minds on a benefit offered by their products that's not offered by competing products. For example, 7-UP is the "uncola" for people who want to drink something different, and Apple computers are for those who "think different."

Small businesses that embrace positioning understand that the marketplace is competitive and cluttered. They know they will be ignored or forgotten by prospects attempting to wade through a barrage of information and marketing noise unless they distinguish themselves somehow.

Positioning means you'll never be confused with thousands of other businesses selling essentially the same thing. This is because you won't allow yourself to be just another "graphic designer," a mere "management consultant," or a humble "wedding photographer." You will use the power of positioning to make your business distinct, meaningful, and indispensable, with the result that your potential customers pick you out.

Standing Apart from the Crowd

In today's ultra-competitive business world, you need to find ways to really stand out. You must develop a strategy that makes your business distinct from your competitors by communicating the value you deliver in a way that is all your own.

Bruce Smith refuses to be seen as just another travel agent. After considering ways to distinguish himself from thousands of other general travel agents, he had a fortunate accident. His wife asked him where they would celebrate their first wedding anniversary. When he gave her a blank look, she set about planning a trip—but wouldn't tell him what she was planning.

Because he enjoyed the mystery leading up to the trip, and the hints his wife gave him, he repackaged his travel service as The Veiled Voyage, selling "destination unknown" vacations to couples and others. The idea was a hit. It radically repositioned his business in a very competitive industry, and developed a memorable brand.

Like Bruce Smith, begin by developing a positioning strategy that distinguishes your brand with a simple message that communicates value to the needs of your target market. If you don't determine your place in the market, the marketplace will simply think of you as one undistinguished business among many.

Your market position evolves from the characteristics of your product. Elements that contribute to your unique position include:

What Benefits Do You Offer? What do your customers get when they work with you? Increased business? More physical comfort? Financial well being? Use this as the keystone in your positioning strategy together.

Does Your Price Point Differentiate You? Is your product a luxury item, somewhere in the middle, or cheap? Pricing can be used effectively to differentiate you from competitors.

Is Your Quality Better? Is your product particularly well produced? What quality controls are in place to assure consistency? What national or international standards do you meet? Do you back your quality claims with customer-friendly guarantees, warranties, and return policies?

Do You Offer Special Services? Customers expect good service— but do you offer something better or different? Do you offer the added value of Web-based or 800-number telephone support? Do you have a guarantee? Is your product customized or personalized? Do you offer quick turnaround or around-the-clock service?

If you are surrounded by businesses offering similar services or products, you must combine a number of features valuable to your target market in order to develop a strong positioning statement.

Start by doing research to understand your current practices, the practices of your competitors, and, most importantly, the practices you will need to adopt to achieve the position you want.

- Do you save people time or money?
- Do you make money for people?
- Do you offer a larger selection?

- Are you more conveniently located?
- Do you offer free installation, inspection, or other services?
- Are you more expensive, less expansive?
- Do you offer better or faster service?
- Do you guarantee the lowest price?
- Do you match the lowest price your customers can find?
- Do you honor your competitors' special discounts?
- Do you offer a stronger guarantee?
- Do you use technology to respond faster to a customer's needs?

You don't need to be completely original in your positioning statement, as long as it offers something significantly different from and superior to that of your competitors.

In the crowded marketplace of boutique winemakers, for instance, Guy Davis stands out because he combines a passion for what he does with a sense of how to get noticed. He embraced a simple positioning strategy—handcrafted wines from carefully selected vineyards—which he implemented by searching out wine grapes grown in places most conducive to their style. In addition to his vineyards in California's Sonoma County, he traveled to other countries, including Argentina and New Zealand, in search of vineyards to pursue his craft in the best way possible.

Soon he was working two harvests a year (the southern hemisphere harvests grapes in March and April) and this translated into his personal positioning statement, "a winemaker for all seasons." The phrase stuck, pleasing his loyal customers and getting the attention of wine writers.

Positioning is power. It creates a strong link in prospects' minds between you and the product or service you've made your own. Then, every time they need your products or services, your company will be the first name that pops into their mind—or even better, the only one. The most important thing to remember is that positioning is not what you do to a product or a service; it's what you do to the minds of your prospects.

Develop a Positioning Statement

Your positioning statement is a succinct promise to the target market that you will provide them with the benefits they care about the most. The trick is capturing that promise in a very short space and in a very compelling way.

Imagine you're in an elevator with a potential customer, and you have 30 seconds to answer his question, "What business are you in?" A positioning statement answers that question in a couple of sentences, clearly stating the benefits you provide, and why customers should choose you over the competition. A positioning statement defines what's important and appealing about your business.

Here are some examples:

- We are an accounting firm specializing in nonprofits in Houston.
- We are an all-organic grocery delivery service.
- We help professional service firms attract more clients.
- Our design firm specializes in refurbishing Victorian homes.

Keep your positioning statement short, focused, and easy to remember. If you can't explain your positioning statement in one sentence, you'll have a hard time getting your fellow-rider in the elevator to remember you after you've reached the lobby.

Evolving Your Niche

The marketplace is always changing, and if you don't want to be left behind, you need to stay plugged in, to be aware of current conditions, and to anticipate trends.

TAX TIPS — CNN LIVE — 9:14ᴀ ET

REAL-WORLD SUCCESS STORY

Ed Lyon Uses Humor to Stand Out from the Pack

Like most people, Cincinnati-based tax specialist Ed Lyon is commonly asked what he does for a living. But rather than reply, "I do taxes," he says, "I'm the funniest tax guy in America." It's an immediate attention getter that has helped Lyon get noticed, and remembered, in his competitive field.

Lyon came into his moniker after compiling top ten lists of humorous tax deductions to promote his book, *The 60-Minute Tax Planner*. His efforts resulted in an appearance on *The Roseanne Show* in April 1999, where the television hostess dubbed him "the funniest tax guy in America." This led to appearances on CNN, CNBC, MSNBC, and Fox News Network.

The name stuck because Lyon made it stick. "I've used it in all of my marketing. It starts a conversation," says Lyon. "When somebody asks me what I do for a living and I say, 'I do taxes,' it does nothing to distinguish me from all the other CPAs and tax preparers. When I tell them, 'I'm the funniest tax guy in America,' it always starts a conversation, even if they say, 'Well, you don't have much competition.'"

"If you had told me when I was sitting in Federal Income Taxation class that I would someday appear on CNN — discussing boob jobs for strippers — I would have told you that something was about to go terribly wrong!" says Lyons. "But my yearly lists of celebrity tax deductions result in media coverage that lends me tons of credibility and a lot of new clients."

REAL-WORLD SUCCESS STORY

Dr. Robert E. Balon
Meets Change Head-On

Dr. Robert E. Balon enjoyed a strong, comfortable niche for many years performing market research for the broadcast radio stations. Then there came the day when he had to recognize that all his expertise couldn't reverse the fact that radio markets were consolidating, and the demand by radio stations for that expertise would be sharply diminished.

"We thought, okay, our business is going to drop by 60 percent in the next two years. Where do we go from here?"

Balon contacted a local Texas restaurant association, and pitched the idea of a column on market research for their newsletter. After that, he organized a trend-analysis conference targeted to the central Texas food and hospitality industry.

Not having the money to totally bankroll the event he envisioned, Balon sought out potential industry partners who could lend funding and credibility to his conference. "I wanted to be the one that the trade press was excited about. I looked at where we're going to present it, how we're going to present it, and how we're going to position it."

Balon partnered with a large, upscale hotel chain and Block Distributing, the largest southwest wine distributor, and got them to underwrite part of the seminar. "It was a win-win proposition: the Four Seasons liked having top local CEOs visiting their space, and the distributor appreciated the opportunity to network with a lot of his clients who had been invited to the free-of-charge conference."

The conference helped the Benchmark Company refocus its target market, and become established as a market research firm that works with the Texas restaurant industry.

Approach market research with an open mind and a willingness to change direction if necessary. It can show you that a seemingly great niche is not predisposed to buy your services, or is already served by a number of competitors. The hardest thing about market research isn't finding or understanding the data, it's that market research can burst bubbles.

CHAPTER 3

The Brand Is You

Martha Stewart, Michael Jordan, Emeril Lagasse, and Dr. Ruth Westheimer—all are examples of the power of personal branding. And though you may not aspire to their level of brand stardom, there's nothing preventing you from doing the same for your small business on a smaller scale.

Today, brands distinguish products and services from many competing choices. That's why all kinds of products and services—from accounting firms to sneaker makers to restaurants—are figuring out how to transcend the anonymity of mere category membership, and attain a unique brand identity.

But isn't branding the domain of soap, tires, and toothpaste? Think again. In "The Brand Called You," an article written for *Fast Company* magazine in 1997, management guru Tom Peters describes how brand equity has emerged over the past few years as a key strategic asset, not just for products, but also for business people and companies of all sizes.

"Charles Schwab was just a broker toiling on Wall Street until he turned his name into a winning brand," says Peter Montoya, publisher of *Personal Branding* magazine and author of *The Personal Branding Phenomenon*. "He made his self-named brokerage service a brand by saturating the media with his name, face, and company identity. Now, millions of Americans recognize in the Charles Schwab name perhaps the best known brand in finance."

Brands have a number of strategic functions, enabling you to:

- Differentiate yourself from your competition
- Position your focused message in the hearts and minds of your target customers
- Persist and be consistent in your marketing efforts
- Customize your services to reflect your personal brand
- Deliver your message clearly and quickly
- Project credibility
- Strike an emotional chord
- Create strong user loyalty

For small businesses, branding is not about slick advertisements. Small-business branding is about getting your target market to see you as the preferred choice. Building a slightly famous brand is not just about what you do; it's about what you do differently from everyone else.

"Branding is about getting prospects to see you as the only solution to their problems," says branding guru Rob Frankel, author of *The Revenge of Brand X*. "You want them to see your competition, and then run your way bellowing, 'Nobody understands me the way you do!' That's what gets them in the door—and keeps them coming back for more."

The Soul of Your Company

Your brand holds your entire slightly famous marketing strategy together. Once created, your brand will be the central theme that connects your business, both rationally and emotionally, to your market. It will convey personality, mystique, and drama. It will become the total aura around your business that cannot be duplicated by anyone else.

Branding is the total integration of everything your company does—including public relations, customer service, networking, newsletters, and word of mouth—that reflects on your company's reputation for quality of products and services within your target market.

Effective brands send a deliberate message that encompasses all aspects of a product or service, including a distinctive logo that appears on stationery, business cards, signage, packaging, advertising, Web site, and place of business. It also ties into prices, customer service, and guarantees.

"When most people think of a brand, they visualize a slogan, a logo, a campaign, a promise, or a product. A brand is much more," says Karl Speak, co-author of *Be Your Own Brand.* "Your company's brand is a powerful relationship fueled by a loyal belief system and knotted to the principle of providing exceptional value."

Whether positive, negative, or indifferent, every company has a brand. Your brand "describes the total experience of doing business with you, or consuming your products or service," according to Speak. Every business needs to evaluate its brand identity against the following criteria:

Relevance to the Market A brand must stand for something that is meaningful to members of a target market. Your brand encompasses the total experience of doing business with you.

Consistency of Behavior Customers must be able to depend on the brand to deliver the same experience every time. Because your market experiences your values through your brand, the only way they will truly become loyal to your brand is through your dedication and consistency.

Relationship-Building A brand is not a logo or an advertising strategy. "The strength of any brand is in the relationship it has between a company and its customers," says Speak. "The stronger the relationship, the more business they will do, and the more likely it is that customers will refer them to their friends and business associates."

Loyalty to the Customer Is Returned The test of a brand is, in fact, the strength of loyalty it generates. If you have a strong relationship with your target audience, then you have a strong brand and a strong business.

Reputation Is Priceless The only way to be successful in business is by establishing a good reputation, and a brand can help you do that. Your reputation works as your strongest marketer by communicating the relationship you have with people who've done business with you, and your target market in general.

The following pages focus on two critical elements that communicate a brand identity: personality and expertise.

Personality Branding

Personality branding is a strategy that showcases your personality and equates it with your business to produce an emotional bond with your prospects. In other words, you put a human face on your business by bringing your personality to the forefront of your marketing and business identity. It's also an opportunity to express your entrepreneurial passion—to show how your background and interests inform the soul of your business.

LILLIAN VERNON®
FAVORITES
Everything Under $20
1.800.545.5426   www.lillianvernon.com

When a company is named after a person, it puts a human face on an anonymous corporate entity. This marketing strategy has obviously worked for Lillian Vernon, a woman who created a very successful personal brand from her kitchen table five decades ago.

Lillian Vernon is one of America's most accomplished and well-known leaders in the catalog industry. According to an *Opinion Research* poll, more than 39 million Americans are familiar with the Lillian Vernon name.

"When I first launched the company in 1951, my marketing plan was simple. I wanted to establish a memorable face behind my company to add a personal touch to our business," says Vernon. "I wanted

REAL-WORLD SUCCESS STORY

Dave Hirschkop Proves That a Little Insanity Goes a Long Way

When you meet Dave Hirschkop at a trade show, don't expect to shake his hand. This is because he'll be wearing a straitjacket while standing before a simulated insane asylum to promote his popular line of "Insanity" hot sauces.

Hirschkop has become a living testament to the power of personal branding. His company, *Dave's Gourmet, Inc.*, steps to the front of the crowded hot sauce category, while his brand identity has resulted in fiercely loyal customers and great media exposure.

"When people eventually meet me, they expect to find a wild man who wants to burn everything in sight," Dave says, "but I'm just a normal guy with a sense of humor who went into my business and created my brand by accident. It was sort of a joke."

Dave's "Insanity" sauces came into existence when he owned a small Mexican restaurant near the University of Maryland. Late at night, a number of Dave's patrons were usually drunk and troublesome. "I discovered that when I'd feed drunks my hot sauce, they either left or became extremely quiet. The hotter the sauce, the faster drunk patrons left."

This gave Dave an idea about how he could become a standout maker of hot sauces in an already-crowded market: make the hottest sauce possible, even hotter than people really liked! Instead of promising sensual pleasure, he promised pain, even danger — but pain that came with bragging rights. Nevertheless, it took him a while to realize that he had to be really

my customers to feel that I am their personal shopper. My persona is the key to maintaining our loyal customer base."

After her catalogs grew in popularity, she created a bond with customers by including a personal letter and photograph in each catalog. Lillian's letters became such an inspiration that Hillary Rodham Clinton once told a group of leading businesswomen that she felt that she knew Lillian Vernon by reading her letters long before they actually met at the White House.

Because customers responded with true curiosity about Vernon's life, she wrote about her dog, which then gained a role in making the Lillian Vernon brand. "Mopsey gets fan mail, has appeared on the

extreme. "At first, nobody wanted the sauce, and we got no respect. We decided we'd really need to hammer people."

When Dave introduced his Insanity Sauce at the National Fiery Foods Show in New Mexico, he made attendees sign a release form before tasting from a bottle that came in a coffin-like box wrapped with yellow police tape.

His Insanity Reserve hot sauce is still the brand leader, so fiery that he doesn't recommend it for human consumption. His best, if unintended, publicity coup happened when a show promoter had a minor respiratory problem after tasting his sauce, and banned him from the show. "That really had a part in our growing popularity," says Dave. "Although you'd have to be insane to eat some of my products, they get people talking.

"I think personal branding works because America wants entrepreneurs to succeed," says Dave. "There are a lot of competitors in hot sauce. We outsell them because they can identify us. We have a certain cachet in our brand."

The more he personalizes his business, the more people gravitate to his products. "People feel like they know me," says Dave. "We get calls at 3:00 AM on our voice mail saying, 'Dave, man, you burned me!' I think my all-American name helps, but it's really because we use our smallness and specialty in ways that corporate giants can't touch."

front cover of our catalog and even has her own page on our Web site," says Vernon. "Our customers like knowing that I'm a happy pet owner."

In 1995, when Lillian Vernon went online, the Internet turned out to be a natural vehicle for selling her products and promoting her brand. "The Web site helped us further promote the brand and reach new people," says Vernon. "Our Web site includes a page called 'Lillian's Corner,' devoted exclusively to my life, complete with a baby picture and the first ad in *Seventeen Magazine* that launched our company."

Lillian Vernon has become a household name, recognized as part of popular American culture and featured on numerous television programs including *David Letterman, Conan O'Brien, Jeopardy!, Saturday Night Live, The Daily Show, Northern Exposure*, and *Roseanne*. Her management team spreads her branding philosophy throughout the company to ensure that everyone from customer service representatives to forklift operators are trained to represent the company image.

"It's obviously gratifying to be in the limelight, but our real reward comes from the four million customer orders we receive each year," says Vernon. "Our company works hard to project a unified brand in our eight catalog titles and two Web sites, and these orders are the payoff."

To Brand Is to Promise

In the information age, brand marketing—the process by which a product creates an emotional connection with its audience, and sets itself apart from the crowd—is more important than ever. Your brand should be your best defense against a cynical world.

Simply put, a brand is a promise. Today's busy consumers don't have time to investigate everything and don't want to be taken. There is more competition than ever. We've seen it all. We've heard every outrageous claim imaginable. And before we are willing to spend our money, we need reassurance.

Against this backdrop, merely doing good work or selling good products is no longer enough. By identifying and authenticating a product or service, branding delivers a pledge of satisfaction and quality. A brand promises value. It gives people something to trust and identify with in a complex world where it's increasingly hard to know what's real and what's not. A brand provides a reassuring aura that not only shows prospects you understand their needs, but that you will deliver value to them time and again.

"A brand is a promise you are willing to keep, to yourself and the clients you serve," says Debra Valle of Marketing u, a virtual university and coaching company for small business owners. "It's doing something consistently and authentically that represents the work you present to the world. This is a formula that is very fulfilling for the small business owner and very attractive to their customers."

Valle, who has been a brand strategist and marketer for Fortune 500 companies, finds that many small businesses believe they're too small to create the kind of distinctive message and look accomplished by Madison Avenue. "It doesn't take a Madison Avenue to create distinction in the marketplace, what it takes is a simple willingness to think like a major brand—and a determined effort," says Valle.

"Most small businesses present themselves to the world as a list of facts and services without heart or passion," she explains. "They are unfocused at best, bland at the worst, because they fail to connect their brands to who they are or those they serve." The problem is that most professionals spend little or no time crafting their brand identity. She believes it is imperative that we intentionally craft our brand, or central message, around our unique passions, skills, and values.

"Your brand must be central to who you are," says Valle. "It must be authentic to you and exclusive to your target market. When you define and live your brand, you live the life you want. You attract the right kind of clients because your brand resonates with desirable clientele. Brands draw from your passions."

Another mistake many small businesses make is to fail to include their clients as central players in their brand identity. Crafting a brand means finding the overlap between your "gifts" and your customers' "ultimate desires." The territory where the two intersect provides fertile ground for a brilliant marketing campaign, and the key to great brand identity.

"When you are focused with the help of your brand identity, you contribute in a way that's genuine and useful," says Valle. "Your

T. Scott Gross Offers Ten Steps to Create a MicroBrand

Branding means owning a tiny corner in the mind of someone you want to influence. T. Scott Gross, author of *MicroBranding*, believes the most powerful brands are those with a personal or local identity, implemented through clever promotions, innovative targeted marketing, and strategic networking.

"MicroBrands are efficient, local, and often rely on individual personality," says Gross. "But it's important not to confuse image with brand. A brand rests solely in the mind of the consumer, and it evokes a whole range of information and emotions. An image can evoke a brand but, by itself, a clever logo does not a brand make."

Gross suggests ten specific steps for you to take in creating your "microbrand," as he calls a brand designed to win you a niche market:

Step One: *Start with Your Own Values*

List your personal values as you perceive them, creating an itemized list that might include such general concepts as integrity, teamwork, and profitability. In twenty-five words or less, describe what it is like working for you from the viewpoint of your employees.

Step Two: *Define the Mission*

The mission statement answers the question, "What is the point of pursuing this line of business?" Good mission statements are meaningful, and short enough to remember easily.

Step Three: *Capture the Vision*

A vision statement answers the question, "How will you know when you have done what you said you would do in your mission statement?" The most important thing about vision is to have one.

Step Four: *Take a Snapshot*

Look at where you are right now. In twenty-five words or less, describe your business in terms of where you are in reaching your vision. Address the issue of awareness and market penetration. What percentage of the market is aware of your brand? What percentage of the market do you currently own?

Step Five: *Identify the Market*

Define your market. Here's an example of the kind of statement you are after: "The ABC market consists of medium-sized companies in the health-care industry. They have high customer contact and have shown a dedication to customer service. They have a history of investing in training. Fun and creativity are characteristics of their operations and marketing."

Step Six: *Create a Persona*

You need a position statement that defines the mental real estate you want to own. How do you want the market to think of you? A good tag line should start the positioning process.

Step Seven: *Give Yourself a Name*

A name has to capture every aspect of what a company does. It is the most important part of the process. Great names are not generic. Generic names encourage generic business.

Step Eight: *Establish Your Logo*

A great logo will immediately create brand recall, while being a positive, accurate representation of the brand promise. Evaluate it in terms of these two points; then list opportunities for getting your logo seen.

Step Nine: *Enter Your New World*

MicroBranding emphasizes strategic networking. You must recognize the network you already have, and use it to define and grow your brand. List the influential people you already know, and then list the important networking events that you need to attend.

Step Ten: *Command Attention*

MicroBranders get others talking about them. Who are the most influential people in your industry? Who do you already know that could you get an introduction? Who might make a good co-marketing partner? This could even be a competitor!

brand helps you know where you're going and how you want to be seen. When businesses make a stand and get behind their brands, business seems to find them."

Trust Opens the Door

If you establish a place of trust and relevance in prospects' minds, you're already in the door. The more people believe in your brand, the more it will spread throughout your niche market without your pushing. If your brand is clear, distinctive, and easily understood, and expresses a unique, compelling benefit that people believe in, it will bring you all the business you can handle.

Expertise: You Have It, So Flaunt It

Branding your business around your expertise means using your knowledge to communicate competence and industry leadership in a manner that is relevant and appealing to your target market. Achieving an expert's reputation transforms you from just another vendor, vying for your customers' limited funds, to a trusted advisor with intimate knowledge of their conditions. In a world where product characteristics are easily copied, or are perceived to be minimal, your expertise communicates your individuality—something that nobody can duplicate.

Not so long ago, expertise was equated with the number of years you were in business, or the college diploma that hung on your wall. That has changed as people have come to be more interested in results. If you can deliver, people will be interested in you no matter how brief your business experience or how bare your walls are of diplomas.

Experts are sought after. They get more business with less effort, and command higher fees. Journalists come to them for information.

Fred M. Tibbitts, Jr.
Will Drink to That!

REAL-WORLD SUCCESS STORY

Frederick M. Tibbitts, Jr., founded Fred Tibbitts & Associates in 1992 to help food and beverage companies reach global markets. Since then, he's strategically cultivated a reputation in his industry as one of the most well-connected and knowledgeable global beverage-marketing experts.

Tibbitts has become slightly famous within the beverage world by becoming fluent in all the details of his business. He monitors global beverage trends on a daily basis while staying in contact with global account managers at hotels and restaurants. He also hosts a series of special events, "Fred Tibbitts Spring & Autumn Dinners with Special Friends," in key markets, including Hong Kong, Singapore, and New York. Guest lists at these events read like a *Who's Who* of the beverage world.

"I'm as much a global beverage strategist as anything else," says Tibbitts. "I constantly update my knowledge of world news and events, and I read everything about the beverage world. I try to see the relationships between seemingly distinct things to see what the future holds. And I maintain a vast human network that adds value to my clients."

His commitment to understanding his niche, which means a total dedication to learning everything about his clients' condition and everything that may affect it, has positioned Tibbitts as the foremost expert within his industry, virtually eliminating competition.

Tibbitts also attracts media attention. He contributes a wine column to *Hospitality International Magazine* in London six times a year, and numerous industry publications have published articles about his company.

"I'm fond of the Buddhist saying, 'When you open your heart to the world, the world opens its heart to you,'" says Tibbitts. "When you know your stuff and put others first, it's a formula for becoming dominant in your target market. I'm living proof."

They are asked to speak at conferences. They out-position their competitors because they know more and are recognized as knowing more.

Marketing guru Dan Kennedy stated, "You don't need someone else's permission to become successful." By the same token, you don't have to be appointed by anyone other than yourself to become an expert in your field. Becoming an expert takes work, but it's within your reach. You don't need a special degree, but you do need a willingness to learn.

Commit to Lifelong Learning

To become an expert, you need a deliberate strategy to help you understand everything you can about your market niche. You don't need to know everything, which is impossible, but you need to be considerably better informed than most. Staying in this position is a process that never ends.

Your future is directly related to how much you develop yourself. You may have the fanciest brochures or an impressive client list, but if you don't continue to invest in your own development, you won't remain competitive. Look for the gaps in your knowledge, and for ways to fill them.

Experts know their fields are always changing. They constantly update their knowledge and look for ways to stay knowledgeable.

Establish and Articulate a Viewpoint

It's not enough just to be an expert. You need to use your knowledge to deliberately distinguish yourself from your competitors. This means determining where your expertise fits in your positioning and branding strategy. Assess what others are doing, saying, and writing about your industry. Your goal is not just to be fully informed, but also to develop a perspective that makes connections between your industry and the larger world.

Jump into the ongoing discussions taking place in your industry. These discussions often can be found in trade publications, industry Web sites, newsletters, Internet chat rooms, and at trade association meetings and events. Your goal is to plug yourself into every possible outlet that influences your niche.

Experts know that they must actively seek out new evidence that impacts their theories and assumptions. Keep on the lookout for statistics, case studies, and research that either substantiates or refutes your thinking. You don't need an ultimate truth, but you do need to articulate your position clearly and have the relevant facts close at hand.

Read Everything You Can

Subscribe to e-mail newsletters, news services, and specialized publications. These sources enable you to take the pulse of your industry. Trade magazines cover all the issues that affect your niche, while providing up-to-the-minute information you won't find anywhere else. If you can't afford all the magazines, you might be able to find them in a library or read back issues on Web sites.

Don't just study the contents of the articles, note who writes them. Because writers often specialize in an industry, you will see their names again and again. These people can become valuable sources of information and potential messengers for your business. Set aside dedicated times to read these publications and clip articles of interest.

Make frequent trips to a good business bookstore, and look for books that address your industry, niche, and type of work. Develop a reference collection you can turn to for immediate, dependable information. Read regularly and act on what you learn. Allocate a budget for books and materials that keep you up to date and advance your expertise-seeking agenda.

You Are the Resource

Becoming a resource within your target market starts with sharing your knowledge. You can give away free information—booklets,

TIPS FROM THE GURU

Robert Middleton Offers Solutions and Information

Robert Middleton of Action Plan Marketing promotes and practices a strategy called "InfoGuru Marketing," based on his observation that giving away your expertise is an effective way to gain trust, attract prospects, and become a center of influence.

"All my successful marketing strategies are based on solutions and information," says Middleton. "For an Internet Service Provider, we created a booklet that promised to untangle the Internet. For the executive recruiter, it was a unique search process that guaranteed client satisfaction. For me, it was giving talks with a focus on attracting new clients. In every case we were offering ideas and information that promised a desired solution."

Middleton now urges his clients to give away solution-based information to leverage their credibility. The more you give away, he contends, the more you are perceived as a partner that clients want to do business with.

"This works because you're providing valuable information and resources and spend virtually no time talking about what you *do* or what you *know*," says Middleton. "Instead you learn what prospects need and determine where they want to go. Then, instead of pushing people away because you are trying too hard to sell them, they are attracted because you have something they want."

reports that make a difference to your prospects, valuable Web-site content—in a way that attracts interest but applies no sales pressure. The more you become known as a source of expert information, the more potential customers trust you. You become part of their world, a center of influence, and because people like to do business with people they know, or know of, you will be their first choice.

Centers of influence are always "present" within their target markets. Visibility is part of their formula, so they cultivate opportunities to be seen, read, and heard by the people who matter most. They make sure their prospects hear from them on a regular basis.

Most importantly, centers of influence "walk the walk" as well as "talk the talk." Their credibility skyrockets because they are confident in what they do and consistent in the messages they send.

Terri Lonier Briefs Novice Entrepreneurs

TIPS FROM THE GURU

Terri Lonier began her first business in 1978, a pottery studio in upstate New York. In marketing her own work, Lonier found that she had a natural marketing flair. Soon she found herself giving workshops to artists on how to market their work. When they started bringing their friends — owners of other small businesses — Terri realized that she could expand her reach and provide business information to the growing ranks of solo entrepreneurs.

Lonier is now the author of five books, including the classic entrepreneurial startup guide, *Working Solo.* Her book was named the #1 choice for solo entrepreneurs by *Inc.* magazine and "the free agent's bible" by *Fast Company* magazine. As the president of Working Solo, Inc., Terri is a recognized authority on the small office and home office (SOHO) market.

As a SOHO professional herself for more than 20 years, Terri knows SOHO from the inside out. "My market niche and resulting brand grew from the fact that I identified an area where I didn't have too many competitors, and I built a brand around it," says Lonier. "When I conceived *Working Solo,* I knew it would be more than just a book. I knew I could develop seminars, tapes, consulting, and eventually an online component around my brand."

An important consideration in brand extension is realizing that markets change, and it is important to analyze your current and future business opportunities periodically. "My interests, like my brand, are always evolving," says Lonier. "Each year I consider my biggest pains and design the coming year to focus on the most promising opportunities."

When *Working Solo* came out, for example, there were a limited number of small business marketing books, and competition was not as fierce. But now, because there's an entire aisle devoted to her market niche, Lonier has decided to carve out a new niche, showing the corporate market how to better market to SOHO entrepreneurs.

Terri still works with SOHO businesses, but she also delivers her knowledge on what she calls a "small business revolution" to major corporations through conferences, the media, and her books and seminars. Terri's insights are regularly featured in such publications as *The New York Times, Wall Street Journal, USA Today, Fortune,* and *Business Week,* and on CNBC, CNN, the BBC, and radio programs nationwide.

"Small businesses must be keenly aware of changes in their marketplace," says Lonier. "I initially drew from my core life pursuits, which all involved working solo, to give birth to my brand. Through my ability to adapt to both the challenges and opportunities of my marketplace, I've been able to use 'working solo' as the core idea and unifying center for everything in my evolving empire."

Brand Extension:
Building on What You've Established

When your brand is established, you can use it to grow your business in new directions. Called brand extension, this strategy is employed by businesses that recognize the possibility of taking a brand name that is well established within a particular niche, and cultivating new customers in neighboring niches. Alternatively, a business can capitalize on brand loyalty to provide new services and products to existing customers.

Barbara Hemphill, for instance, started her organizing business in 1978 by placing a $7 ad in a New York City newspaper. Since then, she's developed a multi-pronged branding strategy that targets both individuals and businesses, offering organizing skills designed to reduce stress and increase productivity.

Her *Taming the Paper Tiger* book series established her reputation as a pioneer in the field of professional organizing. This led to the development of Kiplinger's *Taming the Paper Tiger* software, an endorsement by Pendaflex, and, eventually, the founding of the Hemphill Productivity Institute, a company employing more than 70 Paper Tiger Authorized Consultants in the U.S. and Canada.

PART II MEDIA STRATEGIES

CHAPTER 4

Media Strategies That Work

When you read about a business in the newspaper or hear about it on the radio, chances are you immediately elevate that business above its competitors. It has solidity and credibility. This is precisely why media relations (usually referred to as "public relations" or simply "PR") is the ultimate "slightly famous" marketing strategy. No other marketing method delivers so much impact for so little investment of time and money.

The public values the media, and so should you. In one way or another, the media reach and influence everyone with a direct impact on your business. Thus, when properly pursued, media strategies will help establish your reputation and build your brand, reaching far more prospects than you could in person.

Getting media attention requires knowledge and effort on your part, but it's not magic. The strategies discussed in the following chapters are designed specifically for small businesses, and they are within the reach of anyone with a basic understanding of how the

REAL-WORLD SUCCESS STORY

Bart Baggett Pursues the Media and Wins

Handwriting analysis expert Bart Baggett has always had a knack for self-promotion. He began studying handwriting analysis when he was fifteen. Soon he was marketing a line of flash cards for personality assessment based on handwriting analysis, first to fellow high school students, then to fellow college students.

But when Baggett decided to make handwriting analysis his adult career, he realized that he needed to do something special to stand out in a profession comprising 30,000 other handwriting experts. He was young and unknown, and he needed an edge. Baggett turned to the media to help him establish his credibility as a handwriting expert and become a mini-celebrity in his market niche.

"I knew then that my young age was against me and that I needed third-party validation as a handwriting expert to succeed," he recalls. "Because I saw that successful people pursued the media, I knew that if I could convince reporters and producers of my abilities, those who read about me or saw me would believe in me too."

Baggett studied newspapers, magazines, and radio and television programs to find out what types of guests were in demand. He then looked for ways to tie his professional abilities to specific media needs.

At the height of the O.J. Simpson trial, he sent out a news release about Simpson's handwriting that resulted in several timely media interviews. He later appeared on *Court TV* to discuss Timothy McVeigh's handwriting, and was recommended by the director of that program to CNN. Over the years, Baggett has appeared on hundreds of programs, including *Howard Stern* and *Montel Williams*. A feature in *Biography Magazine* led to stories in the *London Times*, the *Dallas Morning News*, and others.

Baggett attributed his success to his reputation for being an available, articulate, entertaining, and easy-to-work-with media guest. "I prominently display evidence of my previous media appearances on my Web site," says Baggett. "Now, editors and producers call me because they see my track record and tons of media experience."

media works. For those who take the time to understand and follow the guidelines that will be offered, the results can be spectacular.

The Rewards of Media Exposure

Media Relations, or PR, is first and foremost about obtaining favorable media exposure for your business—but unlike advertising, it's free. And though usually the result of a lot of work, it's hard to find a more cost-effective way to reach potential customers or clients. The rewards are very real. Here are the kinds of results you can look for.

Increased Sales Although PR is often seen as merely an image-building tool, it can directly bring in new clients and customers. When your phone number appears in a magazine article, for example, you generate inquiries and orders.

Instant Credibility The *slightly famous* approach to embracing the media is built on the understanding that everyone is swamped with marketing messages, and with so many alternatives clamoring for our attention, it's hard to know who is authentic.

Advertisers and marketers agree that the more often someone sees your name, the more predisposed they are to buy from you—an effect that grows when your name appears in contexts that imply you are competent. PR works because it associates your name with the authority of the media.

Enhanced Status As a businessperson, you undoubtedly possess special knowledge. But what good is that expertise if nobody knows about it? When your name appears in print or on the air, you acquire an aura of expertise that will get you more business with less effort.

Expanded Reach No matter how much you network or attend meetings, you can only go so far on your own. Public relations can quickly take you to a larger audience, sometimes focusing national attention on a small, local operation.

Continuing Benefits Any media coverage you obtain can be effectively utilized long afterward. Reprints of articles you've written or been quoted in, and copies of audios or videos of media appearances, make excellent marketing materials that are less expensive, and more convincing, than anything you create yourself. Article reprints can easily replace expensive brochures, mailers, and newsletters. You can send out cassettes of a radio appearance to prospective clients, or, if you are quoted in a magazine or newspaper, you can photocopy the article and send it to prospects as a no-pressure means of keeping in touch.

PR Versus Advertising

While the terms *advertising* and *PR* are sometimes used interchangeably, they really refer to quite distinct marketing tools. With advertising, you are purchasing space or airtime in the media. Public relations is the art of getting the media to give you free coverage.

While there are, of course, expenses involved in getting the "free" coverage of PR, especially if you hire an agency or professional to handle the job, for small businesses the relative cost-effectiveness of PR as a marketing tool can be a tremendous advantage.

As important as the cost savings involved in PR is the credibility that it carries. Advertising is, after all, what you say about yourself, and therefore always suspect. In contrast, PR has others talking about you, and because praise from others is far more credible than praise from yourself, a favorable mention in the media of you or your business is much more effective than even the most powerful advertisement. It's an independent validation of your worth.

Why then do so many businesses rely on advertising to market themselves? Because it's something over which they have complete control. When you buy an ad, you choose the publication, select the size of your ad, and determine what it says and when it appears. PR

Anthony Mora Discusses the Primacy of Public Relations

TIPS FROM THE GURU

Most small businesses don't make media relations part of their marketing strategy because they don't fully understand it. In doing so they lose a lot, because PR is the only form of marketing that produces both public awareness and the implied endorsement that comes with appearing in the media as a news story.

"PR is often considered the poor step-sister of advertising — a non-essential activity that's nice to pursue but not a basic business priority," says Anthony Mora of Anthony Mora Communications. "But because media exposure carries a lot of weight with potential clients and customers, it can become the foundation for all of your success. The financial aspect of PR is very appealing — where else can you get that kind of exposure and endorsement without paying for the coverage?"

Mora believes that most businesses don't understand they are worthy of media attention — yet all businesses have a story to tell. "Smaller businesses might think they're too small for national media. That's not true," says Mora. "The golden rule of PR is that you need to think about how you can be helpful to reporters first. In other words, if you do enough favors, and help a reporter on deadline write a really good story, you will become a media darling, and PR will come to you without too much effort.

"To get the media interested in your business, you have to see the value of your expertise, or tell a story that makes readers interested. Stand back from your business and determine what makes you unique. It's a matter of determining what's distinctive about what you do or what you know, and approaching the media with a carefully crafted pitch or introduction."

The secret, says Mora, is presenting yourself as a "resource." This means adopting a long-term strategy of getting yourself seen as an indispensable part of your industry — so much so that when anyone pursues a topic related to your industry, they are doing themselves a disservice by not talking to you.

Because developing this type of media reputation takes time, businesses should not expect too much too fast, and give up on PR too soon. Like any other marketing strategy, PR is an on-going process. You have to do more than get one article in one magazine to make your name a household word in the households that count.

"Don't take rejection personally," says Mora. "Remember that when the media says 'no' to one of your suggestions, they're only saying 'no' to that specific idea, not to your business. They are only saying that what you are presenting to them is not the right fit at that time. The key is persistence. The more PR you pursue, the more you get your name in front of the media, the easier it becomes."

campaigns come with no such control. In particular, you have no say in the message as it actually appears in the media, or even if it will appear.

Even if you attract a reporter's attention and find yourself guiding an interview, in the end reporters print what they think makes for a good story. This does not diminish PR's place as an important investment in your slightly famous marketing strategy, but you do have to understand that results are inconsistent. Experienced practitioners who master PR may get better percentages, but they never achieve 100 percent.

The Media Need You

The world is a big place. Because the scope of what constitutes news is so vast that no media outlet could possibly know about every topic worth covering, they rely on public relations efforts from all kinds of sources, including businesses, to help them spot interesting news stories. People just like you help shape the news because editors and reporters need inside tips, specialized knowledge, and the unique story ideas that come from small businesspeople.

Although many of the stories you read in the papers have been generated by reporters through investigation and research, many others are generated by PR practitioners who have pitched their story to the media.

In the book *Targeted Public Relations,* Robert W. Bly cites a study conducted by the *Columbia Journalism Review* that analyzed a single issue of the *Wall Street Journal* to determine the influence of public relations on the stories that got published. The survey found 111 stories were taken from press releases, and in only 30 percent of the stories did reporters put in additional facts not contained in the original press release.

There are numerous ways for your small business to get coverage. You can, for instance:

- alert the media to story ideas within your industry
- position yourself as an industry expert or commentator
- organize and promote a public event
- tie your business to current issues
- write articles for trade publications
- showcase an unusual aspect of your business

If you offer a story of genuine interest, even if only to a limited segment of readers or viewers, you are newsworthy.

Partnering with the Media

Although PR is free, it is not "free advertising." Reporters are loyal to accurate reporting and genuinely good stories. The secret to success is positioning your business as a media partner. If you make your expertise and experience available where it's needed, you can help the media do its job while getting valuable exposure for your business.

Part of developing an ongoing relationship with the media involves being at their disposal. Because they have daily deadlines, reporters and editors are almost always in a hurry. They expect you to know this and adjust your schedule accordingly. You will be expected to make time for reporters who, at the last minute, want to interview you for a story due that day. Or you may have to make yourself available weekends or early mornings in order to get interviewed on a radio station.

Finally, there are no guarantees in the world of media relations. The media are not obligated to use your articles, interviews, or pitches in stories. This means that even though you spend time helping a journalist, you may not appear in the final story. You may write an article for a trade journal, only to have it pulled at the last minute due to space constraints. You might promote a charitable event with commitments from local television stations, only to have coverage pre-empted by a breaking news story.

These setbacks will happen, and there's nothing you can do about it. But editors, program directors, and journalists will remember your helpfulness. The media need you, their industry news source, because you help make their jobs possible. By being useful and putting a reporter's needs above your own, you will over time enjoy ongoing media exposure and the benefits it provides.

Establishing and benefiting from a media partnership requires a new way of thinking. It's not enough to have good information; you must give the media a reason to pay attention. You must become adept at turning your business or industry expertise into focused stories with built-in media appeal. With a little knowledge and the right attitude, this is a skill you can develop.

The *Slightly Famous* Media Plan

Slightly famous PR strategies are about developing a systematic approach to marketing that embraces the media on its own terms in ways that will directly benefit your business. You need to craft a plan, consistent with your business and industry, that appeals to your market niche and supports your overall branding strategy.

If you've followed the advice of previous chapters, you've established a foundation from which to launch your *slightly famous* PR campaign. Now you need to work on becoming a mini-celebrity.

Strategic Placement

PR can be labor intensive, so it's important to fashion a media strategy that emphasizes the media outlets that reach your specific target market on an ongoing basis. Look for the centers of influence for your audience, such as trade associations or professional groups that regularly address your audience. Are your potential customers more likely to respond if they read about you in the *Daily Bugle*, a trade publication such as *Management Review*, or a chamber of commerce newsletter?

Sometimes a humble trade publication is the ideal spot to reach your best prospects. A highly specialized consulting firm might seek and get lots of coverage in its local paper, but if its customers are distributed throughout the country, and can be reached only through a trade publication, the effort is wasted. Slightly famous marketers are never seduced by media coverage for its own sake. They do not measure success in column inches, but rather by how much their reputation is spread and enhanced among the right people.

Effective use of the media means reaching the right people with the right message.

A Continuous Effort

Because it is central to your slightly famous marketing plan, media relations need to be integrated into your everyday business. Media strategies connect not just to your marketing strategy, but also to the place your business has in the life of your clients, customers, and everyone in contact with your business.

Integrating media relations into your business requires that you:

- Read everything that affects your industry
- Keep your Web site up to date with relevant information
- Keep an eye on competitors' marketing and PR efforts
- Talk to those in your market niche, and use their feedback
- Attend trade shows, seminars, and other events related to your market

By continually immersing yourself in the world of your customers, you can develop a sixth sense regarding PR and how it can help you maintain your reputation in your market. The more you

REAL-WORLD SUCCESS STORY

Anthony Lemme Puts New Wine in Old Bottles

Anthony Lemme, the exclusive U.S. licensee for Vacu-Vin, a $20 pump resealer of wine bottles, knew the traditional way to publicize his company would be to send press releases to the media. Instead, he pursued a strategy to get people talking about his product to such an extent that press coverage would follow. His goal was to create an irresistible buzz around his business among groups of the most likely prospects.

He planned his grassroots marketing strategy before he signed his license agreement. He organized a luncheon and wine tasting for New York City's top 20 sommeliers and wine writers. The idea was to let wine industry professionals sample wines first uncorked, then resealed with the Vacu-Vin. Lemme also started a Vacu-Vin newsletter, which he sent to all of his 175 distributors, that contained tips for success, honors for top performers, and a welcome to new members.

Lemme's efforts were a success. The most influential people in the wine world loved his product, and began spreading the word among New York's biggest wine buyers. This word of mouth made Vacu-Vin the number-one gift item in Bloomingdale's. Within the first year, Lemme had 25 manufacturers' reps, 150 distributors, and sales of around $5 million.

At that point the press was clamoring to find out about his product. Stories in *The Wine Spectator* and *Wine & Spirits* were followed by write-ups in *Good Housekeeping*, *Playboy*, and *USA Today*. "All of a sudden I was a celebrity," Lemme marveled. "It's amazing — I've got banks calling me. Believe me, banks don't usually call asking for your business."

develop a PR mindset, the more you'll see PR opportunities in your customer and client interactions, in day-to-day news and events, and in your dealings with vendors and others who affect your business.

Slightly famous marketers do not see PR as an on-again, off-again activity, nor do they expect miracles after writing an article or being quoted in a newspaper. Media strategies are dedicated not just to creating but also maintaining a visible, credible brand and reputation. This means pursuing PR with the same regularity as paying your rent.

PR is about investing for long-term results. In the same way that you shouldn't expect a small monetary investment to yield a lifetime of wealth, you should not expect a couple of media appearances to turn your business into a success overnight.

Although initial dividends may look small at first, each media appearance will add to your advantage, growing your reputation and increasing your reach.

Tell Your Story

Sometimes the most interesting business story—and the one of most interest to the media—is contained in who you are or how you conduct your business.

"*You* are the news!" says Jill Lublin, co-author of *Guerilla Publicity*. "In public relations, your job is to define and communicate your business in a way that has built-in media appeal. Many times, that can be as simple as presenting your business in light of what you do or how you got there."

Lublin tells about a client with a lackluster job title. "He was an industrial designer—a label that wasn't very exciting," says Lublin, "but it turned out that he ran a very successful company as a virtual corporation. So we presented him to the media as an expert on virtual corporations. This angle proved to be interesting from a media perspective, and caught the attention of several national and local newspapers, and radio and television stations."

You can also gain amazing results by using a personal narrative to humanize your business. Did you overcome challenges that can be directly related to the success of your company? Are you on a personal mission to make the world a better place using your business as a tool? You see stories of this kind in the papers every day, but they always draw readers because they contain a human element.

REAL-WORLD SUCCESS STORY

Steve Mariotti Demonstrates the Power of a Personal Narrative

Two decades ago, Steve Mariotti was on top of the world. He'd received his M.B.A. from the University of Michigan School of Business, had completed a successful stint at the Ford Motor Company, and, yearning to be an entrepreneur, moved to New York City, where he was soon running a successful import-export business.

Then, in 1981 he was mugged by three teenagers in New York's Lower East Side. The event dramatically altered his life.

"The mugging caught me emotionally off guard," remembers Mariotti. "In the months that followed I suffered painful flashbacks. And, being an entrepreneur, I thought, 'Why would these kids rob me for a few dollars when they could make much more money running a business together?'"

He decided to directly confront the worst of inner city life; he became a teacher. While, at first, his students directed their energies to challenging his authority, their attitudes changed when he taught them how to start their own businesses. Suddenly they had an incentive to learn. Their skills and behavior improved, and their grades went up.

Mariotti left the classroom in 1987 to found The National Foundation For Teaching Entrepreneurship (NFTE, pronounced "nifty"). He used his personal experiences as a tool to help him promote NFTE and to recruit others to the cause of teaching entrepreneurship to at-risk youths. NTFE's product is a business-literate young entrepreneur who has experienced buying and selling in the marketplace, and knows how to keep accurate financial records.

NFTE programs are now established throughout the country, and the program to date has worked with over 40,000 low-income young people. Mariotti's inspiring story has played a hand in getting NFTE a lot of media coverage; both he and NFTE have been featured in dozens of major newspaper stories and television programs that have advanced his organization's agenda.

Mariotti has always used NFTE as a banner that can be carried by all who are concerned with the issues facing today's youth. He uses his own personal narrative to inspire others to join the NFTE cause, and made it a centerpiece for his book, The Young Entrepreneur's Guide to Starting and Running a Business.

"My personal narrative serves as an example and brand identity for the entire program," says Mariotti. "I came out of corporate America to do some good, and hope my story inspires others like me to do the same. If I can convince enough people to mentor kids through a NFTE-sponsored program, I'm sure we could experience an economic renaissance of amazing proportions — and possibly fix a few of society's problems at the same time."

Three Dogs, Two Guys, and One Big Media Break Catapult a Small Company to Stardom

REAL-WORLD SUCCESS STORY

Dan Dye and Mark Beckloff didn't know it at the time, but they were sitting on a media gold mine. It started when they became troubled by all the many additives and chemical ingredients in commercially available dog treats — most of them with names you couldn't even pronounce. So they set out to change the world, at least as dogs know it, when they opened the first Three Dog Bakery in 1989.

Their mission was simple: fresh-bake the world's best dog biscuits (with catchy names like PupCakes, Great Danish, and Snickerpoodles), and thereby give dog lovers everywhere healthy, all-natural treats to give their favorite four-legged friends.

Although Three Dog Bakery started as a humble operation, they learned the power of PR one fateful day in 1994 when a *Wall Street Journal* reporter stumbled upon their showroom full of doggie delights. The reporter was so impressed with the business that he wrote a major story featuring the company.

Little did they know that when the story broke a few days later, their lives would change forever. "We unlocked our bakery door that day and the phone was ringing off the hook," says partner Dan Dye. "At one point, the sheer volume of calls caused the line to go dead for a while. People were calling from all over the country, requesting biscuits, flyers, information, anything we could shove into a box and ship to them."

By the end of the first day, Three Dog was six weeks backlogged on mail orders. They were besieged with calls for almost two weeks, and soon were receiving requests for interviews from *People, Entrepreneur, The Oprah Winfrey Show, USA Today, The New York Times Magazine, National Public Radio,* and *The Tonight Show.*

Next thing they knew, the press was clawing at the chance to be the next to interview the young, self-proclaimed "entredogneurs." Naturally, when Oprah Winfrey called, the Three Dog crew jumped in excitement over the possibility of 40 million viewers getting a glimpse of their new creations.

Since then, Dan and Mark have been featured in articles in hundreds of other publications. They've also appeared on *The Today Show, Late Night with Conan O'Brien,* CNN, the BBC, NPR, PBS, and 18 thirty-minute specials aired on the Food Network.

TIPS FROM THE GURU

Alfred J. Lautenslager Asks, Will Your PR Hit a Home Run?

Many business people see marketing as a panacea to all their business woes. Some people implement marketing efforts and expect immediate results. They are misinformed. Marketing is a long-term, persistent, and consistent activity that should never end.

Another mistake made by many companies, organizations, and people is to concentrate on the marketing or PR home run — that one story, event, or customer touch that will bring a bonanza of business.

The problem with these expectations, says marketing and PR consultant Alfred Lautenslager, is that home runs aren't what usually win baseball games; it's usually a collection of singles and doubles that make for the winning score. "The same applies in business, marketing, and PR. It's the little things that make for the success of a business," says Lautenslager "Sure, you may hit a home run occasionally, but you can't go into the game expecting to win that way."

Lautenslager insists that the world of PR and marketing is mainly a game of singles. A press release here, a news conference and a feature article there — these all add up to effective communication of a company's message or brand — not any one event or one communication.

"Marketing is made up of many things. They all support one another," says Lautenslager. "They all work toward getting the job done, just like in a baseball game. Sure, there's a chance every now and then to hit that home run, but looking for it all the time is futile."

Communicating with the media often proceeds by baby steps. You have to get the word out to them about your company, product, or service. This starts the process of awareness among editors and producers of the media.

Jay Conrad Levinson of "guerilla marketing" fame speaks often about how many times a customer or prospect must be touched before he or she takes action. All these touches represent baby steps (or singles, in the baseball metaphor). Marketing is made up of many small things, and so is public relations.

"Think of all the topics you can write a press release about. Get one or two published, and you'll hear prospects and customers saying things like, 'I see you in all the papers,' or 'Every time I turn around, I see your name in print,'" says Lautenslager. "In actuality, this is only one or two publications that are working on the minds of the reader in synergistic fashion. Remember, synergy means adding the small to the small until suddenly, you have something bigger than even their sum — hitting singles to win the game, and taking baby steps to make great strides. PR and marketing work the same way."

Reprinted with permission from Entrepreneur Media, Inc., www.entrepreneur.com

Build Media Appeal

Don't underestimate the value of building media appeal into your business early on. As a slightly famous marketer, you've developed a business and brand that stands apart from others, and you've created an atmosphere of excitement, personality, and distinction for your business. Use your distinction to your advantage, attracting both prospective customers and the media, which is always in search of stories with built-in audience appeal.

Set Realistic Goals

When developing your media strategy, it's important to set appropriate goals. Though sometimes you can hit it big on the first try—and Three Dog Bakery did it without even trying—you probably shouldn't expect to make your first media splash in one of the country's top publications. These tend to be the hardest to pitch, as they receive hundreds of queries a day, many more than they could ever use. Moreover, since your goal is to reach a targeted audience as frequently as possible, you can seek out smaller media outlets, and thereby avoid competing against billion-dollar firms and highly paid PR practitioners.

CHAPTER 5

Attracting Media Attention

While your *slightly famous* media strategy needs to be customized to suit your business and circumstances, certain techniques underlie every effort. This chapter focuses on ways you can create media opportunities, based on a knowledge of how the media work. As with any task, when you know how to approach the job, you're going to get better results.

Building a Media File

The first step in any media campaign is to identify the media outlets, and the key people within those organizations, that reach your target market. The goal is to build a list of newspapers, magazines, newsletters, and radio and television programs where you want coverage.

Your research can begin by asking your clients and customers what they read, watch, and listen to, and where they get news related to your industry. Follow up with a visit to your public library, and familiarize yourself with the media resources available there. The business reference section in large urban libraries will often have media directories that include information on thousands of media outlets. These directories are usually organized by industry, so you can quickly find the media that address your customers. There are also directories that include industry-specific newsletters, professional organizations, and trade associations. You can, of course, purchase any of these directories, but they are expensive.

A few of the most comprehensive directories that should meet most of your publicity needs:

Bacon's Media Source: Bacon's is the bible of the PR industry, providing detailed information on more than 450,000 editorial contacts at nearly 70,000 print, broadcast, and Internet media outlets in the U.S., Canada, Mexico, and the Caribbean.

This multi-volume set provides listings of newspapers, magazines, newsletters, and radio and television outlets, organized by geographic region and industry focus.

Burrelle's: Burrelle's is another popular multi-volume media directory that provides a comprehensive list of print and broadcast media in this country. Although it overlaps with Bacon's, Burrelle's includes many smaller publications that can be useful for your media campaign. Each of the entries for the 300,000 media contacts and 60,000 media outlets listed includes addresses, telephone and fax numbers, e-mail addresses, and Web site URLs where available. Individual volumes within the set include *Daily Newspapers; Non-Daily Newspapers; Radio, Television and Cable; Magazines;* and *Newsletters.*

Writer's Market: This book contains listings for 8,000 magazines that accept freelance article submissions. Available in most bookstores and at www.writersdigest.com, this media directory is valuable for targeting publications that accept (and usually pay for) articles written by outside contributors.

Encyclopedia of Associations: Most businesses should include associations and their newsletters in their media list. *The Encyclopedia of Associations* lists over 81,000 nonprofit, professional, and trade organizations worldwide. Entries contain complete contact information and detailed data on their membership, budgets, purposes, activities, services, organizational structure, affiliates, publications, and convention/meeting activities.

As you do your research, you'll probably be amazed at the number of tightly focused publications that cater to specialized business categories and interests. Get to know your reference librarian, one of the most under-appreciated information resources in the world, and ask him or her to help you locate resources.

Even if you serve only a local market, don't limit yourself to local media. Include publications with a national audience on your media list, and look for opportunities to be quoted in national publications. Even though such media exposure may not lead to direct sales, it can help establish your credibility.

Study the Markets

Once you've compiled the names of potential media outlets, get to know at least a few of the most promising first hand. If they're available locally, buy a few on newsstands, or you can call the editorial offices and request a sample copy and an editorial calendar, which lists the themes of upcoming issues. Create a file area for publications and related media materials, and keep it up to date.

Once you've identified the media outlets that seem appropriate for your business, get the names of key people at each. These are the people on the editorial/news side of the media, the reporters, editors, producers, and writers, not the advertising sales reps or publishers who deal with the business side of a media organization. Look up articles written in the past year or so by their top reporters to learn the specific subject areas they cover, and to better understand their interests and special angles. Pay special attention to those that cover your industry on a regular basis.

Familiarize yourself with broadcast radio and television programs on your list. Listen to programs relevant to your industry to understand their format, and to pinpoint particular programs or segments where your business story might fit. Having studied the media, you will have a better idea about who to approach with what kind of story.

Press Kits and Media Materials

Before approaching the media for any kind of story, you should assemble an introductory package about your business—in other words, a press kit.

Depending on your business and the image you want to convey, the kit can range in elaborateness from a folder with expensive color materials to a simple sheaf of materials paper clipped together. In any case, it should include the following:

- company background information
- news releases with current information about your business
- biographies of company principals
- a simple, one-page summary "fact sheet" about the business
- a sheet of FAQS—sample questions and answers to a mock interview
- photos of you or your business
- articles that you have written, if any
- customer references and testimonials
- a list of past media coverage with samples

A good rule is to keep press kits simple, including just enough information to introduce the media to you and your business, provide necessary background, and make a good impression. Keep in mind that you'll be sending your press kit only on request; a kit sent to a reporter or editor whose interest hasn't already been aroused will probably wind up in the wastebasket.

With the Internet becoming just about universally available, online press kits are becoming more and more popular. An online kit contains the same items you'd find in a traditional press kit, but comes in browsable form, in an area of your Web site called an online pressroom.

Because journalists have the freedom to help themselves in an online press room at their own pace, you should include all kinds of additional material: articles about your company that have run in the media; white papers; company position papers and statements to the press; industry statistics; a company directory with contact information. It's common practice to make many of the extra materials available in an easily printable format, such as Adobe's popular PDF.

Positioning Yourself as an Expert Resource

Journalists rely on good quotes from experts to make their stories lively and interesting. Quotes lend authority to their discussion, and provide a real-world connection to audiences. Being quoted in one story increases the chances that other reporters will recognize your expertise and call you for similar stories. Quotes beget more quotes. Once a reporter is convinced that you have knowledge that can help him write a better story, your name will come up whenever he's looking for a certain kind of information.

Shel Horowitz, a PR consultant, speaker, and author of *Grassroots Marketing*, has been quoted in hundreds of news articles in publications including *Fortune, Small Business, Women's Day,* and *Entrepreneur.*

"The more you develop a reputation as a great interview source, the more journalists will seek you out," says Horowitz. "The more you get your name out there, the more you begin to establish a reputation within the press as a subject-area expert. Because journalists are under severe times restrictions, they value great interview sources, and will seek you out when you prove that you are one of those people.

"One thing people need to know is that the power of publicity doesn't always lie in the *New York Times*. Some of the best publicity is in local weeklies and trade publications, which are easy to break into, and then set the stage for bigger opportunities," says Horowitz. "For me, ongoing publicity has served as a credibility builder. When I say to clients that I've been interviewed in the *LA Times*, or the *Christian Science Monitor*, or the *Boston Globe*, it lets them know that I'm a serious contributor to my industry."

This is the position you want, and it's not difficult to achieve. Following are some helpful techniques for letting the media know that you are available as an authority on a particular subject.

Introduce Yourself

Writers, reporters, and producers cultivate relationships with outside experts. You can become one of these experts by letting the right people know that you exist and making a compelling case for your expertise.

The process begins with you identifying the media professionals most likely to need your expertise—for instance, journalists who regularly write about your industry, or consumer action reporters who might want information on products like yours. Introduce yourself and your qualifications as an expert, and offer to be of help when they write articles in your subject area. You can mention that you'd like to alert them from time to time to potential news stories about your industry.

Approach them as you would a new client, conveying the message, "I am here to solve one of your problems; your readers need this specific kind of information, and I have it." Send that message repeatedly.

Above all, editors and reporters must find you credible. If a reporter is receptive, send a press kit that shows you have the knowledge you say you do, and that you have a reputation for doing outstanding work.

How to Give a Great Interview

You've been asked to give an interview for a story related to your industry. Great! But to be effective, you must take a little time to prepare.

Have — and Stick to — an Agenda

Don't go into any media opportunity without a clear plan for what you want to get out of it. Although you must help the media do its job, don't ever forget that your main goal in your media appearances is to make them work to your advantage. Outline the messages you want to convey. Make sure your interview positions your business in a way consistent with your brand identity, while providing the information likely to get you included in the article.

Although a journalist will set the pace of the interview, you can assume a measure of control by being prepared with the information that you want to convey. Create an outline you can refer to as the interview takes place. Thorough pre-interview preparation will help you stay on track and remember the points you want to get across.

Background Research

Find out as much as you can about the media outlet, the reporter, and the particular story before you give your interview. Have they covered your business and its issues before? Who else will they be talking to for this story? How long will the interview be? Ask to receive a list of sample questions to help you better prepare for the interview.

Ask the reporter ahead of time to describe the nature of the interview. Offer a list of questions to the reporter that you think should be covered; a brief e-mail will do. Then prepare your answers, and have your notes in writing before you when the reporter calls.

Speak Quotably

It's not enough to have information; you must also learn to speak in a way that makes you worth mentioning. You must be able to express yourself succinctly and memorably. Practice condensing your key points into brief, clear sentences. A good quote ensures that you get mentioned in the final story. The better you become at speaking quotably, the more journalists will want to call you.

In addition, the better prepared you are prior to the interview, the easier it is to speak quotably. Anticipate questions and practice your responses. Reporters tend to look for clear, direct statements; they don't have room to print fully developed or carefully modified arguments. Speak in positive statements. Take a stand.

At the same time, don't feel obliged to fill "dead air." Pause to think before you answer. Be conversational and avoid professional jargon. Keep your message simple. Speak in terms that even somebody not familiar with your industry can understand. Most important, unleash your enthusiasm. If you don't seem to care about what you're saying, no one else will either.

Don't Pretend to Know Something You Don't

Always stick to your area of expertise. Don't feel obliged to answer questions if you're not qualified. If you don't know the answer, you can offer to find out and get back to the reporter before his deadline. If you know someone else with the information, or where the answer is to be found, say so.

Pitching Your Story

Editors are gatekeepers charged with allowing only newsworthy stories, meaning those of interest to their readers, to pass through the gate. They hate public relations efforts that simply seek to promote companies and have no inherent news value. On the other hand, if you can offer reader-centered information and a unique story angle, your public relations efforts will be successful.

To repeat, pitching stories to the media begins by seeing your business from the media's perspective. Only when you learn to align your business interests with the media's interests—typically, by coming up with a new angle on your subject—will the media want to consult you, quote you, and write about your business.

There are plenty of ways to prove to the media that your business deserves their coverage, but all of them begin by answering the simple question, "What makes this news?"

Announcements

Open houses, tours, award ceremonies, accomplishments, anniversaries, rallies, and debates all can warrant news coverage if they capture the interest of some important segment of readers or viewers. The test of whether an announcement deserves media coverage is its relevance to the interests of the specific outlet. *USA Today* may not care about events at your local accounting firm, but a local newspaper business editor would very likely be interested in an announcement that your firm is hosting a free tax-preparation seminar for local businesses.

Controversy

The media love controversy. An effective way to get media coverage is to challenge the status quo by taking a stand contrary to prevailing wisdom.

Lee Hull, a financial advisor, challenged an industry status quo when he wrote an article entitled, "Where Are All the Customers' Yachts?" Repeating the advice he gave his clients, the article, which drew a tremendous amount of attention, suggested that investors work only with financial advisors who charge on a pay-for-performance basis, rather than getting a commission on sales, as is common in the financial services industry.

Events

In the 1920s, long before smoking was linked to health concerns, the American tobacco industry realized the social taboo against women smoking in public was costing them half their potential business. They turned to Edward Bernays, sometimes known as "the father of modern public relations," for help.

In what is regarded as the first publicity stunt, Bernays arranged for women's rights marchers to parade down a New York City avenue smoking Lucky Strike cigarettes. The event was a media sensation. Dubbed the "torches of freedom contingent," the sight of hundreds of women openly smoking their symbolic "Torches of Freedom" was viewed as a victory for women's rights. Within months, women were smoking openly, and sales of Lucky Strikes soared.

Publicity events, or stunts such as grand openings and the like, can be used effectively to generate media coverage. You can make your event newsworthy by tying it to a current event or holiday, by involving local celebrities, or, as in the case of Lucky Strikes, by connecting it to a burning social issue.

Studies, Surveys, and Statistics

The media love stories supported by studies, surveys, and statistics. If you can provide this kind of information about your industry, you can easily get attention.

The American Association of Advertising Agencies, for example, in a report called *Advertising in a Recession*, cited a number of studies that show a strong correlation between sustained spending on advertising, even in a recession, and increased market share. The report was cited widely in newspaper, magazine, and online articles.

Similarly, Biz Rate, an Internet e-commerce rating service, conducts surveys on various Internet retailing issues throughout the year. They announce their findings in press releases, offer statistics and background findings for free, and make themselves available to the media to answer questions about e-commerce trends.

A very different kind of business using the same strategy, PGT Industries, a manufacturer of custom-built patio rooms, conducted a national survey and found that 64 percent of all homeowners wished they could add a sunroom. They also found that nearly 70 percent of homeowners who currently have sunrooms consider them "extremely important" living spaces. Here's the core of a news story that could easily find its way into the real estate or family living section of a newspaper.

As a source of reliable statistics, you are a quotable media source. Outplacement firm Challenger, Gray & Christmas exploits this opportunity thoroughly by regularly performing studies on employment in the United States, and sharing their findings with the media. As a result, company spokespeople are frequently asked by major newspapers and magazines to comment on employment trends.

Timely Tie-Ins

Relating your business to breaking news or current issues can be especially effective. In the summer of 2001, media attention was on California's then-critical energy crisis. Solardyne, a Portland-based company that sells solar and wind power equipment, seized the moment by sending out a news release with the heading, "Energy-Strapped Consumers Take Another Look at Solar, Wind Alternatives."

Parenting expert Caron Goode, author of *Nurture Your Child's Gift*, wrote a short article called "What Harry Potter Can Teach Parents About Kids" shortly after the movie *Harry Potter and the Sorcerer's Stone* was released. The article was picked up by a number of media outlets because of the timely tie-in and clever angle.

The more you look for connections, the more you'll see them. You need to make a habit of looking at current events and asking, "How can I hook onto that?"

The Pitch Letter

Whether you're looking for a story on a particular topic, hoping to be interviewed, or suggesting coverage of an industry issue or trend, editors, reporters, and producers will expect you to present your ideas in writing in the form of a pitch letter. Like a sales letter, a good pitch letter will reduce a story to its bare-bones essentials, demonstrate the topic's inherent news value, and inspire a reader to ask for more.

Rules for the Pitch Letter

A pitch should be brief—no more than a page—conversational, upbeat, and confident. It should also include the basic information reporters need to follow up: how to set up an interview, for example, or request a sample product. It should also communicate how the proposed story will appeal to the media's audience.

Following are some important elements of a good pitch letter. (PR professional B.L . Ochman provides more details in her *Tips from the Guru*, below.)

REAL-WORLD SUCCESS STORY

B.L. Ochman on How to Write Effective Pitch Letters

I've been a publicist for the past 20 years and I'm going to share a trade secret with you. I haven't sent out a traditional press release in the last 10 years, but I have placed stories about my clients in the *Wall St. Journal, New York Times, ABC News, The Today Show, Good Morning America,* and just about every major media outlet on the planet.

Editors surely don't need me or any other publicist to write their stories. They need me to point them in the direction of a good story, succinctly give them the facts and sources, and then get out of the way so they can write their own stories. I do those things by writing pitch letters, damn good ones. Here are some guidelines I recommend.

Say Why You Are Writing

Begin with your reason for writing; for example, "I am writing to suggest a story about . . ." or "I'd like to recommend an interview with . . ." Too many times the reason for the letter is hidden several paragraphs into the letter. Editors are busy. If you don't give them an immediate reason to keep reading, you've lost them.

Explain Your Premise in No More Than Two Sentences

Explain what makes your idea newsworthy. Why is this a good person to interview or a good story to cover? Describe your idea's relevance to current events — its connection to an existing trend, or a coming one — or the likelihood that it will interest a broad cross section of the audience.

Explain Your Story Idea in One or Two Paragraphs

Explain how the story would work, what it involves, what role you will play in assisting the reporter.

A Strong Hook Make the first sentences of your pitch letter so interesting, and so relevant to the needs of the media outlet, that a busy editor will give your letter his full attention and read it from beginning to end. Start with your strongest material, and make it irresistible.

A journalist friend who told me he gets a three-foot stack of snail mail and over 150 e-mails a day shared this story with me. "Let me tell you about a letter that typifies the ones we journalists never finish reading. I got one the other day that started off by saying 'I've been on the *Joe Franklin Show*, this show, that show, been talked about by so and so. I've also done this and that.' The next line was 'I'm not a status-oriented person.' There were about eight more pages, but I didn't bother to read them. I just laughed, showed the letter around, and threw it away."

Timing Can Be Everything

Timing is incredibly important. Your chances improve when you can say, "This is a hot topic, and I have a great source." Let's say you're an ophthalmologist and the President is going to have eye surgery. You stand a good chance of getting a phone call for your opinion if your e-mail arrives when the reporter is looking for a resource. At other times your pitch will become a story only if it is an attention grabber. I think of it as the "hey Martha" factor; editors look for stories that would make someone say, "hey Martha, look at this!"

List Topics Your Spokesperson Can Address

If you're pitching an expert interview source, list in bullet form topics he or she can address.

Get It All into 350 Words or Less

Mark Twain said, "If I'd had more time, I would have written less." Edit. Then, edit again. Once you get reporters interested, they will ask you for more information. And then you can give them mountains of background you've researched, because another thing my reporter friend shared with me is this: most reporters hate to do research. If your Web site features a company fact sheet, management bios, relevant photos, and other articles about your company, be sure to include a URL.

A Clear Statement of Purpose Say exactly what you're offering. Are you pitching yourself as an expert interview source? Proposing a feature story about your business, products, or services? Don't make the reader guess why you're writing to him; state the purpose of your pitch letter in the first few sentences.

Relevance After presenting your strongest material in your opening sentences, your pitch letter must go on to explain why your idea is of interest to the publication's or program's audience. Highlight broader themes that relate to your story idea. A pitch letter must make a convincing case that your idea "matters" and has relevance to the media outlet in question.

The Closer State clearly how and when you'll follow up. Following up within a week or two can improve your chances. Even if you don't get a positive response, a follow-up call can elicit valuable feedback that may help the next time you pitch a story.

The Press Release

A press release is a formal announcement of something new and newsworthy—a company launch, new or enhanced products or services, or a customer milestone.

Editors have a love-hate relationship with press releases. Press releases can serve as valuable sources for story ideas. A good press release can be a lifesaver when it arrives at the right time.

On the downside, press releases are often poorly written or useless. Editors complain about having to slog through piles of misdirected press releases that have nothing to do with their publications. They also complain about press releases that arrive en masse, having been sent to thousands of media outlets in one swoop, or that are blatantly promotional pieces with no obvious news value.

"Too many businesses write poorly thought-out releases about non-news events, and wonder why editors never give them a second look," says Darryl Roberts, publisher and editor of *Wine X.* "I get so many media people that approach me with a press release without having taken the time to look at my magazine. They send completely inappropriate materials that do not in any way appeal to our readership. Then, they wonder why I don't give them any coverage."

Bill Stoller on Smashing the Myth of the Press Release

TIPS FROM THE GURU

Bill Stoller is the founder and publisher of *Free Publicity, The Newsletter for PR Hungry Businesses.* A twenty-year public relations veteran, Bill teaches entrepreneurs and small businesses how to achieve maximum publicity with minimal investment. The following comes from Stoller's article, "Smashing the Myth of the Press Release."

Somehow, the press release has taken on a magical reputation as the alpha and omega of publicity. Wanna become rich? Send out a press release. Wanna become famous? Press release. Wanna get on the cover of *Newsweek?* Press release.

Publicity "gurus" are springing up all over the Internet touting the press release as the answer to all marketing ills. Just knock out a release, mass e-mail it to journalists, sit back and wait for Oprah to call.

It's a cruel joke.

If you don't have a story to tell, your press release is utterly worthless. I'm not knocking the press release — it's an important tool. But it's just that: a tool. It's not the first thing you need to think about when it comes time to seek publicity. In fact, it's one of the last. And it's not even absolutely necessary. (I've gotten plenty of publicity with just a pitch letter, a quick e-mail, or a phone call.)

If you worship at the shrine of the press release, it's time to rearrange your priorities. Here, then, are the things that are essential for a press release in generating publicity:

1. **A newsworthy story.** It's the very basis for your publicity efforts. Without it, your press release means nothing. To learn about how to develop a newsworthy story, ask yourself, "Is my company/website/life really newsworthy?"

2. **Learning to think like an editor.** Oh, what an edge you'll have in scoring publicity over all those press-release worshippers once you learn how to get inside the head of an editor. Give an editor what he wants in the way he wants it, and you'll do great.

3. **Relevance.** Tie in with a news event, make yourself part of a trend, piggyback on a larger competitor's story, but, by all means, make your story part of a picture that's bigger than just your company. Stories that exist in a vacuum quickly run out of oxygen.

4. **Persistence.** Sending out a press release and waiting for results is lazy and ineffective. If you really believe in your story, and you believe that it's right for a particular media outlet, you need to fight to make it happen. Call or e-mail the editor to pitch your story before sending the release. If one editor says no, try somebody else. If they all say no, come back at them with a different story angle.

Editors get hundreds of press releases each week. They have one job, and it isn't to please everyone sending in a release—it's to please their readership. Knowing this, you should ask the same question of your press release that editors ask, "Will it interest our readers?"

Formatting Your Release

A press release is really a mini feature story, and should resemble in style and structure actual stories or articles that appear in the publications you are approaching. In addition, there are eight basic elements that every press release should contain.

The Release Statement The words "FOR IMMEDIATE RELEASE" should appear in all caps on the upper left of the sheet or computer screen. This lets the media know your story is current. If you have upcoming news, but want to send the release earlier, note the exact date on which it is acceptable to release the information.

Contact Information A line or two after the release statement, list the name, title, e-mail address, and telephone and fax numbers of the person you want editors and reporters to contact if they need more information. Provide home and cell phone numbers, since reporters on deadline sometimes call after business hours.

The Headline The headline is one of the most important parts of the release, and often the most difficult to write. Because it is competing with dozens of other releases, your headline must be compelling. Keep headlines short and tight. Spend some time studying the headlines in a few newspapers. The headline should appear two lines after the contact information, in boldface type.

The Dateline A dateline conveys the geographical origin of the release, and the date you make your information available to the press, for instance: "Oakland, CA, January 15, 2003." The dateline appears as the first sentence of your first paragraph.

The Lead The first paragraph of your release does a lot of work. It must provide essential information—who, what, where, when, why, and how—and present the essence of your story. A good lead anchors everything that follows, and clearly shows how your proposed story relates to its audience. A "summary lead," the most common and usually most effective technique, relates the news and how it affects people.

B.L. Ochman proposes the following helpful formula. "The lead paragraph of a release should try to state its point in 40 words or less. Of those 40 words, no more than six words should be used to describe what the company does."

Another effective lead style imitates a magazine or newspaper feature story, as in the following example.

Three-Part Series Examines Miners' Courage,
Lack of Progress on Safety

CHICAGO, Sept. 20 /PRNewswire/ — In the shadow of September 11, word on Sept. 23, 2001, of the most catastrophic mining disaster in the U.S. since 1984 went all but unnoticed. One year later, with coal mining back in the news following the successful rescue in July of nine Pennsylvania miners, the *Chicago Tribune* revisits the events that cost 13 men their lives— and the state of an industry that remains plagued by accidents and safety violations.

Body Copy You only have room for a couple of short paragraphs to develop the material introduced in your lead, so keep material in the body of your release short and relevant. Keep paragraphs short, no more than four sentences, and use subheads or bullets so that your release can be read at a glance. You can use quotes from company executives, but only if they add something essential to the story.

GMS
LAZER WORKS

*Laser
Cartridge
Remanufacturer*

*Laser
Printer
Servicing &
Supplies*

*94 Galli Drive
Suite A-2
Novato, CA
94948
415-382-6681
800-829-6264
FAX: 415-382-8218*

Media Contact: Kimberly Hathaway
Hathaway Public Relations
415.563.5972
hathawaypr@aol.com

FOR IMMEDIATE RELEASE

Everyday is Earth Day for GMS Lazer Works
Novato firm saves land by creating remanufactured toner cartridges for
Bay Area businesses

NOVATO, CA – April 1, 2000 - Everyone knows that the paperless office never happened. Paper use is on the upswing, giving rise to another industry–toner cartridges. Each year almost 150 million pounds of empty computer printer cartridges are generated in the U.S., usually finding their way to landfills. About ten years ago, an industry emerged on the heels of print industry giant Hewlett-Packard's creation of the disposable cartridge.

Today, over 48% of all the toner cartridges used in the world are remanufactured. Novato-based GMS Lazer Works was at the heart of this industry's emergence, and helps recycle the over 12 million pounds of cartridges doomed for landfills each year in California alone. Nationwide, over 75 million pounds of toner cartridge waste are saved from landfills each year, the lions share being from environmentally-aware California.

"Our business is service-based," states George Simmons, owner of GMS Lazer Works. "We are also in the print repair business, so our customers have their cartridges picked-up and delivered by a service-person at all times, usually involving a printer repair. When delivering cartridges, customers may receive a free maintenance check on their printers." Simmons notes that his customer's participation in the compatible industry isn't all about the great value-added services GMS Lazer Works provide customers. "People have a genuine desire to feel like they're making contribution to a better environment by using compatible cartridges."

Simmons and partner and wife Ann, are particularly proud of being a recipient of the prestigious WRAP [Waste Reduction Awards Program] Award in September. The WRAP Award is sponsored by the Integrated Waste Management Board of the California Environmental Protection Agency. The business community generates over 50% of the state's trash that fills landfills, this sector's contribution in waste reduction is significant. WRAP recipients like GMS Lazer Works offer a critical product and service that makes it easier for businesses to meet reduction guidelines.

GMS Lazer Works, located in Novato, California for over 10 years, provides compatible cartridges for many brands of laser printers and photo copiers. GMS Lazer Works specializes in the repair and preventive maintenance of copiers and laser printers, and offers same-day service for most calls. GMS is a member of the International Cartridge Remanufacturer's of America (ICRA). GMS offers free technical support, quantity discounts and free pick-up and delivery and to all of their customers. GMS Lazer Works serves the needs of both small and medium-to-large size businesses in the Bay Area.

-end-

For more information contact:
http://www.gmslazerworks.com

GMS Lazer Works
94 Galli Drive, Suite A-2
Novato, CA 94948

The Ending Let editors know where your release ends with either the word "end" or the symbol ###.

Honing Your Style

Well-written press materials get better results than those that are awkward, confusing, or overly complicated. Here are some additional guidelines that will improve your chances of eliciting a positive response.

Get to the Point Don't waste time clearing your throat at the beginning of your release. Skip the company introduction, and go straight to the news that makes your press release relevant. Assuming that editors will not read past the first paragraph unless it's a grabber, put your strongest material first.

One way to achieve this kind of tight writing is to practice "speaking" your main point until you can get it down to one or two clear sentences. Once you have it on paper, build your release around it.

Provide Some Flair You can give your releases a more journalistic feel—making them more like stories than advertisements—by including anecdotes, human-interest elements, and sensory images. Put a face on the facts by telling about someone who's benefited from your product or expertise.

Size Counts Against You Keep press releases to no more than one page. Write concisely, including only the most essential details. Cut out every excess word and be sparing of unnecessary adjectives. If you can't include everything on one page, attach a fact sheet. When sending press releases by e-mail, keep them no more than one screen long, eliminating the need to scroll.

Sending Your Release

Sending news releases en masse is akin to dropping leaflets out of an airplane. Although you might hit an editorial target if you throw enough press releases into the editorial wind, you waste a lot of energy and good will. Editors expect your pitch to address their needs.

If you're targeting several publications, take time to customize different versions, one for trade journals, another for business publications, another for online media, and so on. Wherever possible, go the next step, and craft each news release or pitch letter to the style and needs of the individual outlet you are sending it to.

Before you send anything, contact the publication to determine who is responsible for reading press releases like yours. Also, ask how they prefer to receive press releases—whether by mail, e-mail, or fax. This is not the time to pitch your story. Rather, just get basic contact information to ensure that your release reaches the right person in their preferred format.

While your press release may provide all the information you want to present, you can't assume that editors will read it thoroughly. This is especially true in busy newsrooms that receive hundreds of press releases every day. That's why it's important to include the kind of pitch letter discussed above. Your pitch letter is a summary of your story. When editors or journalists like what they read in your pitch letter, they can continue reading the accompanying release for a more complete treatment of your subject.

Know the Editor's Deadlines Allow enough time between when you send the release and the time you want it to appear. Publications have lead times. For newspapers and broadcast media, this can range from several days to a week. Magazine lead times are longer, anywhere from one to several months.

Keep Your Web Site Up to Date Before sending your release, make sure a journalist or editor can find further information about you and your subject on your Web site. If you are pitching a new product, update that section of your site. If the product is not important enough to be covered in detail on your own site, why should anyone write about it?

Think of yourself as a journalist's assistant. Access to sources, updated facts and figures, accurate and detailed contact information, points of view in opposition to yours—these are all things a journalist needs to do a story. Links to this kind of information on your Web site can score you big bonus points.

King, Brown & Partners Makes the News It Wants You to Read

REAL-WORLD SUCCESS STORY

King, Brown & Partners (KB&P) saw an opportunity to demonstrate their talents and gain a lot of free media exposure at the same time. As a market research firm specializing in online surveys, KB&P orchestrated a media survey during the 2000 holiday shopping season to gauge consumer online purchasing behaviors, both before and after the holiday shopping season.

The campaign and the information it generated got the media's attention. Over 30 media outlets published references to the survey findings, many times running the following press release in its entirety without changing a word.

FOR IMMEDIATE RELEASE

Brand Familiarity Vital to Online Purchasing

SAN FRANCISCO, CA, February 4. An online survey by market research firm King, Brown & Partners (KB&P) revealed that online shoppers were strongly influenced by Old Economy factors last holiday season. Findings among 1178 respondents revealed that brand familiarity and paper catalogs — mainstays of Old Economy marketing — still strongly impact online purchasing decisions.

Shoppers are willing to purchase from unfamiliar sites as long as they have a familiar brand name. A full 71% of respondents bought at sites they had never purchased from before. However, the same proportion (71%) were already familiar with the brand name and almost two-thirds (64%) felt that knowing the brand name beforehand was "very" or "somewhat" important.

Paper catalogs are an important part of the online purchasing process. A full 79% who purchased online this holiday season received a catalog in the mail from an online retailer, and 72% said paper catalogs were "very" or "somewhat" useful when making online purchasing decisions. Nearly two-thirds (62%) who received a catalog bought from the company who sent the catalog. Of those, 89% went to the site to purchase.

To obtain the complete 2000 Online Holiday E-tailing Study visit www.kingbrown.com/pressframe.htm

Following Up

Most PR professionals agree that following up after sending pitch letters and press releases betters your chances of getting coverage. Sometimes, sending a brief note offering to answer questions or provide missing information not contained in the original release is sufficient, but many times a phone call to the person who received your materials is the best bet.

Be warned, many reporters and editors, under constant deadline, do not welcome follow-up calls and may be gruff or annoyed when you reach them by phone. "Nothing sets a writer or editor's teeth on edge more than an eager voice saying, 'I'm calling to see if you got the press release we sent,'" says Esther Schindler in her article, "The Care and Feeding of the Media." "When we're in the middle of a tight deadline, the last thing we want is a phone call that contains no new or useful information whatsoever."

When you make follow-up calls, know exactly what you're going to say before you telephone the reporter. Have it written down in front of you. When you reach an editor or journalist, quickly get to the point. Ask them whether they are on deadline, and if they can spare a moment. Use your instincts. If the reporter sounds rushed, ask when you should call back.

When you reach the right person, remind them who you are and what you sent, and offer to answer any questions they may have. If a reporter rejects your story idea, ask if he or she can recommend someone else who might be interested. When a media outlet responds positively to your pitch letter or press release, send a thank-you note.

Going It Alone Versus Hiring Outside Help

If you're a small business owner single-handedly dealing with all facets of your operation, you might want to consider outsourcing some or all of your PR work. One advantage of working with an out-side PR firm or professional writer is that you can put together a publicity plan for your business and know that it will actually get carried out.

Professional PR firms often work on a monthly retainer that cov-ers a certain level of service, such as a preset number of press releases to be sent on your behalf. But full-service PR firms can be costly, and their results, and the degree of personal attention your small business can expect from them, are sometimes questionable.

Between the extremes of doing everything yourself and hiring a large, expensive firm, it is possible to find independent professionals and small firms willing to work on a project basis. There are also plenty of freelance writers and publicity consultants who can be hired for less money than a full-service firm.

6 Getting an Article into Print

Early in my career, I wrote an article about how to publish articles as a marketing strategy for small businesses. It took only a few hours because I knew the subject intimately, and the results were incredible.

Almost immediately after it was published, I landed a new client, was invited to submit two proposals, and added dozens of names to my mailing list. I reprinted the article as a newsletter, made copies for my marketing kit, and posted it on related Web sites. I later republished the article with minor revisions in other publications, including *SPAN* (a newsletter for book publishers), *Dynamic Business* (a Pennsylvania business journal), *Opportunity World* (a business opportunity magazine), and several others.

Years later, the benefits continue to roll in as prospects read my article on the Internet, recommend it to associates, and hire my firm because I'm an "expert" in targeted public relations strategies. In one instance, a reader who later became a client requested a proposal from my company, even though her company had almost finalized a decision to hire a competitor. "We came across your article, and it made all the difference," they said. "We knew from your article that you could help us."

Not every article you publish will hit the jackpot, but once you start getting your name in print on a regular basis, you'll reap many benefits. An article published in your name gives you instant credibility because it's editorial matter—not advertising—and hence carries the endorsement of the publication in which it appears. Articles help you get taken seriously and attract prospects, sometimes—as in the incident I described above—delivering them right to your door. As an added bonus, article reprints make excellent marketing materials.

You don't have to be a professional writer or seasoned journalist to get your name in print. Whether you're a management consultant or a masseuse, publishing articles under your byline can do wonders for your business. And with more than 10,000 publications in print today, your opportunities are virtually unlimited. You can do it.

Publications Need You

From fillers to features, most magazines you see on newsstands every day rely on freelance writers for at least some of their content. No, you don't have to have a cousin in the publishing world to see your name in print. You just have to learn and follow the same rules as journalists, and one day editors will be calling you.

This chapter provides a step-by-step tour of how to get your work in publications that reach your target market. Once you learn the ropes, you'll find that placing articles in publications relevant to your business is a powerful and effective way to market your services. There are thousands of business, trade, and Internet publications covering every imaginable industry and audience, and many are fairly easy to break into, even for beginners.

TIPS FROM THE GURU

Kimberly Stanséll Describes Her Marketing Mix

Kimberly Stanséll is president of Research Done Write!, a Los Angeles-based consulting and training firm that offers workshops and seminars for entrepreneurs, especially for professional women. Stanséll has written two books, several articles, and a syndicated column, "Bootstrappers' Success Secrets." Since 1992 she has been a noted expert on entrepreneurship, largely because of these publications.

Stanséll has written for dozens of publications, including *Home Office Computing, Entrepreneurial Edge,* and *Self-Employed Professional.* "I write articles based on information from my books, workshops, and networking experiences. As a bonus, I often get paid top dollar to write them," she says. "I've found that having three to six pieces in circulation at any time gives me consistent coverage."

Stanséll credits these articles with expanding her name recognition and promoting her book. "At conferences, people tell me that they read about my book in *Black Enterprise,* or that they recognized it at Kinko's and bought it. I get invitations to participate in events from people who've read my columns and articles. I also get credibility. People automatically assume I'm expensive, which raises my fee even before I open my mouth."

How much of her current business comes from her articles? "It's hard for me to measure, because my publishing affects my business in different ways. The name recognition my column has given me is tremendous."

Stanséll advises that you treat your writing efforts as a component of your overall marketing strategy. "Publishing articles is just one cylinder in my marketing engine," she explains. "My business is to teach, speak, research, and write about issues that are important to entrepreneurs. The articles I write complement my other efforts to create recognition for my books, and attract teaching and speaking engagements."

Your Road to Becoming a Published Expert

Bylined, contributed articles are a mainstay in many business publications. Often written for a small fee—or given freely in exchange for an author bio or byline designed to elicit business—these articles show off the expertise of the businessperson or consultant who authored it.

Start Small

When you begin approaching publications as a potential expert contributor, be realistic. Too often, new writers expect to publish their first article in top publications like *Inc, Business Week,* or *Fast Company.* That's being as unrealistic as a baseball player who expects to bypass the minor leagues and go straight to the World Series. Many of these publications are entirely staff-written, and do not accept contributed articles.

On the other hand, there are thousands of trade, business, and special interest publications with names like *Marketing News, Pharmaceutical Executive, Bay Area Parent,* and *New Jersey Outdoors.* If your business serves the readers of these magazines, these publications want to hear from you. Editors at trade publications are more accessible to you than those at general interest publications, and because trade periodicals provide information that is critical to their readers' businesses, they are often read with intense interest.

Coming Up with Ideas

Coming up with interesting article ideas is often a struggle, but there is no reason to strain your imagination or look for something completely novel. Study your chosen publications, and determine the types of stories each of them seems to favor—then use them as starting points for your own ideas. Look for patterns, trends, and points of discussion.

Save relevant news stories as launching points and ready-made research for your articles. Gather publications that serve your target market, and look for ideas that relate to your business. Look to your own experiences and those of your colleagues and clients—there's plenty of good material all around you. Few story ideas are truly original. A new slant, an interesting angle, timeliness, and focus—these are enough to make a story publishable.

The Difference Between a Topic and a Story Idea

"I'd like to write a story about marketing" is unlikely to attract an editor because the idea is too vague. To turn your idea into a workable story, you need to narrow your topic and slant it to a particular audience. Though it may be connected to larger issues, you need to address a sufficiently narrow range of applications so that you can offer the kind of detail that will be of value to your readers.

"Employee references" is a topic; "Should Employers Be So Tight-Lipped About Former Employees?" is a story idea. To turn a topic into a magazine article requires focus. A 500-word article, for example, requires a laser-sharp focus on one tiny aspect of a subject. A 2000-word article could have a somewhat wider focus, but still needs to be specific.

Take an imaginary walk around your subject the way you would walk around a building. Look at it from a variety of angles and perspectives, and think about how you can slant it according to the demands of different audiences and publications. Editors evaluate an idea by deciding how well it fits their particular publication. No matter how strong your idea or how well you write about it, if it doesn't meet an editor's needs, he or she won't buy it.

How to Study a Publication

Do your homework before you start pitching ideas to editors. Contact magazines and request a sample issue. This is not the time to pitch your ideas! Ask for their writer's guidelines (policies for contributing writers), an editorial calendar (a schedule of editorial topics for upcoming issues), and an index of previously published articles.

Look at a few copies of the publications you've targeted. Study their style to better focus and slant your ideas. Armed with this information, you should be able to get a good sense of the magazine's style and con-

Financial Executive Editor Jeffrey Marshall Discusses the Role of Expert Contributors

TIPS FROM THE GURU

Jeffrey Marshall is the editor-in-chief of *Financial Executive* magazine, the flagship publication of Financial Executives International (FEI). The magazine provides senior financial executives with financial, business, and management news, and with trends and strategies that help them work better, faster, and smarter. Marshall regularly has businesspeople contributing articles to his publication. His advice should be helpful to anyone who wants to work with a trade journal or magazine.

Can you discuss the role of expert contributors at Financial Executive?

Experts play a larger role at *Financial Executive* than at many business publications for one obvious reason: they will write articles for free, a major consideration for a publication with a small budget that simply cannot afford to pay freelancers to fill the magazine. Additionally, business experts bring specific expertise that is targeted and often very useful, especially for complex areas of accounting, tax, and corporate finance.

In your experience, what value do expert contributors bring to the table?

Expert contributors bring depth of field, focus, and, yes, expertise. Ideally, they are current on the latest nuances in their field, and also bring a historic perspective — often knowing what was happening five years ago or 15 years ago. Also, they know the hot buttons in their subject area better than anyone outside it.

What are some things that expert contributors do, in general, that needs improvement?

Most of the time, expert contributors don't have the sophisticated style of full-time writers or the ability to craft a thesis that draws readers into their article. Their phrasing is often formal or clunky, and the organization of their material may be weak. As a result, some articles run considerably longer than they should. The bottom line is that expert contributors should work on being decent writers, or get help.

Also, company experts need to steer clear of talking about their company and how well they do things. Business magazines don't want commercial sales pitches disguised as editorial matter.

TIPS FROM THE GURU

Gordon Burgett on How to Look at a Publication

Gordon Burgett, author of *Sell & Resell Your Magazine Articles*, offers the following advice on how to study publications and approach them with saleable ideas.

Read closely each article in recent issues of the publication you are targeting. As you read the articles, study how they address the basic working questions of who, what, why, where, when, and how. Put yourself in the writer's shoes. How did the writer slant the subject to appeal to the magazine's readers?

Study how the writer carries the main theme through the article. Study the writer's use of facts, quotes, and anecdotes. List every source used, including direct references and quotations. Ask yourself where the writer might have found the facts, opinions, and quotes that are not clearly identified by source in the article.

Concentrate on the lead. How long is it, in words or sentences? Does it grab your interest? Does it make you want to read more? Why? How does it compare with other leads in that issue? Look throughout the article at the transitional words and sentences, and see how the overall article structure ties the treatment together. Is the subject treated chronologically, developmentally, by alternating examples, or just point by point?

How does the article end? Does it tie back to the lead? Does it repeat an opening phrase or idea? The conclusion should reinforce and strengthen the direction that the article has taken. Does it? How? Finally, look at the title. How well does it describe the article that follows? What technique does it use to make the reader want to read the article?

tent. This will put you in a much better position to develop and pitch appropriate story ideas. Remember, the quickest way to turn off editors is to pitch an idea that has nothing to do with their magazine.

Selling to Editors

As a rule, professional writers try to sell an idea before they do the writing; they don't develop an article and send it scattershot to all the magazines they think might be interested. Why not? Because editors want to have input that will help shape the stories they assign. A query letter starts a dialogue between you and the editor that will hopefully land you an assignment; that is, a request for an article of a certain kind and length on a specified topic with a particular slant.

As a matter of policy most magazines do not accept and will not read completed manuscripts because they just don't have the time to look at materials submitted outside their regular ways of working. A query letter saves everyone time. An editor will not have to read a lengthy manuscript that might not be right for the magazine, and you don't spend hours researching and writing an article that may never see the light of day.

The Query Letter

You need to sell to editors just as you would to any client. You do this with a query letter—a mini-proposal that sells your article idea before you write the article. It also sells you, the writer, as someone qualified to deliver on your promise. In some ways like cold calls, they are, nevertheless, the best way to solicit writing assignments from editors who don't know you.

On any sales call, the first moments are the most important. Your query letter is all an editor knows about you. Many good article ideas get rejected because an editor sees nothing in the presentation that says the writer is up to the job. You need to put your best writing into your query letter.

A good query letter presents the facts in a conversational tone with just a hint of formality. Pretend you are telling your story idea to a friend who is slightly senior to you. Avoid exaggeration, but if you have special knowledge of the topic, mention it. If you have a perspective other writers might not have, say so.

Following are some basic guidelines for writing a letter that will sell you and your idea.

The Lead In journalism, a "lead" is a short summary that introduces a news story or magazine article. Also known as an opening, intro-

REAL-WORLD SUCCESS STORY

An Interview with Lisa Tomaszewski, Magazine Editor

Lisa Tomaszewski is the assistant editor of *Physician's Money Digest*. She regularly works with expert contributors, and values their contributions. She also offers advice on how best to work with publications like hers.

Why are expert contributors important to you?

They are an invaluable resource to our readers and a cost-effective way for us to continue providing quality editorial. Many readers even take the next step and contact our contributors for more information or to employ their services.

Are there things that contributors could improve upon?

They need to write helpful articles that provide a lot of useful information, not advertisements for their company. While I understand that expert contributors are motivated by getting a free "plug" in our publication, there's nothing more frustrating than receiving articles that are mere advertisements for the writer's firm, and leave out crucial information to "tease" readers into contacting them.

I once had an estate planning article submitted that said, "You can be hit with an 80 percent estate tax . . . if you want to know how, please contact our firm." Statements like this get cut, or we pull the article from the publication entirely.

Furthermore, an article that provides incomplete information can do more harm than good to our readers. Novice investors may read the "80 percent estate tax" article and take drastic, and potentially illegal, steps to protect themselves. Authors who leave out information are not only a detriment to our readers, but also themselves. No one is going to pursue advice or service from someone whose only concern is their own profit.

duction, or hook, the lead is a paragraph or series of paragraphs that have been carefully constructed to capture and hold reader interest. The lead anchors the central theme, thesis, or organizing principle of an article. A lead must:

- answer the questions who, what, why, when, where, and how
- introduce the article's topic, focus, and slant
- arouse interest, making an editor want to read on

What constitutes a good approach to writing contributed articles?

There are several qualities that "ideal" writers possess. They first take the time to understand the magazine's style and audience. Are they experienced? Will you need to explain concepts to them? For example, you shouldn't use terms like P/E ratio or FICO Score if the magazine's audience doesn't know what they are. My magazine is a finance magazine written for doctors, so the content has to be explanatory, just as a medical article written for brokers would have to be written in "layman's terms."

Good writers also turn in copy that is clear, concise, grammatically correct, and conforms to the style of the magazine. They're willing to crack open that grammar book. Don't count on editors to catch your mistakes; if you do, it will not reflect well on your abilities. If you feel that your writing skills aren't up to scratch, but you still want to submit your ideas, either take a writing course at a local college or hire a PR firm to do the writing for you.

Ideal writers also need to be independent; that is, they don't need to have their hand held throughout the submission process. There's nothing more infuriating than a writer calling me ten times asking me pointless questions about their 500-word article. I edit over 50 articles per issue, twice a month; I don't need every author calling me about irrelevant details. In sum, an ideal contributor will follow instructions and submit a clean, proofread copy on time.

Finally, focus on the reader's opportunity to learn from you, rather than the opportunity for you to sneak in an advertisement. I can't stress this enough. Readers can tell when you are trying to sell them something; this strategy always backfires (not to mention the fact that editors will cut your advertising efforts and you may not be asked to submit again). When your article is published it will reach many eager readers, and you want to appear to be a teacher, not a salesperson.

- present your strongest material at the beginning

Your lead needs to be good enough to distract editors from their daily concerns and make them give their full attention to your idea. You want them to finish the letter and think, "Yes, here's an article that would work for us, and a writer we can trust to write it appropriately."

Write the lead in the same style as the article you're proposing. It can, in fact, double as the first paragraph of the article when you get the assignment. A lead is a stage setter, conveying the tone, style, and voice of the article. Your lead will resonate throughout your query, and eventually your article, as the central principle that holds everything together.

An "anecdotal lead" opens with a short account of an incident or situation that supports, illustrates, or embodies the main point of the article topic you are proposing. Highly popular because they engage our feelings as readers, anecdotal leads are built around a miniature story—for example:

> As Joe Smith watched a tow truck pull his mini van from the driveway of his suburban home, he was speechless, unable to explain to his daughter how he would take her to school from now on. He had lost everything—his house, car, and self-respect. Joe is one of thousands of people each year forced into bankruptcy after overextending themselves in a culture of easy credit.

"Hard fact" leads are packed with statistics, information. They get a reader's attention by revealing a hidden opportunity or danger. Because it is grounded in fact, this kind of lead feels substantial and compelling. When done correctly, readers feel the relevance of the information, and keep reading to find out what they need to do about it. Here's a fact-based lead:

> Did you ever wonder where your tax dollars go? As a small business owner, you should want to see some of them coming back to you. Each year the government sets aside $210 billion in contracts for goods and services, resulting in many millions in procurements daily—all of it up for bid by America's businesses. Federal, state, and local governments need businesses of all types and sizes to provide the goods and services necessary to run the country. Why can't your business be one of them?

A "news peg" is another way to start a query or an article. This is simply some interesting news item on which you can hang the story. Even if you have a story idea that would tie into a topic with a longer shelf life, such as an ongoing political saga or crisis, you might be able to tap into current events in a way that improves its chances of getting accepted.

Alternatively, you can jump right into your subject matter with a "strong statement lead." This can work well if your topic is something your reader is already familiar with. Here's a sample:

> Let's face it—politics is about money. Whoever gives the most stands to gain the most. The average American may give a few bucks here and there to his favorite candidates, but that's small potatoes compared to how much the average corporation shells out every election cycle, both directly and indirectly.

This "point/counterpoint" lead presents a statement of fact, then contradicts it with an opposing fact. The state of tension established between the two then becomes the subject of the article.

> In the 1990s, the home became a hotbed of business activity, combining lifestyle choices, entrepreneurship, and significant profits and revenues. The SBA estimates that home businesses now account for over 50% of all firms in the United States, and generate over 10% of the nation's Gross Domestic Product. But even as more home businesses dot the economic landscape, most continue to face the burdens of local zoning and use restrictions in residential neighborhoods, turning many home-based businesses into underground outlaws.

Just as its name implies, the "atmospheric" lead invokes an image or feeling. This type of lead is especially effective for human-interest stories where the purpose is to generate an emotional response from readers.

Phang-Nga Bay, the idyllic, 400-kilometer body of water off the Andaman Sea in southern Thailand, is one of the great natural wonders of Southeast Asia. It offers warm, emerald green waters, plenty of equatorial sun, and an occasional fisherman casting a net from a long-tail boat. Declared a national park in 1981, the area became famous after the James Bond adventure, *The Man with the Golden Gun*, was partly filmed there, and has since become a favorite destination for outdoor enthusiasts.

Create a Framework You've captured an editor's attention with a powerful lead. Don't let up. Your second paragraph must keep an editor reading, expanding the promise of the first paragraph and placing your idea into a larger contextual framework, as in the following example:

> *Communication with the Click of a Mouse—*
> *How to Start Your Own E-mail Newsletter*

Terry Alton, principal of Computer Wizard in Lincoln, Nebraska, is a popular guy. Each month 5000 people from all over the country await "PC Secrets," his monthly e-mail newsletter of computer tips directed at small business owners. Unlike other consultants who constantly seek new business from strangers, Alton gets himself all the business he can handle without spending a penny on printing, mailing, or advertising.

E-mail newsletters (or e-zines) are an effective tool to help small businesses keep in touch with their clients, customers, and prospects. The overriding goal of e-zines is to provide readers with useful information on a regular basis that creates a win-win situation—readers get news they can use, e-zine publishers establish good will and credibility—an ongoing gesture that builds a bridge for future sales.

Use the third paragraph to explain how you intend to tailor your idea to the needs of the publication. Here's where you discuss the slant and focus of your topic.

In the fourth paragraph talk about your expertise as it relates to the article. Discuss your credentials. Mention sources of information you will use. Be prepared to discuss opposing opinions. List any writings you've published. (If you haven't published before, skip that part.) An exceptional query letter can compensate for lack of experience.

Finally, sign off gracefully. A one-word sign-off statement will suffice: "Interested?"

Sample Query Letter

Query: Barter—Cashing In on an Old Idea

Robert Pritikin, owner of the Mansions Hotel in San Francisco, was having a bad day. His finely plumed macaw had taken sick in the hotel lobby. He needed lots of props for the "miraculous snowstorm," part of the evening's magic show. His magicians needed to be paid. And, to top it off, there was a plumbing leak in the restaurant.

As usual, Pritikin relied on bartering, an idea as old as civilization, to handle these business needs. Through a simple phone call to his barter exchange, Pritikin obtained a veterinarian, props for his magic show, compensation for his employees, and emergency plumbing service—all without spending a dollar in cash.

By definition, bartering is any cashless trading of goods or services. But it's far more sophisticated today than when our ancestors traded chickens for horseshoes; today's savvy business people are, with the help of barter exchanges, swapping hotel rooms for printing, paging services for computer repairs, and advertising space for timeshare condos in the Caribbean.

Part accountants, part matchmakers, today's barter brokers bring their members new business. As a business activity, barter is huge. According to Tom McDowell of the National Association of Trade Exchanges, there are between 400 and 600 barter exchanges in the United States, with over a quarter million members generating the equivalent of billions of dollars in trade revenue each year.

I would like to write a feature article explaining the benefits of barter exchange membership to your readers. I will define bartering: how it started, what it entails, and how it can be used to boost profits. I will explain the basics of barter exchange membership, provide quotes from national experts, and provide reports of experience from business people across the United States who have benefited from bartering.

I am a writer and marketing consultant based in San Francisco. I have been involved with four different barter organizations over the past four years. I am intimately acquainted with the barter industry, and understand the considerations small businesses face when joining an exchange. I have enclosed some previous clips and a SASE for your response.

Interested?

Steven Van Yoder

Submitting Your Query Letter Since your query letter is supposed to be the beginning of a relationship, don't come off like a door-to-door salesman by sending anonymous "Dear editor" letters. Direct your letter to the right editor by calling to inquire which editor handles topics like yours, and make sure you have the correct spelling of his or her name, and the preferred delivery method.

It's also important not to send query letters to competing magazines simultaneously. Create a priority list and propose your piece to the first on the list. If the first magazine rejects it, send it to the next magazine on your list, and so on. An editor who discovers that you've been two-timing him or her will drop you forever.

Be professional in your presentation. Avoid flowery stationery or garish logos. Don't detract from your presentation by calling attention to insignificant details. Editors buy well-presented ideas, not attempts to compensate for basic weakness by ornate packaging.

It never hurts to include samples of any previously published work. The more they relate to your query letter, the better. If you don't yet have clips, just make sure your query letter is as strong as you can make it, and rely on the quality of your presentation to help you make the sale.

You've Sent Your Query Letter. Now What?

One of three things is likely to happen after you submit your query letter.

1. You will receive a go-ahead from the editor "on speculation." This means the editor likes your idea and wants you to write the article, but won't commit to publishing it until approving the completed manuscript. Your chances of getting published are excellent if your article is well written.

2. Your query is rejected. Don't take this personally. Send your query letter to the next editor on your list.

3. You hear nothing. If you have not heard from a publication after a few weeks, send a follow-up message. If after a few more weeks you still receive no reply, call the editor.

Writing the Article

Congratulations! You've sold your idea. Now it's time to gather your thoughts, incorporate the editor's feedback into your plans, and meet your deadline. The editor will give you some idea of how long the article should be, and may also provide guidelines on how to best slant and focus your article so that it appeals to his or her readership. Here are a few guidelines for writing the best possible article.

Outlines and Research

Just as you wouldn't begin building a house without a blueprint, don't begin writing an article without an outline. Without an outline writing can be tough going, an upstream swim. If your outline is complete, you can cruise downstream as you write.

A well-organized outline prevents writer's block. Inspiration goes only so far—you must take the time to get organized, either before you write, when it is much easier, or during the writing, which inevitably makes even a small writing project take twice as long and leaves you frustrated.

Some writers love research, others hate it. Whatever your inclination, writing well depends on researching well. When you have the facts in hand and understand the context of your subject, you will be able to reach out to your readers with a sense of authority.

Formulas Make Writing Easier

Outlines and research make the process of writing easier; formulas can be used to provide an instant structure for articles. Formulas are set patterns for expressing your ideas. Most articles follow one formula or another. Here are some of the easiest and most common formulas that can be applied to articles:

The List Just as it sounds, a list article presents a number of items tied together by a binding idea. "Ten Common Sales Objections" and "Eight Ways to Avoid Workplace Injuries" are examples of list articles that promise an easy grasp of a cluster of facts based on an overall theme.

The Roundup Article The roundup article gathers information around a question or a common theme, and presents it in an organized manner. This format calls for the opinions of various authorities, making the article easy to write and sell. A roundup article is like a conference on paper, bringing together a group of people to talk about a particular topic.

The Case Study Case studies provide extended examples of how someone has met a challenge, sold a product, or communicated an idea. Your own company might be the subject of a case study if you can show you helped a client solve a common business problem.

The How-To This is one of the most common formulas, and a favorite among writers, editors, and readers. Its plan is simple; show readers how to achieve something on a step-by-step basis. Examples of the how-to formula include "Ways to Include Humor in Speeches," "How to Recession-Proof Your Business," and "Strategies to Resolve Workplace Disputes."

Rights and Contracts

If you plan to reuse your work after it's published, you need to understand the basic principles of copyright before you agree to write for a publication. Here are the most common copyright arrangements between freelance writers and the publications they deal with.

First Rights When a magazine buys first rights, it purchases the right to publish the article before it appears anywhere else, and it has exclusive use of the article for the lifetime of the issue in which it appears. When that issue is no longer current, you are free to republish it in any way you choose.

One-Time Rights Under this arrangement, the publication buys the nonexclusive right to publish the piece once. The writer can sell the same article to other publications at any time.

All Rights This means you give a publication complete ownership of your article for a period defined under copyright law. Under this arrangement the publication owns the article, not you, and you'll need to get their permission for any further use of it, including publishing the article on your own Web site. Avoid this arrangement if you plan to reuse your work.

Work for Hire Under this arrangement, you sell your copyright and any claim on your article, forever. They own the copyright, and don't have to give you credit. This arrangement doesn't work as a *slightly famous* marketing strategy.

Electronic Rights More and more an issue with regard to written works that previously only appeared in print, these rights refer to the use of your words on Web sites or CD-ROMs. Many publications will want you to grant them permission to archive your article on their Web site. If you agree to this arrangement, make sure you retain the right to reuse your work in any form.

Always ask the editor whether they will be sending you a contract. It's best not to write anything before you have a signed contract that includes your copyright agreement. Use the contract template found on the Resources page of www.getslightlyfamous.com to finalize the terms of an assignment.

How to Get the Most from Your Articles

In addition to increasing your company's visibility, articles can generate immediate response from readers. Here are some techniques to maximize the results.

The Extended Byline

A byline is the author's name as it appears attached to a published article. An *extended* byline includes not just an author's name, but contact information and/or a short description of the company he or she represents. Extended bylines are common in trade and specialty publications, and if you are contributing an article for little or no money, it is a reasonable expectation.

An extended byline should be a concise but accurate profile of your company, expressing your identity and the benefits of doing business with you. Here's a byline I have used on many occasions.

GET THE WORD OUT! Communications can help you become a recognized expert in your industry. We develop, write, and place feature stories in publications read by your prospects and clients, and can help you get quoted in publications that reach your target market. Ask about our custom tailored Media Interview, Article Coaching, and Strategy Programs to help you harness the power of PR for your business at a reasonable cost. Learn more at www.getthewordout.net.

The Offer

How do you ensure that readers, who are ultimately prospects, have reason to contact you? Draw readers toward your company by offering something free— a booklet, product sample, consultation, special report, or other such enticement—related to your business. You can do this in your extended byline.

Make sure prospects feel that requesting your information will be painless, risk free, and unaccompanied by sales pressure. If possible, let prospects request information by writing or e-mail.

Marketing with Reprints

Savvy marketers get maximum mileage from their efforts by using reprints of their articles as creative marketing tools. Not only do reprints cost a mere fraction of the price of an original brochure, but they carry far more credibility. While a brochure will always be perceived as a sales piece, reprints read like news, making prospects more receptive to your marketing message.

REAL-WORLD SUCCESS STORY

How Jeff Dobkin Promotes Articles Through Self-Syndication

"Every few months, I mail out a packet of 15–20 articles to a list of 100 carefully selected magazine editors whose publications reach my audience of small business owners and direct-marketing professionals," says Jeff Dobkin, the author of *How to Market Your Product for Under $500*. "In an average month, about 10 of the editors publish one or more of my articles, which cover topics like '12 Places to Buy a Mailing List,' and '18 Marketing Assumptions That Aren't True.'" His most popular article, 'The One Evening Marketing Plan,' has appeared in over 50 magazines.

Dobkin makes the articles available for free on a non-exclusive basis to editors, the only catch being that they must include his phone, fax, and other ordering details at the end of the story. This method has paid off very well. In four years of steadily mailing out articles, he has sold more than $400,000 in books (some direct and some through bookstores). In addition, the name recognition he has earned has allowed him to increase his speaking fees to $5,000 per engagement and brought a steady stream of direct-mail copywriting and consulting clients.

"Most of the magazines running my articles are niche market trade magazines (for example, *Office Systems, Mortgage Press*), regional magazines *(Business Strategies of Eastern Ohio)*, or second-tier national publications," says Dobkin. "The two common characteristics are a willingness to run non-exclusive material, and very tight editorial budgets."

Here are more details on his approach:

Develop a list of magazines. Dobkin's first step was to build a mailing list of 300–400 publications that addressed his audience and seemed to be open to running non-exclusive how-to articles.

Here are several ways to use reprints to your advantage.

- Include reprints with proposals. You have a better chance of impressing prospects with your abilities if you are a newsmaker.

- Use reprints to keep in touch. When you publish an article, you can mail reprints to prospects, customers, and clients. Again, you can do this at a fraction of the cost of writing, designing, and mailing a newsletter.

Target the top editor. In the case of small magazines, Dobkin mails his article packet to the top editor listed in the publication's masthead (typically the Editor-in-Chief).

Titles are key. By far the most important part of the article is the title. When drafting each article, Dobkin says he typically begins by writing many possible titles in an effort to find the one that's most compelling.

No fluff. Dobkin's articles average 600–2,000 words, but most are around 1,200 words long and include practical how-to information. He suggests making them easy to read by using subheads and keeping paragraphs short.

Easily editable. Since magazines use articles of varying lengths and need to slant articles for their readerships, many of Dobkin's pieces are lists of tips that can be easily shortened and adapted to individual publications. For instance, "The 23 Best Lines in Marketing" can quickly become "The 18 Best Lines for Marketing Florists" if an editor doesn't have space for the entire list or needs to slant the article accordingly.

Supply multiple formats. Dobkin's typical package includes a set of 15–20 articles on 60 lb. white offset-quality stock. He also includes a black-and-white photo of himself, plus a cover letter that mentions that he'll gladly e-mail the articles or provide the text on disk. The latter options save editors the time and hassle of retyping the article.

Customize articles if they pay. While Dobkin's primary focus is on finding editors who will run his existing articles for free in exchange for a resource box mention, occasionally editors contact him who are willing to pay him to tweak an article just for them — or even write a new one from scratch. His fees vary from $250 to $1,500, depending upon how much customization is required.

Reprinted with permission from Book Marketing Update, www.bookmarket.com

- Frame or laminate articles to display in your lobby or reception area. Everybody likes to do business with a winner. Show your customers and clients how you stand out.

- Turn reprints into special reports and booklets. You can take your article and reprint it in other forms that can be given away as sales incentives.

- Post published articles on your Web site. You can show off what you have done, and at the same time keep your Web site fresh with new content.

- Republish articles in other magazines, Web sites, and newsletters. Make the most of each article you write by looking for likely publications and Web sites that would be interested in reprinting them as is or with a few changes.

- Use reprints as trade show handouts. You can send reprints to key vendors, customers, and clients with a cover letter announcing your presence and location at the show. An effective article can lure prospects to your booth.

How to Become a Columnist

Articles are usually a one-shot deal. Columns, on the other hand, are regular engagements that allow a writer to build relationships with readers. Columns appear on a weekly or monthly basis in newspapers, magazines, and Web sites. They can brand the authors not just as experts, but also as friends, confidantes, and mentors.

Columns are appealing promotional vehicles because of their regularity. Becoming a columnist is not easy; there are fewer opportunities for columns than articles, which makes landing a regular column a competitive contest. But if you succeed, becoming a columnist can turn you into a recognized authority within your target market.

"My column gave me an opportunity to touch people in a meaningful way and enhance my reputation," says former *San Francisco Examiner* career columnist Pat Sullivan. "People would forward my column to their friends and associates and many times I'd hear people say, 'This column really started a discussion in our workplace.' My column also helped me get invitations to speak and even land some new clients."

You don't have to achieve "Dear Abby" status to be a successful column writer. As with any *slightly famous* marketing strategy, your column only needs to reach the right people in your target market to position you as a resource.

Years ago, motivational speaker Bill Hodges was frustrated by what he felt was a constant barrage of negative news in the media. He approached his local newspaper editor, saying that the paper should devote more print space to uplifting news. The editor told Hodges to fix the situation by writing something himself.

A few weeks later, Hodges came back to the editor with thirteen columns on the power of positive thinking. The editor was so impressed he made Hodges a weekly columnist. In the years since, Hodges has expanded the reach of his "Positive Talk" columns, which now appear in 16 weekly papers in 37 countries around the world. With titles such as "Even the Bravest Need a Shove," "The Fear Is False," and "The Art of Human Relations," these columns have brought a tidal wave of speaking engagements and book sales.

Hodges maintains that writing a column is a grueling but ultimately rewarding experience. "I don't generally care what they pay me for the columns, because they're usually worth well over ten times the amount I receive," says Hodges. "The thing that I stress is that consistency counts. Getting my name out there and getting in papers has delivered many benefits. Furthermore, the discipline of writing the weekly columns allowed me to write a book and to put a set of tapes together."

Marketing and selling a column requires work—often more work than writing the column itself. Here are some possible markets.

- **Daily newspapers.** Although competition is fierce, 1600 daily newspapers make this market worth exploring. Newspapers that don't have print space for your column may be interested in publishing it on their Web site. Some newspapers also have online-only supplements to their print versions, including many columns that are online-exclusive.

TIPS FROM THE GURU

An Interview with Jay Conrad Levinson

Jay Conrad Levinson is the author of the acclaimed *Guerilla Marketing* book series. When *Guerrilla Marketing* was first published in 1983, Levinson revolutionized marketing strategies for the small-business owner.

How did you come to appreciate the value of getting your name into print as a way of building your business and reputation?

It happened by accident. I was teaching a course at a local college in the mid-1980s, and my students wanted to know if I could recommend inexpensive marketing books. Because there weren't that many devoted to small businesses at the time, I wrote *Guerilla Marketing*, which not only took on a life of its own, but also became the name of my course.

The book led to speaking engagements and media interviews. Soon, I started writing columns, and though the pay was nominal, it got my name out there along with contact information. Then I was able to take columns I had written and incorporate them into books.

Now, my agent markets my columns to publications that reach small businesses. I don't receive financial compensation, but the name recognition of having my name in print leads to other things. Publishing helped me land a job teaching a course at U.C. Berkeley. And other unexpected opportunities always result from publishing.

When I give a talk, say to a national convention, they always ask if I would write something for their newsletter, and I almost always agree. So my message is always out there, often in publications I'd never even heard of.

What's your advice to businesspeople about using article and column publishing to promote themselves and their small businesses?

- **Community newspapers.** These weekly publications have experienced steady growth, and can make good markets for your column. You might need to "localize" your column, but if the subject is universal, it could be as simple as finding different examples for each market.

- **Alternative press weeklies.** These newspapers are often free, usually urban and eclectic, and sometimes left of center politically. Many are unofficial entertainment guides for their cities.

The easiest way to get into print is through Web sites. Search for sites that match your expertise and industry. Web sites provide one of the most accessible and inexpensive ways to get your message out there. There are about 50,000 newsletters online. These are excellent sources for the beginner. Online newsletters are more willing to say "yes" where magazines might say "no." By publishing on the Internet, you can generate published articles quickly, and move on to bigger things.

What's one of the most interesting things that happened to you as a result of publishing articles and columns?

I have a mind-boggling success story. A *San Francisco Chronicle* reporter wanted to interview me years ago about my book *Earning Money Without a Job*. He was especially interested in my assertion that I've been working a three-day week since 1971. He wrote the article, which included my phone number, and in a few days I received 1,000 orders for the book that translated into $10,000 in sales.

After the interview, the reporter was so impressed by my self-determination that he vowed to quit his job and make a similar move. In the end, the reporter quit his job and went on to found Banana Republic.

What's your advice to people who lack the confidence to get started?

You can do it. There are millions of Web sites out there hungry for material from people who know their stuff. And there's very little downside to it. If you take a little time to learn the ropes and tailor your writing to the needs of others, it's almost rejection-free. And, you can make copies of everything you've published and use them as marketing materials or brochures. Once you get started, and your name begins to appear in new places, it will open up a whole new frontier.

- **Magazines.** Although the sheer number of magazines now being published may seem promising for the aspiring columnist, breaking into magazines is not easy. The best place to begin is to forge a relationship by writing freelance articles that may, over time, prove you are a good bet for a regular column.

- **Internet publications.** Don't reject the potential benefits of reaching your audience via the Internet. What may appear to be an insignificant Web site or eletronic publication could be an opportunity to raise your stature and provide an inroad to your target market.

Read Other Columnists

Find out where your column concept might fit in the marketplace by carefully reading what others are writing on your subject. Being able to articulate how your column fills a unique need in the marketplace will give you an edge.

While you may be the only person writing about tax planning for your hometown paper, there are probably many columnists addressing the same subject in various publications throughout the country. So if you want to go national, you'll have to differentiate yourself from them.

Before you get too far into your column project, run your idea by a few editors. Tell them what you have in mind—your column idea, your selling strategy, and an overview of your column's position in the marketplace. You'll find most editors helpful and willing to give feedback and guidance.

Selling Your Column

If you're serious about pursuing a column, you will need to put together a sales package that includes:

- a cover letter describing your proposed column
- six to ten sample columns
- the copyright terms you are offering
- reprints of published articles
- a biography and business background
- a self-addressed, stamped envelope for editor response

If a publication is interested, they will most likely name a price for the column (yes, you can get paid for this) that will probably range between $30 and $150.

7 Broadcast Media

Dr. Douglas Markham, a Los Angeles-based chiropractor and nutritionist, approached dozens of radio and television producers with the message "Eating Fat Does Not Make You Fat." As a nutritionist who'd recently developed a new dietary system, Markham asserted that the "low-fat, high-carbohydrate diet that has gotten so much attention does not work." Moreover, he said, the studies that promoted these diets were biased, possibly even corrupt, because they had been financed by the food industry.

His message hit a nerve with the media because he touched on what broadcasters are often looking for, controversy. Markham received 25 phone calls from television and radio stations eager to interview him. His media strategy even landed him on *Larry King Live*, where he appeared with one of his celebrity clients who testified that Markham's dietary system worked.

Radio and television producers are always looking for interesting and informative guests, and compelling content that informs and

REAL-WORLD SUCCESS STORY

Mark McMahon Becomes Famous for Charitable Work

Mark McMahon, a cosmetic dentist, made himself a media mini-celebrity with a thriving practice. His financial success was due in part to his doing high-profile *pro bono* work within his community, a strategy that landed numerous radio and television appearances in communities where he worked.

Each Thanksgiving, McMahon established partnerships with local charities, including a homeless shelter and a shelter for battered women, and offered free dental services to their members. Prior to each event, he contacted local media and let them know what he was doing. Several local television stations showed up at McMahon's offices, filmed him treating patients, and later aired the segments on the evening news.

"These events were surprisingly easy to arrange, and every year, they'd help us get press simply by doing these charitable promotions," says McMahon. "Local television news stations loved the emotional element. And it was obviously rewarding to see patients after we'd treated them who'd been in pain for months talking about how glad they were to be relieved of their toothaches."

Another project involved the Delancey Street Foundation, a residential education center for former substance abusers and ex-convicts. "I agreed to treat some of their members' acute dental needs," says McMahon. "I quickly

---

entertains audiences by bringing a fresh and insightful angle to the day's news. You don't have to be a celebrity to be a guest on radio and television shows. All it takes is tailoring your expertise to the needs of particular audiences, and presenting your message in an enjoyable and interesting way.

An Overview of the Airwaves

Broadcast media provides a great way to reach large local, regional, or national audiences. Unfortunately, too many potential beneficiaries of the media are intimidated by radio and television, and think them unapproachable.

appreciated the media appeal of transforming the appearance of these rough-looking guys with terrible smiles."

McMahon captured the event with before and after photos. "These guys had missing teeth and terrible smiles," says McMahon. "So I had a professional photographer capture before pictures of these guys in street clothes with their snarling faces. After I fixed their teeth, we took more pictures, but this time dressed the guys in suits and ties, now looking like lawyers and accountants, with me sitting right in the middle. The media loved it, and it was great seeing these men looking like new."

McMahon's television appearances created a lot of name recognition. "After I did the story on a local television show, I was recognized in my gym by a masseuse who had seen the show," recalls McMahon "She said, 'I was thinking about you this morning while I was flossing my teeth.' She became a great source of referrals."

Radio and television stations rely on interesting guests, including those from the business world, to fill airtime and add authority to their news stories. And they are always looking for businesses and products that offer some novelty or special angle that will grab their audience's attention.

The broadcast media reach the ears and eyes of your target market, delivering these powerful benefits:

- **Greater reach.** Consumers today spend much more time watching television and listening to radio programs than they do reading traditional print media like newspapers and magazines—some studies indicate that the ratio is on the order of 5-to-1 or more.

- **Personal connections.** Unlike print media, where you appear only indirectly, behind a wall of words, radio and television programs enable you to reach out directly and make a more personal connection.
- **Celebrity status.** The more you appear on radio and television programs, the more you'll be seen as a celebrity, which will boost your brand and reputation.
- **Enhanced credibility.** People who appear on radio and television are seen as leaders in their industries.
- **Increased sales.** If you target the right radio and television programs, your media appearances can make you money. Appearing as a guest on a local program that reaches your target market can attract many clients and customers. National television shows like *Good Morning America, Oprah,* or *Larry King Live* reach millions of people.

Understanding What Radio and Television Want

Broadcast opportunities are abundant for experts in everyday subjects such as travel, taxes, health and fitness, parenting, and home safety, to name just a few. Unique products can be good material, and colorful individuals and personalities that offer excitement and entertainment value to broad audiences are always in demand.

Compelling News

You must craft your message in a way that gives it obvious news value. "What most business owners need to do is put themselves in the position of the editor or producer," says publicity expert Paul Krupin. "You have to look at what they do. The key to being successful is to give them news that's better than anything else they have. It's that simple."

Radio and television producers consider items usable when they have broad consumer appeal. Producers particularly want information about current events, new industry developments, and business and product innovations. For example, if you are a local dry-cleaning operator who has embraced the use of non-toxic cleaning solvents, you could generate media exposure through your environment-friendly practices, especially if they challenge industry norms.

Captivating Material

Radio and television producers need material that keeps audiences tuned to their programs. They want guests who evoke an emotional reaction from their audiences. If you can provide material that's so riveting, entertaining, or even outrageous that no one would think of changing the station while it's on, you will be in demand.

Many producers use the term "sexy" when rating the media value of a subject. They ask themselves, "Is this sexy? Does it hold strong appeal?" This does not mean the content is sexual, it means material that is compellingly attractive to their audience. If your business doesn't appear exciting at first glance, look for ways to add excitement, even an outrageous twist, that will make news-hungry producers take notice. Depending on your situation, industry, and personal inclinations, you might dress in an outrageous costume, hold a wacky contest, or stage an elaborate publicity stunt at a public location. Even humdrum businesses can cut through the clutter and get noticed by the media when they develop creative strategies.

Seasonal Appeal

Broadcast media may give you some coverage if your topic is timely or tied to a holiday or seasonal event. Certain broadcast media segments that appear every year are tied to seasons and holidays. For

REAL-WORLD SUCCESS STORY

The Surreal Gourmet Gets Real Attention

Bob Blumer makes a big impression when he rolls into town. Blumer (a.k.a. The Surreal Gourmet) travels in a custom-made Airstream Trailer, a one-of-a-kind kitchen on wheels dubbed the Toastermobile due to the giant sheet metal pieces of toast protruding from the roof.

As one of today's most imaginative food personalities, Blumer is a good example of how any business can make itself interesting, exciting, even outrageous, and enjoy a lot of media attention.

Blumer designed the Toastermobile to promote his third cookbook, *Off the Eaten Path*. "When I'd seen Airstream trailers in the past they always reminded me of the shape of an old classic toaster," Blumer explained. "So when I was getting the trailer ready for the tour, I thought, 'why not?' and had two 12-foot-wide pieces of 'toast' installed on top."

Blumer became a food personality when he published *The Surreal Gourmet: Real Food for Pretend Chefs*. It was an instant hit that established his brand and earned him a loyal following. "The success of my first book made me live up to my own moniker of the surreal gourmet," says Blumer. "I saw the potential to get a lot of publicity on television shows that are always looking for interesting people."

It's a strategy that's paid off. His 30-city, three-month book tour for *Off the Eaten Path*, fueled by Blumer's knack for showmanship, not only got a lot of media attention on CNN, QVC, *Entertainment Weekly, People*

example, radio and television programs regularly provide tax tips in April, and discuss educational products during the back-to-school season. Look for ways to tie your business to these "evergreen" calendar events.

Be on the Spot with Your Expertise

Radio and television stations don't have the time, money, or staffing to fill every second of airtime themselves. Almost anyone with inside understanding of some widely interesting subject area can present himself as an expert to radio and television audiences.

Michelle Burke, author of *The Valuable Office Professional*, created a

Magazine, and over 100 daily newspapers, it also helped him land his own show on the Food Network.

Now, whether he's traveling the country in his Toastermobile for the Food Network, designing a surreal meal for the Salvador Dali Museum, or creating a supermodel diet for RuPaul, Blumer continues to build his personal brand identity in ways that make the media take notice.

"In the world of cooking, I've carved out this one little niche that is very unique and attractive to the public and the media," says Blumer. "Because I so passionately and completely live my brand, and go out of my way to make it fun and interesting, the media love it! I make their job easy by developing my own surreal bag of tricks and culinary theatrics."

Blumer's trump card is salmon fillets poached in the dishwasher and topped with a brightly flavored cilantro sauce. According to Bob, "Not only do the media love it, but you can cook salmon, wash the dishes, and have your plates warmed all at the same time."

niche that helped executive assistants more effectively work with their bosses. Each year, she pitched herself as an expert on media stories related to Secretary's Week, and got several interviews on radio and television programs that in turn generated book sales and established Burke as a leading figure in her industry.

Media Kits

A media kit, including the pitch letter and press release discussed in chapter five, is a standard tool in any publicity campaign. In addition to these basic elements, when approaching broadcast media you should include:

A List of Interview Questions A list of interview questions is an important part of any broadcast media kit, particularly for radio programs where the question and answer interview format is standard. Many radio producers don't have time to research products, guests, and issues for upcoming segments, and rely on the questions you provide as the basis for the show. You should list the questions in order of importance to assure that your main points are covered in case time runs out.

A Biography Create a personal bio to introduce yourself to the various people at the media outlet that you'll be interacting with. Keep your bio short, no more than 200 words. Support your statements with credentials, educational background, or professional experience that boosts your credibility. Write your bio as a broadcast producer would want it read on air, tight and concise.

Visuals When approaching television, you should include your photo and/or a photo of your product.

Video Footage (B-roll) Often, television stations would like to cover your story but don't have the resources to videotape your business on location. In such cases, they rely on video footage—B-roll, as it's called—provided by the subject of the proposed story. Your provision of B-roll increases your chances of getting on the air by making it possible for television producers to create stories without sending a film crew.

You create B-roll video footage with the help of a video production company that specializes in your business, product, or event. Once it's created, the video company edits the footage into several television-friendly segments, ready to be sent to appropriate producers. The footage can then be broadcast by the station or network, with a voice-over provided by you or a news anchor.

The cost of creating B-roll ranges from several hundred dollars to several thousand dollars. Its creation is best left to professionals; it must be shot in a format suitable for broadcast (producers rarely use VHS format). Generally 5–7 minutes of B-roll is sufficient, and this much usually takes a half day to create.

Your product offering and individual situation will determine if it's right to make this type of investment. If your story includes something such as a new product or manufacturing process, for example, you may be able to tell your story better visually.

Video News Releases (VNRs) A video news release is a two- or three-minute-long, professionally produced video in the format needed by news programs. It may be distributed through local and national news outlets, or even more widely via satellite broadcast organizations. With a professional voice-over, it provides a dynamic, visual press release that can be used "as is" by a broadcast outlet. If you are creating B-roll, you will have the raw footage to produce a VNR as a by-product when the B-roll is edited, and this can be archived for use at a later date.

Television Press Kits Sample footage on VHS tape is fine for inclusion in a television press kit. If you've been on television previously, or had some successful speaking engagements, include tapes of these events in your media kit. This sample footage shows producers that you are "ready for prime time."

For Radio Press Kits An inexpensive five-to-ten-minute audiocassette interview should be included in your radio media kit. Radio producers need to know that you're an articulate, engaging guest. If you haven't been a guest on a radio broadcast previously, create your own mock interview by using your well-crafted interview questions. Professional videotape suppliers generally carry audiotapes that can be purchased in 15- and 30-minute lengths. Finish them off with professional-looking computer-generated labels. You can add the plastic cases or simply tuck them into your press kit as is.

Identifying Broadcast Opportunities

How do you determine which broadcast media are right for your business? You are probably already familiar with the radio and television programs that reach your target market. Look closely at the types of topics that get airtime on them. Pitch programs that pertain to your geographical area. Look for programs likely to feature guests and segments related to your business. Here are a few considerations to keep in mind:

Local Media: Your Best Bet Again, you are probably already familiar with most of the programs you want to be on. You watch the local newscasts and have a favorite morning show. You listen to radio talk shows or the latest gardening tips while driving. You've probably seen or heard other businesses tell their story and wondered, "How did they get on this program?" This section answers that question.

Determine the Station's Format First, find out which radio or television programs have guest segments. Some stations limit programming to what is termed "hard news." This means that there are no guests, only interviews usually done at the site of breaking news.

Newscasts or programs that feature guests conduct interviews either in the studio or in the field. This means that either you would travel to the studio and be interviewed on a set, or a reporter would come to your place of business and interview you on-site. Once you've learned which radio or television programs book guests, you can target those that are a fit for your story.

Do You Have a Local or a National Pitch? Most *slightly famous* entrepreneurs have a story that is locally or regionally focused, so if you're typical, your business and your customers are limited to a geographical area considerably smaller than the whole United States. However, you may be an exception; you may have a product or service that is available nationally, meaning your broadcast opportunities are much greater.

Regional Considerations Consider regional factors when targeting radio and television stations. Is the area urban or rural? Is the population conservative or liberal? If your product or service is impacted by these factors, keep this in mind when pitching producers. Some stations producing nationally syndicated programs have Web sites providing information on past guests and subject matter.

Radio Versus Television

There's no formula for determining which broadcast media should be part of your campaign. Obviously television is more suited to a visual presentation, but radio often dedicates more time to a presentation or interview, so you have a greater opportunity to tell your story. Here is a more detailed discussion of the major attributes of radio and television.

Radio

Radio is generally considered a more forgiving medium than television. Radio interviews usually offer larger time slots to tell your story. You can be interviewed in your office, your home, and even your car if your story is related to breaking news.

Radio producers generally have longer lead times than television producers, so you may have more time to prepare for your appearance. Understanding the overall time constraints in radio programming can help you better target those programs appropriate to your business.

Drive Times Radio has two "prime time" slots, the morning drive time (roughly 5–9 AM) and the evening drive time (roughly 4–7 PM). The audiences in these slots are mainly commuters. The formats are news, traffic, and short guest interviews that are often rebroadcast throughout the entire drive time slot.

REAL-WORLD SUCCESS STORY

How Alex Carroll Scored Huge Book Sales Giving Radio Interviews

Alex Carroll's battle against traffic tickets began more than ten years ago when he took his first job as a courier driver and accumulated ten moving violations over four years. Because the company allowed drivers only one ticket, Carroll had two choices: beat his tickets or lose his job.

Carroll challenged his moving violations in traffic court. To his surprise, he managed to beat 8 of his 10 tickets. From this experience the idea for writing a book, *Beat the Cops*, was born.

Lacking money to spend on promoting the work, he began looking for very cheap — or better, free — ways to promote his book. Radio was the answer. Discovering that the thousands of radio stations across the country need approximately 10,000 guests a day to fill their programming schedules, he decided to create a morning drive radio tour to target audiences trapped behind the steering wheels of their cars during commute hours.

Alex started conducting interviews on smaller radio stations before moving up to the really large radio stations, those with over 100,000 listeners. He created a press kit, pitched himself as a guest, and quickly established himself as a radio personality, reaching national radio audiences several times a month.

"The best part is I didn't even have to get out of bed," says Carroll. "Radio stations would call and wake me, then I'd do the interview and go

Other Time Slots Non-prime time slots are the longer stretches between the drive times. Midday programming audiences are often largely of retirement age. Travel, food, and leisure subjects are often the best subjects for these slots. However, there are many business and consumer issue programs in these time slots as well.

Evening programming may lean towards authors, public issues, or the arts. If you are a therapist, attorney, or artist, these time slots may be your best targets. Weekend programs typically deal with health and fitness, parenting, gardening, and other home-related topics.

Local Radio Programming Local radio is usually simple to approach. You can easily become familiar with the content because it's available on a daily basis, and most local radio stations want to

back to sleep. I'd wake up later and see that 200 to 500 orders worth thousands of dollars had been placed by listeners while I slept."

Since writing *Beat the Cops*, Carroll has been featured on ABC *News with Sam Donaldson, E!, The Learning Channel* and *Howard Stern* — and has been a guest on more than 1,200 radio shows worldwide, selling over 100,000 copies of his book.

Carroll has become a vocal opponent of speed traps, insurance surcharges, and unfair tickets. He was a leading spokesperson for the National Motorists Association during their successful campaign to repeal the 55 mile per hour speed limit.

The secret to effective radio publicity, says Carroll, is targeting the types of shows that make sense for your business and message. Carroll also stresses that radio publicity requires both persistence and phone calls. "You can't just send your press release everywhere and expect good results," says Carroll. "One month, I booked 77 interviews by making 1,500 phone calls. You have to keep calling until you reach the right producer."

Most important, successful radio guests see themselves as partners in the programming process. "When you decide to do radio, you're in show business," says Carroll. "You've got to be able to come up with great ideas for shows and make yourself intriguing.

"Can you help people save time? Can you make them rich? Can you tell an amazing story? Can you make listeners laugh? If you can engage listeners and keep them from changing the channel, producers will welcome you and you'll enjoy considerable sales as a result. If you have secrets or tips that make people say 'Wow!' then you have an entrée to radio."

keep their finger on the pulse of a community, so they make themselves accessible to local people with messages to deliver.

National and Syndicated Radio Programming If your story has national appeal, you can pitch to national and syndicated programs. These programs usually have a specific focus, such as health, parenting, travel, or personal finance. It's easy to identify which ones may be best for your pitch. National programming generally has long lead times, and the programs may be taped weeks or months in advance of the actual airdate.

Radio as the First Step to Broadcast Radio is a great medium for first-timers. For many it may be the most appropriate broadcast vehicle, but even for those aiming for a television appearance, it can serve as a good stepping stone. It gives you the opportunity to polish your story, and get a feeling for being interviewed. You can hear what your voice sounds like when telling your story, and learn the difference between being interviewed and carrying on a normal conversation.

The Lure of Television

Television is best for stories and products that beg for visual demonstration. It is also ideal when you have a physically attractive spokesperson to convey your message. Television interviews can be conducted in television studios, your place of business, a customer's location, or possibly a tradeshow or other commercial event.

Unlike radio, television affords little margin for error. Television cameras not only capture but also magnify your every gesture and nuance. However, if done well, television appearances offer some of the most powerful broadcast opportunities available to the *slightly famous* entrepreneur.

Local Programming You are most likely familiar with the local television or cable programming in your area. Once you have watched the programs to determine which shows have guests, identify your targets and move on to pitching the producers of those programs.

Carol Watson-Brand began rock climbing at age 40. She earned certification as a walking instructor and created a fitness program called *Carol's Challenge*. This program trained small groups for climbing expeditions from Mt. Whitney in California to the peaks of Nepal.

Because *Carol's Challenge* was so unusual, she got herself booked on a local morning television show for four consecutive Fridays, demonstrating exercises meant specifically for backpacking-related strength building. Carol was later interviewed for a cable television program produced for climbers.

National Television Before you approach producers at national networks like ABC, CBS, and NBC, or cable news networks like CNN, CNBC, and CNN Headline News, gather information about their shows. Investigate their Web sites. Most producers or programming departments can provide audience demographics. Within the framework of these national networks, there are several possible opportunities for *slightly famous* entrepreneurs.

Newscasts News programs are half-hour to one-hour programs that cover breaking news, sports, and other subjects. Guest formats vary from show to show, so make sure you understand the formats of the particular shows you want to appear on. Generally, business segments are aired on morning news, midday news covers leisure or human interest-related subjects, and evening news covers a broad, general range of subjects.

Morning Programs Morning programs offer numerous opportunities for businesses and entrepreneurs. This type of programming is usually aired in one-, two-, or three-hour segments, and generally appears on independent stations that run parallel to the nationally broadcast morning shows. Interviews are conducted either in-studio or in the field.

Magazine Format Programs This type of programming is usually aired in the afternoon or early evening, between the evening news and nightly prime-time programming. Segments may be longer, and have more entertainment or human-interest focus. Generally, there are no business segments, but if your story has entertainment value, this could be a great vehicle for it.

Pitching Your Story

Big radio and television stations don't go looking for guests. Guests come to them. You need to introduce yourself to producers, usually with an initial phone call that you follow with e-mail, snail mail, or media kit. Many producers prefer the initial pitch via e-mail. In the Resources section on page 249 you will find a list of media directories that includes their preferences.

When you pitch producers, the first step towards being a guest is coming up with something that makes the "facts" about your business or product interesting. Here are three ways to grab a producer's attention.

1. **Be controversial.** Producers love anything that gets their phone lines going, and nothing does the trick like a highly provocative statement.

2. **Be entertaining.** If you can make people laugh and tell them fascinating stories, you'll always be in demand as a guest.

3. **Be informative.** Give people useful, timely information. Give them information that makes them say, "Wow! That's amazing! I didn't know that!"

If you are targeting news shows, target the assignment manager, assignment editor, or the assignment desk. This newsroom gatekeeper will route stories of interest to the appropriate producers or reporters. Don't try to talk to anchors or anyone else who appears on the air.

The AM Desk is responsible for the morning and noon news shows. There is usually an early-morning meeting of all of the producers at which they determine which camera crews will go to film particular segments. If you have a newsworthy event coming up that day, get the pitch to the AM Desk early, even the night before. The night person will make sure they see it.

The PM Desk is responsible for the evening and late night news shows. The producers usually meet in the afternoon, between the noon and evening news, to determine which segments to film. While most evening news programs provide extensive coverage of national news and local breaking news, newscasts often end with a light human-interest story filmed in advance.

It's critical to target the right person at any program you approach. Most television and radio programs have at least one producer who's responsible for booking guests. A program that airs daily books many guests, and will probably have several producers who book guests, each responsible for one or more specific segments. Whenever possible, tape shows and note in the credits the name of the person responsible for producing segments relevant to your story. For all other programs, you can determine the appropriate producer for specific segments or programs through any of the media directories mentioned in this book, or by contacting the station.

Radio and television newsrooms operate at high speed. When you're ready to call a producer, have your pitch down to a few sentences. Don't dive into a pitch; instead, ask the producer if they are on deadline. If they're too busy to talk, ask for a convenient time to call them back, and whether it's all right to fax or e-mail your pitch.

If the producer asks to hear your idea, give your pitch directly in a few words. Examples:

"The hottest trend in _____ is _____. This is a subject very popular among your viewers/listeners."

"The new tax laws are stumping even seasoned CPAs. I can inform your viewers/listeners on these complicated new guidelines."

"There's a demanding exercise fad called _____ which is causing lots of injuries. I can show/tell viewers/listeners how to properly execute this new routine."

There's no substitute for being familiar with a program. Radio and television producers appreciate it when you take time to understand

TIPS FROM THE GURU

Donald Moine on Using Previous Radio and Television Appearances

Dr. Donald Moine, co-author of *Ultimate Selling Power*, is a pioneer in sales psychology who has appeared on more than 100 talk radio shows and several television shows in the U.S., Canada, and Australia. His secret? He uses prior media appearances, including articles that appeared about him in newspapers, to generate interest in other media outlets.

"The *Los Angeles Times* interviewed me on November 29, 1992, and published an article about some of my work," says Moine. "I then took the article, reproduced it on two pages, added some potential interview questions, and sent it out to about 150 talk radio shows."

Moine's campaign generated better results than the original newspaper story, helping him get booked on more than 30 shows. Some of them gave him a full hour of radio time and took call-in questions. Many shows let him mention his phone number and the name of his book. "A few interviewers even commanded their listeners, 'Folks, go out and buy Dr. Moine's book today!'"

Moine's strategy works because media outlets have a follow-the-leader mentality. "If they see that another highly respected news outlet has done a story on a given topic or person, and if it looks interesting and of value, they are likely to follow along and jump on board," says Moine.

their format. If you've come across radio or television segments or guests that have dealt with topics similar to your own, you might mention it when you pitch your own story.

Interview Tips

Preparation is key to any broadcast interview. The mantra is *practice, practice, practice.*

Practice your interview questions in a mirror, tape yourself on video or on audiocassettes, practice in the shower, and make your family and friends watch or listen to you.

Beg, borrow, or steal a video camera to tape yourself if you are doing television. Pay for it if you have to. You've got to have concise, sound bite responses to the questions you'll be asked by your interviewer.

A poorly prepared interview is easy to spot. The subject looks nervous and ill at ease, either answering too hastily or giving protracted responses without a clear focus. A seasoned guest delivers crisp, concise responses, and appears relaxed and at ease with the host or anchor. If you're well prepared for interviews, you'll be less nervous, better inform audiences, enjoy a more natural exchange with the host, and present your business in the best possible light.

Rehearse

Find a partner to play the part of the host as you go through practice interviews. For radio, tape your practice interview on an audio recorder, and have your partner use a stopwatch to time responses. For television, obtain a video camera with a tripod, and besides timing your responses, watch yourself later for distracting gestures or nervous tics. Your partner should ask your interview questions off-camera, usually sitting next to the recorder so you are looking at each other. This gets you accustomed to not looking directly into the camera.

When reviewing practice interview tapes, listen for awkward delivery; notice hand gestures, become aware of how fast or slowly you speak, and above all, count the number of times you say "Uhm." (Your "coach" should be on the watch for "uhm's" too.) Buying time with "uhm's" is a bad habit that even a seasoned radio professional may fall prey to from time to time. It will distract from and muddy your message. It is said admiringly in media circles that Bryant Gumbel has never uttered an "uhm" in over 20 years on the air.

Anticipate Questions

Most producers provide a list of questions that will be asked by hosts. These questions often mirror your interview questions, but you should be prepared for possible deviations from your prepared questions.

Try to anticipate interview questions that might occur on the fly. Although you may be well prepared, your host may not be, or may not adequately understand your subject. In this situation, being prepared to deal with common misconceptions about your subject will help assure the interview goes smoothly.

If you are asked questions that stray from your subject, take a deep breath, think for a second about your response, and try to restate the question to fit your prepared responses. If the question is stated in such a way that it's not possible to do so, keep these points in mind:

- Don't be defensive
- Stick to key points that you can quickly articulate
- Maintain friendliness
- Use colorful anecdotes
- Avoid jargon
- Ask the host to clarify if you don't understand a question

Develop Sound Bite Responses

It's important to master the art of short responses, because long, rambling responses may be edited out or edited in a way that changes your meaning. A good response to an interviewer's question should take no more than 30 seconds. You may not think this is long enough to answer a question, but if you take longer than this, your listeners will stop hearing what you are saying.

At least some of your responses should take the form of a sound bite, a very short comment or phrase, anything from a few seconds to 10 or 15 seconds long that is designed to be memorable. This is the exact statement or phrase you want viewers or listeners to hear and remember.

Some Extra Radio Guidelines

Here are a few extra guidelines that are important to remember when doing radio interviews.

For interviews done in the studio be sure to:

- Arrive at least 15 minutes early
- Get the direct telephone number of the producer or sound engineer in case of emergencies
- Bring your media kit or interview questions, even if you've already sent them to the producer

For radio call-in interviews you should:

- Call from a quiet area
- Let anyone around know that you cannot be disturbed
- Have a glass of water handy
- Disable call-waiting on your telephone
- Turn off the radio to avoid feedback
- Keep pets out of the area

Look Your Best on Television

You want to look your best on any televised appearance. Take that one step further and make sure you feel good. Don't try to squeeze into something that doesn't fit because you think it makes you look slimmer. Don't wear a fabric that may irritate or be too hot under studio lights.

Here are a few basic appearance guidelines for television:

- Don't wear prints, stripes, or patterns. These tend to "vibrate" on camera.
- Don't wear a white shirt or blouse; they glare. Creams and blues look good on camera.

- Women should avoid wearing excessive jewelry; anything that creates a sound is distracting, and will be picked up by the microphone.

- Avoid the perspiring anchor disaster, as seen in *Broadcast News*. Men should ensure that their foreheads and noses don't shine by using powder. Practice at home with loose, matte-finish powder. Place tissues around your collar to avoid getting any on your clothing.

- Women who don't wear makeup should use matte powder and lip-gloss at the very least.

- Do a dry run on your makeup; hire a professional if the situation warrants.

- Don't appear in a new hairstyle or hair color unless you've had a chance to wear it at least a week before the interview. If you don't feel you look great, your lack of confidence will be conveyed during your interview.

- Pull your clothing tight behind and under you as you sit in the interview chair. Do this after the microphone has been run under your clothing (a production assistant will do this for you). Men, ensure your shirt is wrinkle-free in front; your jacket is tightly smoothed (yet comfortable). Women, ensure your clothing is tightly smoothed, but loose enough to shift in your chair effortlessly.

- Don't look at the camera, unless instructed to do so. Keep your gaze at a consistent place, usually towards the host. You will be directed on this just before airtime.

- Don't hit your microphone. Practice hand gestures that avoid the left side area around your heart, which is usually where the microphone is placed.

During the Interview

Keep your energy up. A lively, energetic guest will get lots of bookings. When you come across as lively and stimulating, not only will the radio show love you, but so will the audience.

As noted in previous chapters, it is important to conduct your interview as an opportunity to share information. What will you give your audience? Hosts and producers hate it when they ask a guest a question and the guest responds, "Oh, that's in my book," or "You'll find out if you come to my seminar." Never hold anything back. After all, the simple fact of being on a show confirms your credentials.

If you are appearing on radio, the host will introduce you and, with luck, mention your company name; if not, it's your job to mention it in your responses. Practice an opening response to your introduction that easily flows into mentioning your company name: "That's a good question; we at ABC Company feel that..."

If you're on television, a graphic of your name will appear at the start, end, and possibly in the middle of your segment. At the end of a program, either radio or television, try to interject your name again. It may not always be possible when ending, as commercial breaks may abruptly end an interview, but be ready.

While your 800 number may not flash during a telecast or be given on the air, most stations provide their guests with the equivalent of a reader inquiry card. When interested viewers call the station about someone they saw or heard on the show, the station will usually provide a contact name and phone number. Many stations post this information on their Web sites for a brief period of time.

Get a Tape

This is relatively easy if you do an in-studio interview. Just bring a cassette or VHS tape with you, and have it brought to the sound engineer in the booth. Some stations may not do this, but most will be happy to. If you've been interviewed remotely, you may have to purchase the footage from the station or a duplication service. Fees for this may range from $75 to $150. Keep in mind, this footage will not be broadcast quality, but can be used as a learning tool and is also valuable when pitching other programs.

This chapter was co-authored with Kimberly Hathaway of Hathaway Public Relations in San Francisco.

PART III REACHING OUT IN ALL DIRECTIONS

CHAPTER 8

The *Slightly Famous* Web Site

With most *slightly famous* marketing strategies, you are an actor on someone else's stage: a contributor to a magazine, a speaker at a conference, or a guest on a radio or television program. But when you have a Web site, you are the writer, producer, director, and star of your own show, with the opportunity of becoming a minicelebrity reaching a large number of people.

A Web site is also a powerful branding tool that tells your story, showcases your expertise, and puts a human face on your business. A Web site expands your reach. It's a platform from which you can reach thousands of prospects. It can also create new profit centers, and literally make money for you while you sleep.

You need a Web site if only because people today expect you to have one. Not having a Web site these days is like doing business without a phone or fax machine. This chapter will help you create a Web site that advances your *slightly famous* marketing strategy, attracts new business, and dramatically expands your market by building a loyal online following.

REAL-WORLD SUCCESS STORY

How a Professional Speaker Clicked His Way to Success

A few years ago, speaker, author, and Internet marketing expert Tom Antion decided to learn Internet marketing techniques that would help him book more speaking engagements. By systematically pursuing this goal, he's developed a powerful Internet presence that attracts plenty of speaking opportunities, and earned him a reputation within the speaking industry as an Internet marketing guru.

"I'm not all that computer literate, nor do I want or need to be," says Antion. "I just know where to click to make money, and that's all I, or any other businessperson, needs to care about."

Antion uses the Internet to sell a line of products, seminars, teleclasses, and e-books on Internet marketing. Not only that, his speaking fee has gone from $5,500 to $10,500 per day, and he regularly speaks at conferences on Internet marketing (one audience bought $52,000 worth of his products after just one of his speeches). In addition, he publishes the speaking industry's largest e-mail newsletter, having signed up more than 100,000 subscribers in just two years.

Antion also leverages his online marketing to establish greater visibility and credibility within his target market. His site ranks high on most major search engines. He encourages hundreds of related sites to link to his Web site, which serves as an endorsement and traffic-generating tool. All of this tends to convince people that Antion knows what he's talking about, a fact that draws audiences to his events in droves.

"I wouldn't cold-call anybody if you put a gun to my head," says Antion. "That's why I cultivated a lot of visibility and credibility online, and sell my

Master of Your Domain: Make Your Business Web-Centric

Your Web site can become the flagship of your slightly famous marketing strategy, achieving its full potential when you fully integrate it into your business. A Web site is not a static, online brochure you create and forget about; properly set up and maintained, it becomes a virtual branch office and around-the-clock salesperson.

As a resource for your industry, your Web site can feature lots of useful information, including articles, links, downloadable files, cus-

knowledge from my Web site. I learned that people do not hire a professional speaker or a marketer per se, they hire an expert. I merely use the Internet as another tool to demonstrate my expertise in a way that attracts prospects and opportunities."

Antion has succeeded because he makes his Web site the center of his marketing activities, while using e-mail to affordably reach his target market. His many articles, which he publishes on a variety of Web site, help him grow his online mailing list.

"The best part is that I don't have to beg for business!" says Antion. "My Web presence is so well-established, and my credibility so much beyond question, that my reputation draws prospects to me. I now land speaking engagements directly from my Web site, and sell tons of products and get participants for my mentor program. Because prospects see my name hundreds of times in search engines, or read my articles on other Web sites, they call me ready to do business."

The most spectacular testament to Antion's strategy came when his Web site helped him land a job as spokesperson for Switchboard.com, one of the most heavily visited Web sites in the world. "A journalist for the *Miami Sun Sentinel* subscribed to my e-mail newsletter," recalls Antion. "After reading several issues, the journalist was apparently convinced of my expertise, and interviewed me for an article about Internet marketing."

Soon after, a representative from CBS read the article. "CBS just happened to be looking for an Internet marketing spokesperson for an upcoming business seminar series," recalls Antion. "Because of that article, prompted by my e-mail newsletter, CBS offered me the deal and I beat out thousands of Internet experts. It was the easiest six-figure deal I ever landed!"

tomer resources, and anything else of use to your target market. Its also one of the most effective channels for establishing strategic alliances, facilitating co-promotions, promoting online classes and seminars, and reaching a global audience.

Design: Keep It Simple

First and foremost, your Web site is a marketing tool, not a design showpiece. Web users are notoriously impatient. They want information, and they want it quickly.

A simple Web site design is easy to navigate, and avoids fancy graphics and theatrical elements that look impressive but serve no marketing purpose. Excessive embellishments can actually work to your disadvantage by slowing down your Web site and driving away impatient viewers.

As you consider your Web site design, write down adjectives that describe the ambiance you want to create. Make sure your Web site is aligned with your overall branding strategy. Use colors that evoke the feelings and moods you want to convey. Consider your business style and the way you want to be perceived. Your Web site design needs to match expectations about your type of business. If your site sells high-end financial services, you must convey a professional image.

If you choose to work with a professional Web designer, look for someone who possesses a solid understanding of marketing (both on and off the Internet), design, and technical know-how. Avoid Web designers who are primarily artists with little understanding of marketing. Also, avoid technical wizards who want to impress the world by loading your site with spectacular bells and whistles at the expense of usability.

Choosing a Domain Name

Choosing the right domain name is critical; it needs to be memorable, it must differentiate you from competitors, and it must support your brand. The perfect domain name describes what you do, and is simple enough that people can type it in easily on their computers, and pass it along to friends. The maximum length for domain names is 67 characters, but for marketing purposes, the shorter the name the better.

Here are some of the most common options for choosing an effective domain name:

- **Your own name.** If you are a solo professional, such as a writer, attorney, or fitness trainer, this is the most direct approach. Using your own name is also effective when you establish yourself as an expert. Speaker, author, and marketing consultant Larry Chase uses his own name to brand his Web site, larrychase.com. If you are seeking to develop personal brand recognition, then—assuming your name is easy to spell and pronounce—naming your URL after yourself makes sense.

- **Your company name.** If your branding strategy revolves around promoting your firm, use your company name as your URL. Of course, the requirement of easy spelling and pronunciation applies. If it's too long, try shortening it to something manageable that still suggests your full company name. For example, the Small Press Action Network opted to use an acronym for its URL, www.span.org.

- **Your main concept or idea.** Sometimes, it makes sense to name your URL after your core business concept or solution. Author and simplicity expert Janet Luhrs' domain, simpleliving.com, clearly expresses the central theme of her books, her speaking engagements, and her publication, *The Simple Living Journal.*

When acquiring a domain name, it's good practice to also reserve names that are closely related to your chosen URL. If the name of your company is Spring Advertising Services, make sure you acquire spring.com, spring.net, and spring.org, then go a step further by getting springmarketing.com, .net, and .org. There's no reason you can't have more than one Web site or have multiple domain names pointing to the same site.

The Web site of a small, non-computer business will usually reside on a dedicated Web host, a computer owned by a service company that specializes in storing (and possibly maintaining) Web sites. For this reason, when registering domain names, it's imperative to protect your ownership and control. If you have a third party, such as your Web host company, register your domain name(s), make sure you are listed as both "registrant" and "administrative contact." This assures that you maintain full control over your Web site should you need to switch Web-hosting companies.

Web Pages and Navigation

Make it intuitively easy for visitors to find their way around your Web site. Imagine yourself as a first-time visitor as you consider your Web site's navigation scheme. The first rule is not to burden the visitor to your site—especially the first-time visitor—with excessive options.

Developing a user-friendly Web site should not constrain good design, but it needs to be an integral part of the design process. According to Gerry McGovern, co-author of *The Web Content Style Guide*, your navigation scheme should:

- Help readers quickly find what they are looking for
- Let readers know where they are at all times
- Provide context
- Be consistent
- Provide feedback and support
- Never surprise or mislead a reader

Because navigation is an aid for visitors, start your design from their point of view. Involve people in the design process who represent your customers' or clients' point of view. Find out what they want from your site.

The Home Page: Your Virtual Kiosk Easy navigation begins at a home page that functions as a virtual lobby or kiosk. This is where you orient visitors to your business, and guide them to subsequent pages of your Web site. If your home page doesn't grab visitors' attention and make them want to enter and explore your Web site, you risk having important pages go unviewed, regardless of the toil that went into their construction.

Because your home page is the first thing visitors will see, it must speak directly to your target market, letting them know they've come to the right place. Keep the message on your home page down to a few paragraphs and boldly convey the core benefit of your business. Focus on the keywords, features, and images that will capture the attention and interest of your target audience.

Provide a summary of your ultimate business benefit. This will help visitors decide whether your Web site contains information relevant to their needs. Be as direct and clear as you can. A travel site might say, "Are you a single mother who needs help planning your next family vacation?"

Next, describe how your company provides the answer to that question. Using the above example, your next line might read, "A Mother's World is a travel service that works exclusively with single mothers. Our unique focus helps single mothers enjoy fun, educational vacations with their children."

Finally, state how your company is the best choice for visitors, promising what they will find throughout your Web site when they dig deeper. "We help clients plan exciting, hassle-free trips within the United States, and provide a range of travel options to meet your needs and budget. Our site is filled with useful information to help you plan your next vacation."

By delivering value in the form of relevant content, you guide visitors through your entire Web site to your e-mail sign-up pages, and—ultimately—your services.

About Us Once visitors get a picture of who you are and how you can help them, you need to show how your business is uniquely qualified to help them. You can do this by:

- Positioning yourself against your competitors
- Highlighting your approach or process
- Emphasizing your experience
- Featuring or demonstrating your expertise

Staff Profiles Visitors need to know and trust the people behind your site before they put their faith (and their dollars) in your business. Staff profiles give visitors reassuring background information about the qualifications of the human beings behind the Web site.

List in order of importance the most relevant qualifications or experience of each of your principals and other key staff people. List everything about them that sets you apart from competitors. List the professional affiliations and anything else that makes a case for their experience and expertise.

Products and Services Provide a description of all the products and services you offer, with enough detail for visitors to see the benefits and value of each. Depending on the price and complexity of the items you offer, you may need to provide separate pages with highly detailed descriptions, specifications, and pictures.

For example, if you are a martial arts instructor offering a variety of programs, you might provide separate pages for programs aimed at children, teens, and adults. By focusing on individual client groups, and emphasizing the benefits that apply directly to each, you'll attract more customers.

Clients, Customers, and Case Studies To earn visitors' trust, it helps to name customers you've already served. You can accomplish this to some extent just with a simple list of past clients, but it is more effective if you go on to provide details about how you've helped those clients and customers. If you present a lengthy list, you can create subheads for different categories of customers.

Case studies are great for conveying to visitors how you achieved favorable results for your clients and customers. Choose situations that are broadly representative of your target market. Describe the customer's situation both before and after they worked with you, and be very clear about the results you achieved for them. You want your potential clients and customers to put themselves in the place of past clients and customers, and see themselves receiving similar benefits.

Testimonials Develop a dedicated testimonial page and keep it constantly updated. Ask satisfied clients to describe how your organization solved a problem for them. Because they don't come directly from you, these stories have greater credibility.

In addition to, or instead of, a testimonial page, you can place customer testimonials throughout your site. You can put them in the margins of individual Web pages or intersperse them in stretches of sales copy.

Articles Because content is king on your *slightly famous* Web site as it is everywhere, you should include articles you have written or that are about you. Such materials demonstrate your expertise. If you have more articles than will fit, include a list. This makes a case for your expertise and also attracts Internet keyword searches. (See below for more on this.)

You should also consider including articles and columns from "guest experts" who can address issues that are important to your readers. By inviting others to help you create a compelling Web site, and publishing thoughtful pieces written by others who are respected, you make your site a valuable resource.

Resources and Links Whenever possible, include pages with valuable information—either in full or in the form of links to other sites—and update them regularly. This gives visitors a reason to return to your Web site even when they're not ready to buy. You might have links to all the professional associations in the area, or links to related business services. You might offer a list of relevant books, with key excerpts from the best of them—in short, any resources that your visitors might find useful.

Press Room Many Web sites fail to provide the kind of fast, basic information journalists are looking for. That means lost publicity opportunities, since harried journalists looking for information will quickly move on to another source or subject.

In contrast, a well-designed Web site with an easy-to-use press center will attract reporters who are writing about your industry or community. To design a Web site that meets the media's needs, keep these tips in mind:

- Provide a direct link from your home page to your press center.
- Give reporters what they are looking for: press releases, media clippings, and other information that facilitates their research.
- Make company facts and information easy to find and read.
- Prominently display contact information and include phone, fax, pager, and cell phone numbers, as well as e-mail addresses.
- Offer the names of people in your company who are expert in particular subjects.
- Include links to relevant sites, including industry organizations, clients, and governmental agencies.
- Invite reporters to register to receive future company news and updates.
- The Haddon Group, an IT consulting firm, fulfills these requirements by offering a list of areas on which they can provide industry commentary, some samples of their work, and articles and white papers that demonstrate their expertise.

Contact Information As mentioned above, make it easy for visitors to contact you. Your contact information should contain an e-mail message form so that visitors can send you a message without leaving your site, your e-mail address, phone number, fax number, postal mailing address, and any other relevant information (like the best times to call you).

Include contact information on every page of your Web site, and make sure it's visible. Nothing is more frustrating than searching a Web site in vain for a telephone number or other basic contact information. As a test, ask others to find such information on your site, and see how long it takes them to find it.

You might also offer visitors a questionnaire they can complete before you contact them. This simultaneously demonstrates your ability to diagnose their needs, and the fit between the visitors and your business. Construct your questionnaire around situations or scenarios. Ask questions about common problems, and help visitors see the benefits of your business in light of their situation. Make sure you respond promptly.

Newsletter Sign Up Once someone has visited your site and liked it, don't lose contact with them. Many new visitors, even those who have enjoyed and benefited from your Web site, will forget about you unless you capture their e-mail addresses and stay in touch. So it's important to have a vehicle, such as an e-mail newsletter, to make that possible.

"Think of your Web site as your car or vehicle. It can take you where you want to go with your marketing," says Robert Middleton of Action Plan Marketing. "Then think of the e-mail newsletter as the gas for that vehicle. Without gas, the vehicle may look beautiful, but it simply won't go very far."

Create a page that offers your latest newsletter, along with a simple sign-up form on each page of your site asking for visitors' names and e-mail addresses. Motivate visitors to join your e-mail list by offering something free, such as a special report or article. Your goal is to be able to continue to market to them with their permission, and keep the door open for them to become customers or clients.

TIPS FROM THE GURU

Dr. Ralph Wilson on Making Your Site Trustworthy

Web users worldwide have been buzzing for years about the insights of Dr. Ralph Wilson, aka Dr. Ebiz. A widely acknowledged Internet guru, he's given hundreds of thousands of people Internet marketing advice since 1995 through newsletters, e-books, articles, seminars, and his book, *Planning Your Internet Marketing Strategy*.

Wilson realized early on that trust was paramount if consumers were to use the Web as a commercial resource. Creating Web-site credibility, and overcoming what Wilson calls "the central problem of fear and distrust," is key. You need to overcome the fact that, as he says, "You can't shake hands with a Webmaster."

"Tell your story," Wilson suggests. "Rather than a corporate-sounding 'About Us' section, provide insight into the people behind the company, their passion for the business, their struggles to achieve success, and their plans for the future." Developing a chatty, person-to-person rapport gives you an advantage over larger, impersonal business entities.

Wilson also suggests including a photograph of the business itself, when applicable, and getting involved with trust organizations, such as the Better Business Bureau; if you can, display their logos. Include any awards you've won. Also, promise that all visitor information will be kept confidential and never sold to third parties.

Wilson emphasizes that writing articles and providing expert content plays a large part in establishing visitor trust, and has helped him grow his e-mail newsletter relationship with his more than 120,000 subscribers. "Publishing instantly makes you an expert, and expertise instills trust," says Wilson. "Not even a politician could easily shake 120,000 hands, yet I do it figuratively a couple times a month."

Writing for the Web

The main thing people seek from your site is to know if you can provide something they want. Don't waste their time (and yours) with anything else. Rather than provide entertainment and flash (unless that's the nature of your business), help people get the information they want when they need it.

Strip away the glamour of the design and technology, and you're left with words. Your Web site lives or dies by the quality of your writing—specifically, your ability to write in a manner friendly to online readers. People rarely read Web pages word for word. Internet readers are skimmers, and that means that information must be presented in short chunks that stand on their own.

Here are some strategies for writing effective Web copy:

- Highlight keywords, phrases, and sentences.
- Use immediately intelligible subheadings, not "clever" ones.
- Use bulleted lists for groups of short, related items.

Develop only one idea per paragraph.

- Use the inverted pyramid style, starting each page and section with the most vital information first, followed by supporting ideas.
- Reduce the word count to half or less that of conventional writing.
- Avoid overtly promotional claims, such as "hottest ever."

While practicing tight writing, don't overdo it to the point of stripping your personality and voice from your Web copy. The best Web-oriented writing is done in a conversational style that creates a personal bond with readers. Web users want to experience the person behind the Web site. Don't be afraid to write using your own voice. We all love stories. Use them to personalize your writing, and help readers latch onto and remember your narrative and, ultimately, your business.

Marketing Your Web Site

The Internet is billions of pages large, so it doesn't take too much analysis to appreciate that the chance of someone finding your site by accident is close to zero.

There are three ways people will get to your site. First, they come to it because you can tell them the URL, either directly or through your advertising. Second, they find it through a link on another site. Third, they find it through search engines.

The best place to begin promoting your Web site is within your existing contact network. Plaster your Web site address on everything that represents your business or touches your buying public—your business cards, invoices, letterhead, and yellow pages ads. It's also worthwhile to announce your Web site through a mailing to vendors, associates, and business contacts.

Don't merely tell people that you have a new Web site, offer them an incentive to visit: a free report, a sample product, a free teleclass, anything with perceived value. You can provide extra motivation to people by offering special benefits that carry an expiration date.

Search Engine Strategies

Search engines are a major source of Web site visitors, but to optimize their effectiveness you need to understand how they work. Search engines do not search millions of Web sites anew each time someone orders a search. Rather, they search their existing indexes of Web sites, which have been ordered by keywords. When users type their search terms and hit "search," search engines scan their indexes, returning links to those Web sites whose listed key words match the search terms the visitors used.

Search engines form their indexes in a couple of ways. Most "crawl" the Web with electronic "spiders," scanning millions of sites to collect keywords. This collecting and cataloging of information enables them to make some sense out of what would otherwise be the chaos of the Internet. Search engines get some keywords by scanning the contents of sites, and some from the keywords explicitly submitted by site owners for inclusion in search engine databases.

To make the most of search engines, you must optimize your Web site before you submit such information to them. You must also employ tactics that ensure Web spiders find and catalog your site accurately. Most major search engines allow you to register your site free. You can simply go to each major search site, click on the button marked "Add Your Site" or "Submit URL" or something similar, and fill in your site information.

It's important to regularly monitor your search engine listings to make sure they are working to your advantage. Getting and staying listed in search engines is part art, part science that requires ongoing testing and detective work. It's a continual battle to keep your site indexed on the major search engines. Some experts suggest that you resubmit your site once a month.

Choosing Keywords Keywords play a central role in ensuring that prospects find your site. Search engines use the number and relative importance of the keywords associated with a site to determine whether a site will be found by a given search. When people search for topics related to your Web site, you want to rank high in the search findings. For this to happen, you must optimize your chances by ensuring that the best search phrases and keywords appear in various areas of your Web site, including title pages, section headings, and site descriptions.

Determining keywords related to your business is pretty straightforward for you. But you will still need to test your assumptions about the words that are most likely to be used by prospects. This requires a little detective work. An easy way is asking people within your target market to suggest words they'd be inclined to use when searching for businesses like yours. The results may surprise you.

You can visit competitor sites to study their keyword usage. (You can view a Web site's meta tags by bringing up the site page, and then looking in your Web browser under View/Source. This will show you the meta tags they are using.) You can also compare the relative ranking of various sites by looking them up with popular search engines. See the Meta Tags section on page 159.

Finally, there are several online services that provide keyword analysis based on the most popular search terms.

The most important place to include keywords is in the body text of your pages. It is the percentage of keywords within the total number of words of your individual pages that constitutes what search engines call their "density". Keyword density matters in different ways to different search engines; most prefer a per-page keyword density of between 5 and 7 percent.

Site Description Once you have a list of keywords, write a site description that makes use of them. For example, if you're an attorney specializing in bankruptcy cases in Chicago, your list of keywords might be:

- Bankruptcy
- Chicago
- Attorney
- Bankruptcy attorney
- Consumer bankruptcy

Make sure that your description both reads well and includes your strongest keywords. Starting from the above list of keywords, a good description might read, "Bankruptcy attorneys specializing in consumer bankruptcy in the Chicago area."

Page Titles You need to give titles to all pages on your Web site, with special attention to the home page. The title is something that you program behind the scenes in HTML code, the language that describes how text should be formatted when a browser displays it on the screen. The tags are simple but play a very important role in your search engine strategy.

The title of your home page is given extra attention by search engines seeking to catalog your site. You need to make sure it includes the keywords you want to have associated with your site.

Page titles are what visitors see at the top of their Web browsers. A sample page title might look like this: "Chicago Law Firm Specializing In Consumer Bankruptcies."

Meta Tags Meta tags are also descriptions that work behind the scenes in HTML code. Although visitors won't see them, they play an important role in determining how search engines treat your site. There are two fields of meta tags to address.

The "description" is a short description of what your site is about. It goes a bit further than your site description and page titles. The keyword meta tag is a place to list additional keywords related to your site. This is where you will pick a few additional words to expand your description in a way that gives users more opportunities to find your site through the search engines.

The following examples display how meta tags might appear on a Web site:

META NAME="description" content="We are a Chicago-based law firm specializing in consumer bankruptcies.":

META NAME="keywords" content="bankruptcy, bankruptcy attorney, filing bankruptcy, Chicago, Chicago attorney, Chicago bankruptcy, consumer bankruptcy":

Pay-to-Submit and Pay-Per-Click Search Engines

Everything was once free on the Internet, but many online businesses, including many search engines, are now charging for access.

Yahoo!, one of the first and still one of the most important search engines, charges a fee to include your site in their database. Unlike "spider"-driven search engines, Yahoo! is a directory. Instead of trawling the Internet and organizing its findings, Yahoo! uses live people to evaluate Web sites and decide whether or not to include them in their directory.

Yahoo! now uses a pay-for-consideration strategy. If you want your site to be listed in Yahoo!, you must pay them a few hundred dollars just to be considered. There are no guarantees that they will actually list the site, and the fee is nonrefundable. Despite the fee, Yahoo! is still a great place to list your Web site. You have a good chance of being listed if you submit a well-designed, genuinely useful Web site, with smartly optimized keywords.

Another new concept is that of pay-per-click search engines, which allow Web sites to bid on keywords, and in effect buy their way to the top of the list of sites found when people search on those keywords. These search engines operate on a commission basis: you determine a dollar amount, list your site, and bid for keywords related to your site. You pay a deposit against future click-throughs. When users search on your keywords, your site comes up higher in the listings than those who've paid less or nothing.

The pay-per-click strategy is becoming more popular. It can work for you if you select good keywords, optimize your site to encourage sales, and bid on keywords for reasonable prices. What's reasonable? That depends on how much traffic the engine brings to your site, and the number of visitors who turn into paying customers.

Monitoring Results

There are many software programs to help you keep track of the various aspects of your Web marketing efforts. Some help you determine the types of keywords people are using to find your site. Others show you where people are spending time within your Web site, and at individual pages.

By taking advantage of the many tools available to track your Web marketing efforts, you continually perfect your marketing strategies and Web site to build a powerful Web presence. Such tools can also save you a lot of time and money by showing you ineffective keywords, those that nobody is using in search engines. You can also learn where people go on your site, and revamp areas that are getting

Joe Vitale on the Power of E-mail Marketing

REAL-WORLD SUCCESS STORY

Joe Vitale is president of Hypnotic Marketing, Inc., and author of *Spiritual Marketing*. As a writer and marketing consultant, he's moved much of his business online. He uses the Internet in a variety of ways to sell his products and services. "The Internet is my home these days. Over 90 percent of my business comes from the Internet," says Vitale.

Vitale was once told that if he could create a mailing list of his own with 10,000 names on it, he'd never have to work again. He began to believe this advice when he made $25,000 in one week with one e-mail sent to a list of 8,000 names.

When Vitale determined to make his book *Spiritual Marketing* a bestseller, he contacted other Internet entrepreneurs and offered to split profits from book sales if they sent an e-mail offer for the book to their subscribers. Vitale sent 8,000 e-mail messages asking people to buy his book from Amazon.com on either of two specified days. In return, he offered free access to marketing articles posted at his Web site that were normally available only for a fee.

With the help of his online friends, Vitale's online marketing tactics paid off. He sold 5,000 copies on his two specified days, plus an additional 2,500 to date. "I was easily able to drive people to Amazon.com, and by becoming the best-selling book for two days, I got a lot of attention."

The undiscovered gold, according to Vitale, isn't in merely putting up a Web site, but in using e-mail to connect with people and exploit opportunities. "My best advice is to start befriending people online," says Vitale. "Build your list, make friends, offer fair deals, and prosper. You might try Web seminars, e-consulting, e-products, and who knows what else."

"E-mail levels the playing field. You can reach anyone with a simple e-mail and a little searching. I've managed to get testimonials from celebrities, start relationships with famous people who are now my friends, make win-win deals, create entire products, and much more, all with simple e-mail. The Net is new. We don't know the rules, and in most cases there aren't any. Think big!"

Seth Godin Unleashes the Power of Viral Marketing

REAL-WORLD SUCCESS STORY

Word-of-mouth is one of the oldest ways businesses become successful. Viral marketing, a new twist on the old idea, is word-of-mouth conducted at Internet speed. Given its nature, viral marketing is a natural for promoting your slightly famous Web site.

"Sometimes it seems as if everyone you know is watching the same television show, reading the same book, or talking about the same movie, Web site, or television commercial," writes viral marketing guru Seth Godin in an article in *Fast Company*. "It usually happens because an idea spreads on its own, not because a company behind a product spends a ton of money advertising it." Viral marketing imitates this phenomenon by encouraging Internet users to pass marketing messages to others by e-mail, thus raising brand awareness exponentially.

Godin put this idea to the test with his book *Unleashing the Idea Virus*. Published initially as an e-book and later in print, it became one of most successful e-books of all time when he made it available for free from his Web site (www.ideavirus.com) prior to publishing it as a hardcover a few months later. More than 100,000 people downloaded his e-book, and many more forwarded it electronically to friends. Not only did the success of his e-book validate Godin's theories, it secured enough advance orders for a hard copy version that justified a 28,000-copy print run, a distribution deal with a major publisher, and translation deals with publishers in Brazil, Japan, and Korea.

little attention. Your Web host may be able to provide these functions as part of its package.

Keep in mind that the world of Internet search engines is complex; the material in this chapter is just an introduction. Several excellent books on the more technical points of Internet marketing are widely available and you should take their advice seriously.

The Online Sales Cycle

In addition to its marketing value, your Web site is a sales tool. But because skepticism runs high in the world of online commerce, you'll need to earn visitor trust over time in order to realize sales.

Godin believes that any viable commercial concept can become an idea virus as recipients become "infected" and pass it on to others. "This wasn't all premeditated. I did almost nothing fancy to make this work," says Godin. "The bottom line is that it doesn't take cash to distribute a book anymore. You can now build an asset on the Internet, and then transfer it through a publisher, distributor, or partner."

He offers the following advice for creating successful Internet viral marketing campaigns:

- Create an online experience that offers your users something completely new, something they can't get offline.
- Fill the vacuum in the marketplace with your version of the idea so completely that competitors will first have to eliminate your virus before they can unleash one of their own.
- Get permission from users to maintain an ongoing dialogue with them, so that you can build a relationship that gives them a beneficial experience and gives you a profit stream.
- Continue creating noteworthy online experiences to spread new viruses. Always begin by infecting your core audience.

"The future belongs to marketers who establish a foundation and process where interested people can market to each other," he writes. "Ignite consumer networks and then get out of the way by offering something new and valuable that will attract people to your Web site and get them talking."

This means turning one-time visitors into subscribers who either return to your site on a regular basis or sign up for an e-mail newsletter.

Successful Web sites give their online visitors a reason to keep coming back by providing fresh, evolving, up-to-date content. They also provide a sign-up button or banner on every page. The easier it is to respond, the more subscribers you'll get.

Many visitors will need an inducement to move from an anonymous visitor to a card-carrying member of your *slightly famous* world. Offer them something valuable in exchange for their e-mail addresses. Give away free e-books, reports, articles, or anything else of obvious benefit. Downloadable files—particularly those offering timely content, such as special reports—have high perceived value, and cost you nothing to deliver, while offering your online visitor a good reason to give you an e-mail address.

CHAPTER 9

Stand and Deliver: Speaking Strategies

Harriet Schechter, founder of The Miracle Worker Organizing Service in San Diego, is the author of three books, including *Let Go of Clutter,* that have been published in five languages. She has been interviewed on *Good Morning America* and numerous radio and television programs, and has been quoted in hundreds of publications including the *New York Times, USA Today,* and the *Atlantic Monthly.* Harriet's media exposure has played a large part in her success, but she points to her public speaking and seminars as primary causes of that success, helping her get nearly 75 percent of her business.

"I founded The Miracle Worker Organizing Service in 1986, and by 1988 was presenting speeches and seminars," says Schechter. "I had not planned on becoming a speaker; it was something that evolved. After I spoke to local organizations like the Lions Club, Rotary, and Kiwanis, my business really took off. Soon I was offered paid speaking engagements, and was prompted to become an author because audience members kept asking me if I had a book."

Public speaking is the perfect *slightly famous* marketing method, because it showcases your knowledge in polished form to people who are interested in hearing it. A person who takes the podium is seen as somebody with something worth saying—something audience members would like to know themselves. Speaking can be the fastest, easiest, and cheapest way to establish yourself as an expert, and it gives you tremendous credibility that increases over time. When done well, a speech can help you close sales before you leave the room. Having heard you speak, people feel they know you personally, and are more confident about hiring you.

Get on the Program

Speakers are in great demand—especially those willing to speak for free. Dottie and Lilly Walters, authors of *Speak and Grow Rich*, estimate that there are over nine thousand speaking opportunities a day in the United States. Clubs, organizations, and associations are eager to establish relationships with speakers who present useful, interesting material to members at meetings, seminars, conferences, and workshops, and you don't have to be a seasoned speaker to get started.

Even so, just because it's easy to get booked somewhere as a speaker doesn't mean it's worth doing. Before you commit yourself, try to find out about the audience. Most organizations can answer these questions:

- Are audience members really members of your target market?
- How many people are likely to show up for the talk?
- What kinds of speakers have recently presented to the group?
- If expenses are involved, will the organization reimburse you?
- Can you hand out materials and/or gather audience contact information?
- Can you sell your books or other materials at the talk?

It takes time to prepare your speech, travel to a speaking venue, and give a talk. Before you pursue a speaking opportunity, or accept an invitation to speak, make sure it has a high probability of benefiting your business.

Here are a few of the most common venues for promotional speaking.

Service Clubs Clubs like the Kiwanis, Lions, and Rotary provide ample opportunities for speaking. Start with organizations where you're already a member.

Chambers of Commerce Local Chambers of Commerce typically have several program meetings each month that require outside speakers. These cover a number of topics of interest to local businesses, from marketing and sales to technology.

Industry Associations Every industry has at least one association, such as the Council of Realtors or Financial Women International. These groups have monthly meetings and quarterly conferences and conventions, most of which utilize outside speakers.

Professional Associations There are several groups not specific to a particular industry, such as Leads Clubs International and American Business Women's Association, that are always looking for speakers.

Continuing Education Programs Teaching a class is a great way to gain credibility in your community. Continuing education programs, adult education programs like the Learning Annex, community colleges, and university extension programs provide opportunities.

Hold Your Own Event You can host an event in your office, in a rented hotel room, or in a conference room at the office of a friend. Such an event allows you to showcase your business in the best way possible.

Online Chats and Teleconferences You don't have to be personally present to give a talk that reaches your target market. Online chats and teleconferences, using your own or others' Web sites or telephone lines, can help you reach a lot of people eager to hear your message.

Approaching Speaking Venues

Once you've compiled a list of potential speaking venues, do whatever you can to become familiar with your targeted organizations. It's always helpful to attend a few meetings to determine whether the organization prefers individual speakers or panels. Read the organization's newsletter to familiarize yourself with member concerns and interests. Then choose a few topics you can tailor to that audience.

Contact the program chairman for each group on your list. Ask to be considered for speaking opportunities and describe how the group will benefit from your talk. Keep in mind that many programs are scheduled from six to twelve months in advance.

Send the program chairman an introductory package, including a cover letter naming other groups that have sponsored your presentations, and citing comments from attendees (when applicable), a personal and company biography, and any other materials that validate your expertise. Briefly describe one to three potential speaking topics, so as to give meeting planners a choice. Each topic should highlight your expertise, while allowing for opportunities to tell stories about your work.

The National Speakers Association notes that most speakers rely on word of mouth to land repeated speaking engagements. Even though it takes some legwork to land your first speaking engagements, the more you speak and the better you become at it, the more you will be in demand.

Preparation

According to the *Book of Lists*, speaking in public produces more fear and anxiety than any other activity—death comes in only seventh.

Roseann Sullivan
on the Power of Public Speaking

REAL-WORLD SUCCESS STORY

Ever since she unexpectedly won a speech contest during a summer school session, Roseann Sullivan has been hooked on communicating effectively. Today, she coaches corporate CEOs and conducts workshops for organizations on how to communicate more effectively. Her clients include Hewlett-Packard, Pepsi-Cola, Apple Computer, and Clorox Company.

"Too often, beginners don't realize the benefits speaking will bring to their businesses, and how much they have to contribute," says Sullivan. "Years ago, when I booked speakers for the Learning Annex, my job was to find independent business owners who could speak about hot topics. I'd approach people and say, 'You have a booming business. Wouldn't it be nice to share it with people?' The response I'd always get was, 'What would I possibly tell people?'"

Eventually, she'd talk them into it, and they would give their speech. And time and again she would see them generate prospects and sales as a result. "That was when I recognized the power of speaking," says Sullivan. "Even if there are only five people in a room, you never know what will come of it because each of those five people knows five people and so on."

The most important thing to remember is that you don't have to be a great speaker to get started. "If you can just get up there and do a decent job you will immediately position yourself as an expert," says Sullivan. "The value of speaking is that it gives people a taste of what you offer in a nonthreatening environment. I hired my caterer because I saw her doing a cooking class, and my house cleaner when she gave a presentation at a Chamber of Commerce."

The good news is that the more you speak, the easier it becomes. Public speaking can be both rewarding and enjoyable.

Although you don't have to be a master orator to be effective, you do need to take time to prepare your speech; you want to avoid damaging your reputation by appearing disorganized, inarticulate, or uninformed. Spend time practicing to build your confidence and abilities. Remember that all great speakers worked to develop their speaking abilities. Martin Luther King gave countless sermons at small churches before his famous "I Have a Dream" speech.

"Speaking before a group about your business is the cheapest, best way to market your product or service, and expand your customer base," says Patricia Fripp, a Certified Speaking Professional (CSP) who started with a career in the beauty industry more than 25 years ago. Since then she has gained a reputation as an award-winning speaker, author, sales trainer, and in-demand speech coach. "I started talking about my business at organizations such as Rotary, Kiwanis, and Optimists. I didn't have any public speaking experience, so I studied the pros."

Her practice paid off. Since 1980 she has spoken to over 100 groups every year. This includes Fortune 100 companies and major associations worldwide. The National Speakers Association, with more than 4,000 members, elected her their first female President in 1984. She has since received every mark of prestige given by the NSA, including membership in their Hall of Fame, and their highest honor, the Cavett Award, considered the "Oscar" of the speaking world.

Fine-tuning your public speaking skills will also improve your performance in other areas, such as conducting meetings and making sales presentations. Every time you speak with confidence, style, and ease, you enhance the reputation of your company, attract more business, and generate credibility for yourself.

Toastmasters (www.toastmasters.org), an international nonprofit group that helps people speak more effectively, is a great resource for aspiring speakers. For a nominal fee, members learn how to speak to groups in a supportive environment. A typical Toastmasters club is made up of 20 to 30 people who meet once a week for about an hour. Each meeting gives everyone an opportunity to practice.

You can further hone your speaking skills by participating in networking groups that require you to talk about your business. These groups usually give members plenty of opportunities to introduce themselves at meetings, give short business presentations, and profit from audience feedback. Practice the basics: planning what you want to say, using positive body language, pacing your speech, and interacting with your listeners.

Your Public Speaking Engagement

Larry Bird, the basketball great from the Boston Celtics, was known to dribble the ball for hours on a basketball court in order to identify the dead spots on the floor and avoid them during the game. On the day of a speech, good speakers, like good athletes, arrive early to become familiar with the room, microphone system, slide projector, and audiovisual equipment. Nothing detracts from the beginning of a presentation as much as testing the equipment by asking the audience, "Can you hear me?" or "Would someone adjust the focus on the slide projector?"

Before the speech, greet guests at the door as they come in to become familiar with the audience and make yourself less nervous. Once you interact with people, you can visualize conversing with them as friends rather than as strangers.

Write Your Own Introduction

Don't leave your introduction in the hands of the meeting planner. Prepare your own introduction, send a copy to the meeting planner, and bring another on the day of the speech. Keep your introduction short, no more than one minute in length, and craft it in a way that creates an interest in your subject matter and establishes your expertise. Your goal is to inform and arouse interest, not to give an exhaustive (and exhausting) infomercial.

Nine Rules for Strong Presentations

1. **Effective speeches come in three segments—beginning, middle, and end.** Create your speech around this simple formula. Introduce the scope or nature of your topic in the begin-

ning, go into more detail, background, or illustrative stories or examples in the middle, and point out conclusions, or issue a call to action, at the end.

2. **Don't read from notes.** Excessive note reading while speaking keeps you from creating a bond with the audience. Use hand-written notes only as an outline to keep yourself on track. Have written bullet points to capture main ideas. They're easy to see and will jog your memory. The briefer your sentences, the eas-ier the speech will be to deliver. Practicing your speech before-hand will make you more confident and less reliant on written notes.

3. **Use a microphone when necessary.** A microphone not only adds volume, it also invests you with an aura of authority. Make sure you have a microphone available for your talk if the size of the room and audience warrant it.

4. **Start with a story.** Launch your talk with a short personal story about an incident related to your business. Make sure the story "humanizes" you, so as to develop a reservoir of good will that will extend to the rest of the speech. For example, "Today, I want to talk about the five most common mistakes people make when starting a consulting firm, and how I made every one of them."

5. **Use client examples.** Use client examples to illustrate the main points of your talk. Describe a problem a client had, and what you did to help. This gives your audience a greater under-standing of what your firm does, and shows in a positive light how you serve clients and customers. Using client examples in your speech is also a sales tool that encourages audience mem-bers to imagine themselves as your clients.

6. **Ask your audience questions.** Good questions engage the audience and help provide direction and momentum for your

talk. By asking the right questions, you can determine the concerns and interests of your audience, and tailor your presentation to those concerns. By asking for answers from the audience, you also encourage people to become involved.

7. **Body language sends a message.** If you look confident, the audience will perceive you that way. When you want to emphasize a point, use simple, understated gestures.

8. **Make regular eye contact with audience members.** This will help you draw listeners into your speech. Nodding to emphasize points helps you make a connection with the audience. If audience members nod when you nod, you make an instant bond.

9. **Your voice is an instrument of persuasion. Use it that way.** Don't rush your delivery. This can be difficult if you are nervous, but take time to gather your thoughts. Try to set a relaxed, conversational pace. When you make a particularly relevant point, emphasize it by pausing before and after the point.

Concluding the Talk

Be prepared to answer questions. In fact, encourage them by seeding the audience with questions. Have a few prepared questions on $3'' \times 5''$ cards, and give them to a few carefully selected members of the audience before you speak. Have these individuals ask the questions on the cards if there's a dead spot during the question-and-answer session.

The time immediately following a speech is critically important for promoting business. Don't be in a hurry to pick up your slides and leave after it is over. Make yourself available to the audience. If you have books, booklets, or other information products to sell, now is the time. When audiences have just heard you speak, they are usually primed to take your advice and move to the next step. Make it easy for them, and profitable for you, by selling information products at the back of the room.

Creating Promotional Opportunities

Since your main purpose in speaking is to build your business, you need to go into each speaking engagement prepared to maximize your return.

Ask the group if they will seek media publicity for your talk. If not, ask if you can supply a press release of your own to appropriate media. Because most organizations have a newsletter, ask them to publish an article by or about you, mentioning your speech, either before or after your talk—or both! As an alternative, you can ask them to include your brochure or other materials related to your company in their next mailing. Point out that this will help to boost attendance at the meeting you'll be speaking at. Develop handouts that have value for your audience, and make sure they include your name, address, telephone number, and Web-site address.

Speaking engagements are a way to gather prospect names, addresses, and e-mail addresses. Offer an incentive, such as a free book or consultation, to get people to drop their business cards in a box. Tell them that you would like to send them your free newsletter—or something else that might have value for them—and that they can unsubscribe at any time.

Audience members may not need you today, but if you make a good impression and continue to send them something on a regular basis, you will build a list of prospects that will grow and bear fruit for years to come.

Seminars

An experienced public speaker who bills himself as "The Mole Man," pest-management expert Jeff Holper promotes his business,

Caterina Rando on Handouts That Get You Clients

TIPS FROM THE GURU

Caterina Rando, international speaker, life-and-business success coach, and author of *Learn to Power Think,* suggests creating "tip cards" to give out at the end of each talk. As its name implies, a tip card contains useful information, but it is formatted to be posted in homes and offices. Once on the wall it's a constant reminder of your talk. The following tips are excerpted from her special report, *Attracting Clients with Ease.*

- Always have something to give audience participants when you speak. Audience members will forget you when they walk out the door if they don't have a part of you to take home with them.

- In addition to the information you conveyed in your talk, consider giving participants an article you have written on the topic. This makes you look like an expert. Always have your brochures and business cards displayed for the taking.

- Include a flyer on your upcoming seminars or a schedule showing where you will be speaking next.

- Put your business name, address, Web site address (URL), and phone number on the bottom of each sheet of paper you give your audience.

- Use an evaluation form to ask audience members for feedback on how your presentation can be improved. While you have to be pretty thick-skinned to do this, it can be helpful.

- Use an action sheet. This is a sheet that asks audience members what action they are going to take now that they have heard your talk.

- Ask audience members for their contact information. You will at least get their e-mail address if you offer to send them your monthly newsletter or articles.

- Ask qualifying questions to help you determine if you should follow-up with an individual. For example, "Do you or does your company use (fill in the blank with your product or service)?" or "Would you be interested in a complimentary consultation to discuss (fill in the blank with your product or service)?"

- Hold a drawing to make sure everyone turns in their forms; give away one of your products or services, or a book of interest to audience members.

Holper's Pest & Animal Solutions, through a workshop for home-owners. To standing-room-only crowds at home shows, trade shows, and wildlife conferences, his program, Holper's Terminator University, offers ten easy steps to dealing with moles and other rodents that invade lawns and gardens. These workshops are a way for Holper to sell his many books, reports, videos, and mole traps.

Bringing a group of prospects together in one place is an efficient way to generate leads and sales. You can charge an admission fee, but you won't get as many attendees. So you have to decide in advance on whom you want to attend and what their attendance is worth to you. And remember that people who have paid want, expect, and deserve more.

Whether for free or for the cost of a ticket, people attend seminars because they want to learn something. They understand that you're there because you have a product or service, but they don't want to feel pressured to buy. You may sell home security systems, for example, but the seminar should focus not on your products, but on benefits such as "safety" or "peace of mind." Useful information is the key. People feel cheated and trapped if you present biased information that amounts to little more than a sales pitch for your company. In contrast, if you inspire trust by giving away some of your knowledge—and thus demonstrating your expertise and fair-mindedness—attendees will turn to you when they are ready for more help.

The easiest way to launch a seminar is through a local organization, community college, or continuing education program. These institutions have positive reputations that will boost the credibility of your seminar, plus they have the infrastructure for making the event happen, catalogs, mailing lists, and meeting rooms. These institutions will also be able to give you feedback on what kind of response you are likely to get.

Trade associations or other industry groups are often willing to promote seminars to their members, if the seminar topic is relevant to their membership. If you can get such an association to sponsor the event you have gone a long way to establishing credibility.

Join with Others for Panel Discussions

Partnering with related businesses to create discussion panels and group seminars lets you share the cost and labor involved in organizing an event, while at the same time creating value from the consumer's point of view. Moreover, if you're not an experienced speaker, taking part in a panel or team presentation reduces the pressure on you.

The ideal panel comprises people from related businesses and professions, but without much overlap. An accountant, for example, could team up with a retirement planner and an accounting software expert for a seminar about small business financial strategies. If each partner can attract attendees from among their clients, then they all can benefit from referrals.

If you're in charge of the panel discussion, make sure everyone is clear about what the discussion is supposed to cover. You don't want to be too general, nor do you want to cover the same points. It's also important to enforce time limits. A panel can quickly fall apart when one person talks well beyond the appointed time limit. Ideally, a 50-minute panel discussion with four panelists would give each panelist 10 minutes to speak, and then have 10 minutes left for questions and discussion from the audience. Have somebody in back of the room hold up a "one-minute" sign, a "30-second" and a "stop" sign that everyone on the panel can see.

Be clear about how you will handle questions from the audience. One common method is to take questions at the very end. Try to make sure that at least one question goes to each person on the panel.

REAL-WORLD SUCCESS STORY

Steve Dubin Learns the Power of Seminar Partnering

Steve Dubin of PR Works embraced partnering when he helped a Boston-based moving and storage company plan a joint seminar to reach business prospects.

He advised the moving company to partner with related businesses to create a more valuable seminar with more crowd appeal, rather than go it alone. The result was a panel of "relocation experts" for a Home Buyers and Sellers Seminar that included a mortgage broker, a real estate attorney, a realtor, and the moving company.

The seminar was a success. Not only did the moving company and its partners generate leads, they now hold their seminars on a regular basis, and attract free media coverage to help promote them.

"I've found that teaming up with a group of related businesses generates more interest among potential attendees," says Dubin. "Bringing together a broad-based panel of experts, instead of one company sponsoring a seminar, gives people a sense that the event is truly an informational opportunity and not a sales pitch."

Here's a press release that Dubin used to promote this seminar:

For Immediate Release

Contact: Steve V. Dubin, PR Works
sdubin@prworkzone.com, (781) 878-9533

Teleclasses

Teleclasses are, in essence, virtual classrooms created with an automated conference call system called a "bridge line." Students register for a teleclass, receive the virtual-classroom telephone number, and call it at the appointed hour to get connected to the host and other attendees in a format that is part lecture, part interactive classroom.

Teleclasses are a great way for businesses to provide information to prospects, clients, and customers all over the world, with minimal cost and effort. Unlike seminars and other meetings, they eliminate the need to travel. Both hosts and participants can attend from their

FREE SEMINAR ON BUYING AND SELLING YOUR HOME IN TODAY'S MARKET

MILTON, MA. Humboldt Storage and Moving continues its series of FREE seminars on "Buying and Selling Your Home in Today's Market" on Monday, October 18, from 7–8:30 PM at the Braintree Sheraton Tara, Exit 6 off Route 128 (across from the South Shore Plaza).

Expert panelists will outline the necessary steps to selling your home at an optimal price, as well as "buying smart" in today's market. Acquiring bank-owned properties will be emphasized.

This ongoing series is sponsored by Humboldt Storage and Moving, one of Boston's oldest and largest relocation firms, and an award-winning United Van Lines agent in Lower Milton Falls.

The seminar moderator is Howard Goldman, President of Humboldt Storage and Moving. Panelists are Claire Garrity of Coldwell Banker Residential Real Estate, who will give the inside scoop on buying and selling homes; Attorney Kenneth K. Quigley, whose topic is "How to Look at Equity in your Home"; and Mary Ellen MacInnis of the Salem Five, who will advise sellers on "How to Obtain the Best Mortgage for the Next Residence."

At the conclusion of the seminar, there will be a question-and-answer period, followed by complimentary refreshments.

Attend this seminar and get information on the housing market from the people who really know. Please R.S.V.P. by calling Claire LeSage of Humboldt Storage and Moving at (617) 696-9500.

offices, their favorite easy chair at home, or even by mobile phone while on vacation. Teleclasses make it easy to connect to prospects all over the world.

Business coach and teleclass leader Michael Losier took his first teleclass three years ago and was impressed with the potential for this type of meeting. Because it was so convenient and so much fun, he decided to try running one himself, and set up a teleclass about exhibiting at trade shows. "I had 60 students in my first class, which was very profitable, and many later hired me as a consultant," says Losier.

Since then teleclasses have helped Losier expand his market, and gotten him a stream of international clients. "After just six months of teaching teleclasses I was able to leave my desk job. I ended up writing two books on my teleclass courses, thanks in part to the feedback my students gave me. I also became a teleclass trainer to leaders across the globe."

According to Anne-Marie Rennick of Learningbyphone.com, teleclasses offer an alternative to live presentations and seminars that doesn't put added stress on people's already jam-packed schedules. "Teleclasses enable you to bring together 10, 20, or 100 people to listen to you talk about your business for an hour, allowing you to engage them and display your mastery," says Rennick.

Rennick's teleclasses generally meet once a week for three to four weeks, with each meeting lasting 55 minutes. "This gives students a chance to absorb a topic in bite-sized pieces, like a short college course, with time in between classes to apply what they've learned."

Many businesses are also offering free teleclasses as an affordable way to connect to groups of targeted prospects and attract new business. "A lot of businesses offer a free initial teleclass to attract people and build a list of prospects," says Rennick.

As in any class, the quality and effectiveness of the experience depends on getting people to participate and interact. And by their very nature, teleclasses are more interactive. They make it easier to participate, because in a roomful of strangers, many attendees are too shy to speak up.

That's why teleclasses often experience increased participation among attendees. They are highly interactive, more like tele-discussions, which make it easier to share and be heard, to ask questions and get answers (they also, of course, make it easy for the very shy to just sit and listen as if they were hiding in the back row of a classroom). "In teleclasses, there's no worry about body language, or turning red when you speak," says Rennick. "Participants are more free to engage in the teleclass."

Josiane Feigon, TeleSmart Communications

REAL-WORLD SUCCESS STORY

During the economic slowdown that started around 2000, many companies slashed their training budgets. This affected Josiane Feigon, president of TeleSmart Communications, whose traditional sales-skills training seminars, directed at sales and customer support professionals, became an easy target for budget cutting.

"The economic slowdown really hit my client base," says Feigon. "As they tightened their belts, it became much more difficult for managers to justify bringing me on-site. They were very reluctant to invest their salespeople's time, pulling them off the phones or out of the field, to travel to training."

But Feigon realized that her clients needed her training more than ever. So she started offering teleclasses as an alternative to on-site seminars. She reformatted her previous multiple-day, 3-hour seminars into a series of 60-minute teleclasses, and used the same delivery principles that made her successful with her on-site training.

"I've always been a big advocate of the telephone as a primary business tool," says Feigon. "And I've always been committed to teaching people to sell by phone. It makes perfect sense to replicate the same environment where salespeople work. Now, I create a memorable experience without being face to face. I time each activity, question, and learning objective to make an impact immediately — within seconds."

Feigon owns a 10-seat license on her telephone bridge line, and places a limit of 8 participants on the sessions. Before the session, she gets a list of attendees, sends out e-mail reminders before placing each call, and offers fifteen 60-minute topics, following the same formula to deliver each.

"My main goal is to engage the team immediately, and keep it going until the last minute," says Feigon. "All the skills I teach are designed to be tested the moment the participants get off the phone. I want to get the salespeople 'addicted' to this type of training. I've designed 3-, 6-, and 12-month teleclass plans that would ideally be incorporated into every training schedule."

Feigon continues to expand her use of teleclasses, constantly looking for improvements. "I don't think we've even begun to scratch the surface of this type of technology," says Feigon. "I constantly attend different teleclasses to discover new possibilities. Teleclasses are the answer to so many issues today. It's had a big impact on my business and quality of life. I'm traveling much less, practicing my trade with clients around the country from my office."

One of Rennick's popular teleclasses covers how to design, conduct, and market a great teleclass. "It's the longest running and most popular of my classes," says Rennick, who usually has from eight to twelve people taking part in her class. She supplements phone time with a manual. "I use that manual as the backbone of the class—then we're all on the same page, so to speak."

10 Info-Products: Create Multiple Income Streams

If you run a small business providing services only, your ability to earn is limited by the number of hours you have available—once you're fully booked, that's it. Information products are especially appealing, therefore, to service businesses whose only saleable asset, otherwise, is billable hours.

It may take some effort to turn your skills, knowledge, and advice into products, but once you've done it, you've created assets that can then be sold and resold over and over again. If you create and market information products that are in high demand, you can literally make money while you sleep.

Anybody Can Be an Info-Entrepreneur

You don't have to be a high-end consultant or established author to produce information products; anybody with special knowledge can use that knowledge to create saleable products. And these products, in turn, will advance your *slightly famous* marketing strategy.

REAL-WORLD SUCCESS STORY

Bill Brooks Reaps Multiple Rewards Through Products

Bill Brooks, CEO of The Brooks Group, a sales training and consulting firm, is the author of nine books and over 150 information products that appear in a wide variety of formats: audio tapes and CDs, videos, CD-ROMs, DVDs, books, manuals, and Internet training systems.

"One of the great things about developing information products is they position you as an expert in whatever niche or segment you want to establish yourself," says Brooks. "The more knowledgeable you are, the more perceived value you have with prospects. Information products position you as an industry leader by distilling your wisdom into concrete form."

According to Brooks, successfully embracing information products begins by taking an inventory of everything a company can provide their target market. "We market training programs for salespeople," says Brooks, "and in working with them we realized they needed advice for overcoming objections, staying motivated, and better managing their time. We address these topics in e-books, manuals, CDs, and special reports."

These information products have generated handsome profits for Brooks' company over the last 25 years. In addition, he also uses these information products as "premiums" to attract new prospects.

An exterminator, for example, can produce a "termite-proofing" report for homeowners, and offer it to prospects on a Yellow Pages ad or his Web site. A kickboxing instructor can develop a video training program that can be sold through local gyms to generate income and attract prospects for live training. A corporate communications consultant can develop an employee training program and workbook that can be sold to companies that don't have their own training programs.

Establish Credibility

Why do so many of the most respected business pros make sure that their names appear on books, articles, and other information products? Because having their names on a dust jacket, the byline of a white paper, or an audiotape training course has a way of convincing people that they know what they're talking about.

The added prestige of being an information-product developer lends you the kind of credibility that allows you to increase your hourly rates and project fees. Information products also let prospects sample your approach, your expertise, and your skills before they hire you. Businesses that produce and market information products regularly report that prospects not only buy those products, but also are more likely to inquire about additional products and services.

Expand Your Market

If you're a practitioner selling customized services to individual clients, you're excluding people who can't afford to hire you one-on-one. You are also limited to working with those in your immediate geographic area.

Turning your expertise into a product lets you serve all those potential customers who can't afford your personal-consulting rates, or who live outside the area you can easily travel to. You can expand your market because your information products provide a range of options at different price points. A small service business, for instance, could offer a one-on-one consulting package priced in the thousands of dollars, an online training course for a few hundred dollars, and a book priced below twenty dollars.

The result is a business that has "something for everyone," and converts many smaller prospects, who would otherwise pass you by, into paying customers. And although you make less per sale on these clients than you would for in-person service, you can make many more such sales.

What Products Are Best for You?

Here are some of the most common information products, along with production tips and suggestions for including them in your *slightly famous* marketing strategy.

REAL-WORLD SUCCESS STORY

David Garfinkel Gains Independence and Respect

David Garfinkel, president of Overnight Marketing, is a long-time copywriter who became an information product entrepreneur. Garfinkel developed information products related to his copywriting expertise because he knew that many business marketers wanted to learn to be better copywriters.

His home-study copywriting course included an audiocassette album and workbook. He also created a Web-based tutorial, and wrote an e-book devoted to advertising headlines. Garfinkel then partnered with others to get the word out, and created an online marketing campaign. "I put together structured sessions that teach people how to be their own copywriter; I give them what they need to know to do what I do.

Garfinkel credits his information products with helping him establish a widespread Internet reputation. "My information products have positioned me as a go-to guy about selling information online," says Garfinkel. "People also want to joint venture with me for projects.

"Having products puts you into a whole other category. You are seen as an instant guru. Not only do you get more respect, people don't argue about your prices or question your abilities. I now pick and choose my clients, and almost all of my prospects come through the reach and reputation I've established with my information products."

Booklets

Producing a booklet is one of the simplest ways to turn your knowledge into a saleable object that is easy to create, and inexpensive to produce and distribute. In particular, the ever-popular "tips" booklet is easy to write, and suited to almost any business topic. A common 8.5" by 3.5" booklet, which fits easily into a standard business envelope, can be produced for less than a dollar a copy, and sold for anywhere from three to ten times that amount.

The process of creating such a booklet is simple. You choose a subject and title (such as *151 Travel Tips* or *20 Ways to Keep Your Car New*), and jot down every fact and idea that comes to mind about that topic. After you have accumulated enough material to fill an eight- or 16-page booklet, group your tips under appropriate headings, and

Paulette Ensign's Booklet Journey   REAL-WORLD SUCCESS STORY

In 1991, long-time professional organizer Paulette Ensign, now the president of Tips Products International, spotted an offer for a free booklet called *117 Ideas for Better Business Presentations*. Upon seeing it, her first reaction was, "I could knock out something like this about organizing tips."

Ensign began collecting ideas for a booklet about business and household organizing tips. The result was not one but two 16-page tip booklets, *110 Ideas for Organizing Your Business Life* and *111 Ideas for Organizing Your Household*. Ensign printed 250 copies of each.

She sent review copies of her booklets to magazines and newspapers, inviting them to use excerpts as long as they included an invitation to readers to send her $3 plus a self-addressed stamped envelope for the booklet. Several publications accepted her offer, and the orders started dribbling in.

Ensign continued to cast "seeds" all over the place, targeting publications through library directories. In February 1992, a 12-page biweekly newsletter with 1.6 million readers ran nine lines of copy about one of her booklets, which resulted in 5,000 orders.

"I distinctly remember the day I went to my post office box and found a yellow slip in my box that said, 'see clerk,'" remembers Ensign. "There was a tub of envelopes that had arrived that day, about 250 envelopes as I recall, all with $3 in them."

Some "very wonderful" things began to happen as Ensign sold her booklets. A seminar company hired her to record an audio program based on her booklet. A manufacturer's representative ordered hundreds of booklets to send to his customers, and she began licensing reprint rights for her booklet, including one deal with a mail order catalog company that resulted in an agreement to print 250,000 copies.

---

create a table of contents. There you are. If you're a proficient editor and designer, you can prepare the whole piece for the printer, but for most businesspeople some production help at this point is probably in order.

Video, Audio, and CD-ROM

Audio and video products are well suited to presenting certain kinds of information, and can deliver benefits by allowing prospects to see

REAL-WORLD SUCCESS STORY

New World Library Publishes Print and Audio

New World Library offers a model that many small and mid-size publishers would be happy to emulate. With a strong line of self-help, inspirational, and New Age titles, the company's audio line brings in 15 to 20 percent of their total sales revenue. Over the years they have had two titles that sold over a quarter of a million copies in audio: Shakti Gawain's *Creative Visualization*, with steady sales over almost 20 years, and Deepak Chopra's *The Seven Spiritual Laws of Success*, which sold that many in less than three years.

With rare exceptions, the audio line is adapted from books that the company has originated. All the presenting is done by authors, and while New World Library jobs out the recording, the editing is done in-house. A major key to their success with audio has been their ability to promote a book and its audio version as a package. Finding it difficult to promote a stand-alone audio cost-effectively, the company includes both print and audio versions in every advertisement, listing, and press release. Author appearances naturally help in the sales of both products.

For both print and audio distribution, New World Library works with Publishers Group West, and even though retailer orders go through wholesalers, the company supports retail sales through active marketing efforts. They mail almost 4,000 catalogs to bookstores, New Thought churches, and specialty shops, and have identified a core list of about 700 stores that account for most of their business. In addition to the retail sales, New World Library actively pursues other markets for their audio line. They license audio rights to audio clubs such as Columbia House, Audio Book Club, and Doubleday Direct, and they sell to direct mail catalog houses such as Audio Editions and Audio Adventures.

New World Library's success in the audio field reflects consistently high-quality content in a subject area that has been popular since the inception of spoken-word audio, and steady efforts at marketing. Above all, they have built up a niche identity that serves them well in either format. Publishers considering their own line of audio must attend to these factors.

Excerpted from The Complete Guide to Book Marketing *by David Cole (Allworth Press)*

and hear you. Selling for prices ranging from $29 to $99, audiotapes can be highly profitable. Videos are usually priced between $30 and $150, but cost more to produce. A commonly sold form of audio is the taped talk recorded live at a workshop. While not always of the highest sound quality, these tapes are great ways to convey information in an easy-to-absorb format, and it's a format that people have learned to rely on.

Izzy Kalman, a school psychologist and psychotherapist, developed an audiotape called "How to Stop Being Teased and Bullied Without Really Trying," which he sells from his Web site for $19.95. The tape is a way for Kalman to offer low-priced help to children and their families, bring in some income, and cultivate potential clients.

Special Reports and Downloadable Files

Tip sheets and special reports provide highly specific, immediately usable information. They are also profitable and easy to produce. An environmental consultant, for example, could compile a tip sheet listing businesses that sell office furniture made from recycled materials. That consultant could also develop a special report titled *Reducing Indoor Air Pollution by Going Green,* which could be sold from a Web site or used as a marketing and sales tool.

Creating tip sheets and special reports is relatively easy. Tip sheets can be easily produced in a word-processing program, and reproduced on a laser printer. Special reports, which can run anywhere from five to sixty pages, go into greater depth about a subject, and can be sold or given away as marketing incentives.

As the number of potential clients and customers with Internet access increases, tip sheets and reports are increasingly being distributed as electronic files. Distributing information by e-mail and posting on Web sites is convenient for everyone. Information providers eliminate the need to print and mail documents, and

REAL-WORLD SUCCESS STORY

PinkMonkey Sells Downloads to College Students

A relatively new Web-based business, PinkMonkey.com (www.pinkmonkey.com), is now selling downloadable *Literature Notes* (study guides similar to the well-known Cliffs Notes), *Test Preparation Guides*, and *Course Guides* ("concise reviews of introductory-level course work such as Biology, Chemistry, Physics, Algebra, Geometry, Trigonometry, Calculus, Economics, Statistics, US History, World History, Government and more"). Files are stored and downloaded in PDF (Portable Document Format), a popular format for all kinds of Internet documents; it is read with Adobe's Acrobat Reader, a program available free via the Web. Both Windows-based PCs and Macs can access these files. The materials are competitively priced, easy to access, easy to download, and easy to pay for via credit card.

Free from the burden of maintaining a printed-book inventory, and serving a technologically sophisticated student audience, this company offers a model for creating electronic materials that may well compete successfully with their printed counterparts. PinkMonkey also benefits from the fact that the materials they are selling are relatively short, thus avoiding both the present resistance to reading book-length materials on-screen, and the need to print out a full-length book.

Excerpted from The Complete Guide to Book Marketing *by David Cole (Allworth Press)*

recipients enjoy instant access to information that might take several days to arrive by mail.

E-Books

Homer McDonald, a long-time marriage counselor in San Antonio, Texas, spent years dreaming of seeing his name on a book jacket. He specialized in working with couples on the brink of divorce, and he knew that a lot of people would like to know more about his successful strategies for avoiding marital breakups.

But when McDonald's marketing consultant, Dean Jackson, suggested that he might be better served by writing an e-book about his

Jim Edwards Teaches Home Sellers to Go It Alone

REAL-WORLD SUCCESS STORY

Jim Edwards had spent eight years as a mortgage broker when his wife suggested that he write a book about what he had learned. He considered approaching a major publisher, but ended up writing an e-book based on his real estate expertise. He called it *Selling Your Home Alone.*

Edwards set up a Web site devoted to the book that included a sales letter clearly explaining the benefits. Then, he used a number of devices to drive traffic to his Web site, including search-engine key-word strategies, joint ventures, and pay-per-click ads.

"In 1997, when I put my first book on the Internet, I had absolutely no clue what was going to happen," says Edwards. "Five years later, this same e-book sells consistently month after month, and now makes enough money to cover my house payment, two car payments, and the electric bill!"

Edwards emphasizes these elements in the creation and marketing of a successful e-book:

- Target your audience clearly.
- Find out exactly what they want and need that's not offered elsewhere.
- Help readers get quick results.
- Put your e-book on CD-ROM to distribute offline.
- Learn everything you can about marketing online, and be ready to adapt.

subject area that could be sold from his Web site, he was intrigued. In a period of 40 days, they distilled McDonald's years of experience into an e-book called *Stop Your Divorce*, which they sold as a downloadable file from www.stopyourdivorce.com.

Through search-engine key-word strategies, and partnerships with other divorce-related Web sites, McDonald has sold over ten thousand copies of his e-book since 1998 at $79 each. Not only was the book profitable, it has helped him convert a hefty percentage of book buyers to paying clients. "Some subjects beg to be sold online," says Jackson, the co-author. "Because our market niche is so specialized, and because we discovered that people on the brink of divorce seek help online, we did quite well developing this as an e-book."

Although e-books can be extremely profitable, they don't carry the credibility of a conventionally published book. Also, because they are outside the mainstream book distribution system, there are only a few places, other than your own Web site, where e-books can be marketed. Nevertheless, e-books, especially as problem-solvers, have shown they can work. Successful e-books have been published that address financial issues, relationships, emergencies, and emotional distress.

If you are self-publishing, e-books also offer some major advantages—no printing bills, no trucking, no packaging, no postage, and, at least for now, no sales tax. Readers get instant delivery. To create e-books, you merely need to convert your finished manuscript into a Web-acceptable format, such as PDF, HTML, or RTF files. These files can be read by most computer users right on their screens, and printed out on their own printers if they wish. As noted earlier, a popular program, Adobe Acrobat, is compatible with both Macs and PCs, and allows authors to encrypt e-books to avoid piracy.

Books

Having your name on a book can be an immense boost to your business. Of all information products, a book has the greatest potential to open doors.

"A book provides you with more credibility than anything else you can do: more credibility than an audiotape, a videotape, a seminar, a screenplay, or a song," says self-publishing expert Dan Poynter. "People place a higher value on a book than on a tape—even though the same amount of work may have gone into their production. The fact is, authors are highly valued in our society."

After spending 16 years working as a flight attendant for a major airline, Elliot Hester recounted his experiences in a book with plenty of attitude and self-deprecating humor, *Plane Insanity: A Flight Attendant's Tales of Sex, Rage, and Queasiness at 30,000 Feet.*

"My plan was to start as a travel writer, because I had free flights," says Hester. "I wrote stories about the places I'd traveled to, and sold them to several newspapers. Later, I used my work to land a travel column for Salon.com."

After his book was published, Elliott appeared as a guest on more than 150 radio talk shows, including *Fresh Air, The Savvy Traveler, The Today Show,* and *Inside Edition.* His success also helped him land a second book deal that paid him to travel around the world for a year, and chronicle his journey.

Finding a Publisher While certainly the info-product with the most status, a book is also the most difficult to develop. The traditional route is to go through a publisher who handles production, marketing, promotion, and distribution. Although publishing your book through a high-profile publishing house carries a lot of credibility, it's not a guaranteed road to riches. It takes a long time for your book to hit the shelves, and for most books royalty payments are usually small and slow to arrive.

Just to be considered, you must write a detailed book proposal, a table of contents, sample chapters, and a market overview. You will also need to develop a marketing plan for your book that addresses the competition; makes a case for you, the author; and outlines what you will do to promote the book once it's on the shelves. You then pitch the proposal to potential publishers on your own or through a commissioned agent.

If a publisher decides to take you on, as a first time author who is unknown, you will probably receive an advance against future sales in a range of $2,000 to $10,000. After the book is completed, you can expect to see it in print in 12 to 18 months. Payment to authors comes from royalties, typically 10-15 percent of the publisher's net revenue from the book, payable twice a year.

TIPS FROM THE GURU

Robert W. Bly on Why Every Guru or Would-Be Guru Should Write a Book

Bob W. Bly, a direct mail copywriting expert and author of 50 books, became a widely recognized marketing expert largely by writing and publishing books on his area of expertise. "I tell virtually every self-employed professional, as well as many small business owners, to define their niche specialty, write a book about it, and get it published," says Bly.

"Nothing has been as helpful in establishing my own career and generating a steady flow of business than the many books I have written on my specialties of direct marketing, business communication, and more recently, Internet marketing."

Bly points out that writing a book is part of larger strategy that brings a host of benefits. Here's what he says:

- In writing a book on a subject, you are forced to do additional research to fill gaps in your knowledge. Your knowledge therefore increases, making you a better authority to your clients.

- Writing a book also requires you to organize your material in logical sequence. Doing so increases clarity of presentation in all your communications, including individual consultations with clients.

- A book can serve as the basis for a profitable seminar or workshop. The chapters of the book become modules of the seminar.

- Potential clients who read your book will call you to inquire about the services you offer, and will be predisposed to hire you.

- Associations will ask you to speak at their conferences for handsome fees if you are the author of a book that interests their members.

- Listing yourself as the author of a book is an impressive credential on your Web site, brochure, and other marketing materials. It increases your status.

Big New York publishers are good at getting books into bookstores; they have sales reps who visit the stores, and a well-established pipeline. But even if you've placed your book with one of them, you will need to put forth a lot of personal effort promoting your book. Large publishers devote most of their promotional

- You can give copies of your book to potential clients to familiarize them with your methodology and convince them that you are an expert in your field.
- You may be called upon to serve as an expert witness on your topic in court cases, at a handsome day rate.
- Editors will ask you to contribute articles to their publications.
- The media will want to interview you as an expert in your field. This can lead to appearances as a guest on radio and television shows.

"I specialize in writing direct mail packages," says Bly. "A few clients began asking me to write Internet direct mail and e-mail marketing campaigns. I liked this niche segment of Internet marketing for several reasons. And it has less competition than Web site development, which was already overcrowded."

Seeing an opportunity, Bly wrote a proposal for a book on Internet direct mail. He sent it to one of his publishers, NTC Business Books, and they gave him a contract to write the book. "During the next six months, I wrote e-mail marketing campaigns for clients. I read everything I could get my hands on about e-mail marketing. I also interviewed numerous e-mail marketing experts and users about what was working for them to research the book. And of course I wrote the book," says Bly.

The result? He became the foremost authority on Internet direct marketing.

"I now knew how to do it, and was doing it, at nice fees, for both new and existing clients," says Bly. "The interviews I had done, which I would not have gotten had I not been writing the book, showed me techniques that increased the effectiveness of my e-mail campaigns. And when the book was published, it cemented my reputation as a leading copywriter in the e-mail marketing field. Many factors contributed, but the book was certainly the catalyst and driving force that gained me early entry into this new niche market."

Excerpted from Become a Recognized Authority in Your Field, *Robert W. Bly (Alpha Books)*

resources to their superstar authors whose books are likely to sell hundreds of thousands of copies. If their books are not to disappear in a frighteningly short time, lesser-name authors must usually fend for themselves.

For most authors with a specialized topic, the best bet is to look

REAL-WORLD SUCCESS STORY

Nancy Mueller Learns the Work, and Payoff, of Publishing a Book

Cross-cultural communications specialist Nancy Mueller had been conducting workshops about international business for many years when she decided that a book about finding work overseas would bolster her credibility.

Mueller bought a book about writing book proposals, followed its advice, and contacted an agent. While the agent was enthusiastic about the project, he couldn't convince any of the top ten publishers to publish it. Not one to give up easily, Mueller started searching on her own. She eventually found a small publisher and landed a book contract for *Work Worldwide*.

"Even though finding a publisher and writing my book was a lot of work, it's established my credibility and positioned me as a global career expert," says Mueller. "The media regularly call me, and I appear in newspaper articles and radio interviews. My book is like a business card that makes selling myself easier. Being an author means I get taken much more seriously.

"I found that there weren't good resources about international career strategies, and it was a subject I obviously knew very well," recalls Mueller. "I felt my how-to approach was different enough from other books on the subject that a book would go over well."

for a publisher with a history of publishing on that topic. A specialty publisher who is focused on your niche will already have established relationships with the people you most want to reach, and your book will be a more valued asset to that publisher. To find these specialized publishers, check your own bookshelf, and go to a library or bookstore to consult *Books in Print*, a multi-volume reference listing all the books that are currently available for sale.

The Self-Publishing Alternative According to Dan Poynter, author of *The Self-Publishing Manual*, self-publishing has many advantages over traditional publishing, the most compelling being greater financial returns for the author. "When you self-publish, you keep all the profits," says Poynter. "Additionally, you get into print quickly, own the copyright, and take all applicable tax breaks.

"Self-publishing is good business. But aspiring authors need to realize that while writing a book is a creative act, selling it is a business," says Poynter. "Some people can do both, while others are more creative than businesslike. You have to ask if you want to be a publisher. Do you have an office, the time to conduct the business, and a place to store the books?"

While authors often feel there is greater prestige in being published by an established firm, this is an argument that self-publishing advocates dismiss. "No one cares who published your book," says Poynter. "Nobody goes around saying: 'I love HarperCollins books. I buy everything they publish.' Potential buyers want to know if a book will solve their problem and whether the author is a credible person. They never ask who is the publisher."

On the downside, self-publishing can be expensive. You pay up front for all the production and distribution costs, and if your book doesn't sell, you'll be stuck with the leftover inventory. However, if your book is successful, you'll not only have the satisfaction and advantages of being a published author, you'll make more money.

Marketing and Selling Information Products

If there's a real need for certain information, and you do a good job of addressing that need with an info-product, that product will sell. Develop a plan tailored to your own goals and disposition. Be realistic and start small. Consider your available time, long-term goals, and production budget before embarking on any information product.

Test the Waters

Don't fall in love with your idea for a book, booklet, or tape series at the expense of the most important part of any successful info-product—a qualified, targeted market that is likely to purchase the product. According to Gordon Burgett, author of *Publishing to Niche Markets*, targeting means knowing specifically who will buy your product, why, how much they will spend (and won't), how they will hear about it, and what your promotion must say to get prospects to make a purchase.

Ask a lot of questions. Contact associations, editors of industry newsletters and magazines, and others who are intimately acquainted with your market. Talk to people who represent your typical buyers to determine their degree of interest in your proposed products, and make sure you have ways to reach them that are effective and affordable.

Price your products to be profitable, but not in excess of the value that customers will perceive in them. Know your costs. Study the marketplace. Ask around. Find out what similar products are going for and determine how your prospective product compares.

Promotion Ideas

Announce your products to your existing client base. List them on your Web site. Create flyers, and include them in all your mailings. Take samples with you to networking events, trade shows, and speaking engagements. As you conduct your daily business, look for every opportunity to announce your products to the world. For instance, you can:

- Sell products "back of the room" at speaking engagements.
- Sell products through workshops.
- List your products in catalogs and directories.
- Sell through dealers and wholesalers.
- Solicit volume sales to trade associations, book clubs, and business groups.
- Cross-promote products with those from other businesses.
- Cultivate free media exposure for your products, saving you money in promotional expenses. But remember, you need a news angle.

Earthworks Press Customizes Books for Utility Companies

REAL-WORLD SUCCESS STORY

Earthworks Press, the publisher of the bestselling *50 Simple Things You Can Do to Save the Earth*, provides an immensely successful example of how to package a book for premium sales.

Having already sold a huge number of their lead title for premium use by companies that wanted to be identified as environmentally sensitive — mostly in response to inquiries from the companies themselves — Earthworks decided to develop spin-off titles for industries in particular need of educational and promotional materials.

At the top of Earthworks' target list were energy companies. Earthworks knew that these companies had been mandated by their governing utility commissions to allot money for conservation projects, and were in need of appropriate materials. With this need in mind, Earthworks approached their regional energy supplier, Pacific Gas & Electric, with two prospective titles, *30 Simple Energy Things You Can Do to Save the Earth* and *25 Simple Things Kids Can Do to Save Energy*. Earthworks offered PG&E the opportunity to customize the books for their audience, developed a working relationship, and eventually wrote an order for 500,000 books.

Building on this success, Earthworks' special marketing staff then made cold calls to over 100 energy suppliers and simply asked for the person in charge of environmental affairs. They used the book developed in conjunction with PG&E as an introduction, and ultimately made sales to about 25 companies, with orders ranging from 5,000 copies to 500,000 copies.

Each company received custom-produced books of either 64 or 80 pages, and paid a price per copy that depended on the quantity they ordered, and how much the book was customized for their use. Since the energy suppliers used the books as part of their educational efforts — giving them away free to customers, at Earth Day fairs, in school programs, and at appliance centers — none of the books carried a cover price, nor were they ever sold through retail outlets.

Excerpted from The Complete Guide to Book Marketing *by David Cole (Allworth Press)*

"The simple fact that your book or other information product is newly published doesn't make it news," says David Cole, author of *The Complete Guide to Book Marketing.* "To turn your information product into a newsworthy item, you need to develop a hook on which you can hang your story—something that people want to talk about, hear about, and read about."

Position your products within the larger context of the overall topic or problem they address. If you can tailor your products to the needs and interests of particular media audiences, you can get your info-products into the public eye without spending a fortune on advertising. Write articles based on the subject of your information products. This is a way to get a free mention of your products along the way in trade and business publications, association newsletters, and Web sites.

Get your products reviewed by the media. If you have a book, e-book, or anything that may be of interest to the public, send it, with a brief cover letter, to editors in charge of reviews at appropriate newspapers and magazines. Favorable reviews serve as third-party endorsements for your info-products.

Expand Your Offerings

Once you distill your wisdom into a book, booklet, or audiocassette, look for ways to broaden your product line. Go deeper into a subject with products that command a higher price, or round out an expensive product offering with a handful of reports or tip sheets. Your goal is to maximize your income by offering your knowledge at many price points, so as to have something for every need and budget.

With a Web site, you can develop an affiliate marketing strategy to get other businesses to help you sell your products by agreeing to sell theirs on your Web site. Affiliate programs are commission-based sales programs that can produce additional income streams. When you sign up as an affiliate or reseller, you can earn money for doing—well, just about nothing other than maintaining your Web site, which you were doing anyway.

Mark Joyner Builds an Online Sales Army

REAL-WORLD SUCCESS STORY

Mark Joyner, CEO of Aesop.com, is like the mayor of a sizable city. If you count the 650,000 people who receive his e-mail newsletter, and his almost quarter-million affiliate sales partners, you arrive at a population close to 1 million people who have joined Mark's self-created online empire.

Mark has found a very inexpensive way to build a huge sales network: by growing his mailing list. Through his mailing list, and via the regular newsletter he sends to those on it with information related to Internet marketing, Joyner can count on a cheap, easy channel to reach a qualified target audience of prospects interested in Web marketing.

Joyner takes great care to ensure that his e-newsletters' content is pertinent, high quality, and worth readers' time. This makes readers more receptive to the direct marketing messages they contain. "People don't like to have their time wasted," he says. "The e-newsletter has to be what you promised, and it has to be interesting, or people will get your newsletter and ignore it."

He also gives away free e-books about search engine tactics and Web marketing as an incentive to subscribe to his newsletter. "It works incredibly well. I still give them away today," says Joyner. "And when you get your foot in the door and give people a reason to trust you, eventually they'll buy your products."

Mark's huge affiliate program positions him to make even more profit from his mailing list by reselling related products from other authors and other content providers. Very simply, he pitches related products to his subscribers, and when a sale is made, Mark and his partner share the profits.

He recently teamed up with marketing author David Garfinkel to promote that guru's new e-book, *Advertising Headlines That Make You Rich*. Through their affiliate relationship, Mark reviewed the book in his newsletter, *Killer Tactics Journal*, and provided a link to Aesop.com, where it could be purchased.

Two hundred and fifty *Killer Tactics Journal* readers bought the book, and Aesop received $12 out of the $27 price, netting the company $3,000. While that may not seem like much, the campaign took very little effort to produce. "When people click through, we're making money on those sales," says Joyner. "The actual hard cost of this campaign was zero dollars, and the man hours, maybe a couple of hundred dollars."

Here is where persistence comes in. "You have to be willing to try out different things, and accept that most of what you try will fail," says Joyner. "If you keep trying, you'll hit on some winners. You should assume that your first round out of your gun is going to be a dud. Accept it and keep firing!"

11 Strategic Partnerships

Everywhere from corporate boardrooms to Main Street America, savvy businesses are partnering with related businesses, even competitors, to forge mutually beneficial alliances.

According to *The Economist*, alliances now account for 18 percent of the revenues of America's biggest companies. Strategic partnerships can include co-op advertising, cross-promotions, sponsorships, and cause-related marketing. And while each represents a different twist on the concept, all involve combining the efforts of two or more organizations to enhance the results for all those who participate.

Whether partnering with a manufacturer, members of your local merchants association, or a company that offers products or services complementary to your own, the potential to form profitable relationships is around you all the time, and can become a core element of your *slightly famous* marketing strategy.

Partnering can help you create inroads into new markets by combining your skills, resources, and capabilities with those of other businesses. When Susan Grant, an executive recruiter in San Francisco, decided she wanted to tap into the biotechnology industry for clients, she looked around for professionals in related service fields who were already established within the sector, and would be open to joint marketing efforts. She hooked up with Carol Cherkis, a mergers and acquisitions consultant, and the two decided to collaborate on articles for relevant industry trade publications. They developed topics that needed their combined expertise, and pitched them as a team to those publications. The result was an article co-authored for *Pharmaceutical Executive* magazine, titled "Mergers & Acquisitions: Plugging the Brain Drain."

Consider your own business challenges. Maybe there are business expenses you can share with others: for instance, warehouse equipment or administrative costs. Or perhaps, like Susan Grant, you can partner with another professional to reach prospects for both your businesses. Sometimes you can ride on the coattails of another, already established business to build market awareness and credibility.

Where do you find potential partners? Talk to your suppliers to identify worthwhile businesses that already serve your target market. Ask trade associations, chambers of commerce, and the Better Business Bureau; talk to board members and staffers who are knowledgeable about your industry. Once you identify businesses that serve your market, look for ways to pool talent, capital, and experience to reach mutually beneficial ends.

Partnering with Competitors

For some, partnering with competitors is akin to sleeping with the enemy, but others have made it work for them. You can enjoy competitive alliances that are both emotionally rewarding and financially profitable. Competitive partnerships can sometimes open up opportunities for creating synergy and enjoying a larger potential market-

TIPS FROM THE GURU

Ed Rigsbee on Creating Successful Partnerships

Strategic alliances are commonplace among large corporations, helping them successfully compete in the global marketplace. Smaller companies can derive the same advantages of strategic partnerships by building win/win relationships with other businesses.

"The key is finding partners with the same core values before you start building a relationship," says Rigsbee. "You need to help your partner develop emotional ownership in the partnership. Without emotional ownership, any commitment will rest on a shaky foundation."

Rigsbee compares the act of establishing long-term relationships with partners to forging a strong and enduring marriage. To ensure that your partner relationships are built on a solid foundation, Rigsbee offers the following pointers.

The getting-married jitters. You must successfully deal with the fears and issues in synergistic alliance partnering. Sensitivity and understanding of your potential partner's situation are crucial at this juncture. Talk about both the upside and the downside with your intended partner. Talk about how you might deal with the relationship if things do not work out. Plan an exit strategy. Getting fears and issues out on the table rather than hiding them in the dark will serve all involved well.

Where are you going to live? Discuss your individual and combined marketing areas. Selecting the alliance's geographic marketing area and the service/product mix is no easy task. You'll need to pay close attention to both the small and large issues. Might you share warehousing or delivery facilities, or possibly even employees, to overcome personnel conflicts?

Who does the chores? Allocation of alliance partner responsibilities will make or break the relationship. Too often this is the area where unrealistic expectations of one another manifest themselves. Be clear about who will be doing what, and put it in writing. It is too easy to forget your commitments six months, a year, or a decade later.

Time to tie the knot. The partnering agreement should be in writing. It should contain detailed explanations of the authority, expectations, and responsibilities of each partner. This document will be your road map for a successful alliance relationship. When in doubt, you can refer to this "Partnering Charter."

Oh no, divorce! You tried, but it didn't work out. This sometimes happens. No reason to feel like a failure, or declare that you'll never again be in a relationship. In dealing with separation issues, be the bigger person, and again meet your partner more than halfway. Otherwise the rage and anger will fester, and you will become embittered. If there is "community property," dispose of it fairly.

The "Group of 8" Contributes to All Its Members

REAL-WORLD SUCCESS STORY

When eight professional speakers needed a way to get speaking leads, they put their heads together. The result was the "Group of 8," an informal leads exchange group consisting of eight professionals who meet regularly by phone to share leads and business development strategies.

"We take turns interviewing one another on an individual basis," says Mandi Stanley of Mandi Stanley Speaker Services in Memphis, Tennessee. "The idea is to spend about 30 quality minutes on the phone and find out the who, what, when, where, why, and how of each other's businesses, so that we intimately understand each other's areas of expertise."

Even though all members are professional speakers, and are nominally competitors, they still find plenty of opportunities to share leads with one another. "Even though we're all speakers, we do not speak about the same topics, and have different areas of expertise," says San Francisco-based Romanus Wolter of Kick Start Your Dream. "There is some overlap, but we are all different enough that it's not like anyone is stepping on anyone's toes."

The group meets every three weeks by telephone conference call to commiserate, brainstorm, and share tips and leads about potential speaking engagements. Between calls, members send one another information and leads about speaking opportunities as they arise. Even though members are spread around the country, they schedule time for personal connections with one another at national speakers' conferences and other events.

"Because the speaking industry is filled with so many potential opportunities, more than any one of us could keep track of individually, we alert one another to opportunities we'd miss otherwise," says Christine Holton Cashen. "One of our members is from Canada, and has introduced us to a number of Canadian associations where speaking opportunities exist. This is an area that many of us would probably not have explored on our own."

place. Such was the case with the Sonoma County Woodworkers Association mentioned in chapter one.

Setting up strategic partnerships with similar businesses can also help you target larger accounts. This is what a cabinet manufacturer did when his company was given a chance at what was for him a huge contract from Disney World. The problem was that he lacked the resources to complete the job within the required ninety-five days. The solution was a strategic alliance with three of his competitors that enabled him to land and complete the $2.5 million contract—something he could never have done on his own.

Co-Branding Alliances

Co-branding is about marketing two or more complementary products together, thus allowing each partner to "piggyback" on the reputation of the other in an expanded marketplace. In a successful co-branding relationship, companies share costs and command more attention than either could individually.

Cause-Related Partnerships

Altruism. Corporate responsibility. Philanthropic image. These are a few ways to describe cause-related marketing, an activity in which businesses join with charities or social causes to market an image, product, or service for mutual benefit.

Other things being equal, many consumers would rather do business with a company that stands for something beyond profits. By identifying with a cause and letting the media know about it, you can benefit from this impulse. One of the easiest ways is to establish a relationship with a charitable organization.

Johnny "Love" Metheny is a slightly famous nightclub owner in San Francisco with a string of local ventures to his name. Whenever he opens a new club, he shares the limelight with a local charity. "I have a history of including the Leukemia & Lymphoma Society in my grand openings," notes Metheny. Beyond these events, Metheny volunteers time to the cause, serves on its board, and was voted Man of the Year for the Society in 1991. So, while beneficial to his business, his association with the organization is more than a marketing ploy.

Ikeda's Country Market Co-Brands Itself up the Food Chain

REAL-WORLD SUCCESS STORY

Developing co-branding partnerships with a variety of businesses has helped Glen and Steve Ikeda, owners of Ikeda's Country Market and Ikeda's Tasty Burgers, grow their business well beyond its local roots. Nestled in the Sierra foothills of California with a modest 6,000 square feet of space, the company has built its annual revenues from $150,000 in 1970 to more than $4 million today.

The Ikedas' involvement with co-branding began when they started buying high-end produce from farms in the surrounding area. They approached Perry's Farms in Sacramento, which had developed a strong reputation for its tomatoes, and arranged to feature Perry's Farms tomatoes by name in their store while the Perry's Farms outlet store sold Ikeda products. It was an arrangement where each brand benefits from the reputation of the other. The Ikedas have also fostered relationships with many local restaurants and a gas station, and, much further afield, the Big Island Candy Company in Hilo, Hawaii, which all sell Ikeda food products.

Glen Ikeda offers advice to anyone considering a co-branding relationship: "Pick the right co-branding partner. Make sure it's someone who shares your commitment to quality and the co-branding concept. Then monitor the relationship to ensure your brand is used appropriately, and not exploited beyond the parameters of the agreement. Remember that it is your brand, and you are its steward."

Cross-Promotions: Working Together to Get the Word Out

Cross-promotional marketing strategies align businesses that serve the same target market, but do not directly compete with each other. Cross-promotional marketing helps you reach a larger audience with less money and effort by pooling resources—time, money, ideas, and contacts—with others.

"The goal of cross-promotional marketing is to reach more people, more frequently, with messages that position your product or service in favorable way," says Kare Anderson, author of *Walk Your*

Talk: Grow Your Business Faster Through Successful Cross-Promotional Partnerships. "You are looking for partners who will help you do that."

Cross-promotional marketing can help you to:

- Stand out in a crowded marketplace.
- Conserve cash.
- Generate more reasons for customers to buy.
- Show support for community causes.
- Reach more prospects.
- Build credibility.

Anderson cites six local businesses that joined forces one Valentine's Day for a weeklong promotion. A bookstore hosted cooking demonstrations by the author of a book on romantic meals, using cookware from the local department store and food from a nearby deli. Finished meals were displayed, with offerings from the local florist, candy store, and card shop. There was even health information from the local Heart Association!

"Cross-promotion offers the most credible, cost-effective way to attract more customers while spending less," says Anderson. "The costs go down as the number of cross-promotional partners goes up."

The trick is to spot opportunities that already exist within your business network, your neighborhood, and your community.

Evaluating Your Cross-Promotion Quotient

If the examples given above have whetted your appetite enough to make you give these techniques a try, your first step is to take an inventory of the intangible assets that make you an appealing cross-promotional partner—your customer lists and relationships, your standing in the community, and your business location. If these have value for you, they will be valuable to other businesses as well.

The second step is to look for equivalent assets in potential part-

How a Travel Agent Cross-Promoted Her Way to Radio Stardom

REAL-WORLD SUCCESS STORY

Fanny Pettijohn, owner of Malachi Travel Group in South Field, Michigan, learned how creative thinking can lead to huge rewards when she orchestrated a very successful cross-promotion with a local radio station. "I worked for 20 years at the Bahamas Tourist Office. But when I went into business for myself, selling leisure and incentive travel, I quickly learned I'd have to create my own opportunities — that I'd literally have to go out and make things happen."

In the dead of the Detroit winter, Pettijohn seized the moment. She contacted the sales manager of a local radio station, and pitched a jointly sponsored listener-appreciation contest offering free trips to Jamaica.

"I needed to get my name out to my community, and radio seemed to be the best way to do that," says Pettijohn. "I told the station manager I would assemble a team that included the radio station (who would give free advertising), a Jamaican tour company (who covered airfare), the Jamaica Tourist Board, and a hotel that provided accommodations."

The results were phenomenal. The highly publicized event was promoted on the radio every morning for a full month. The station gained listeners, and the tour operator and the tourist office got tons of valuable exposure and thousands of dollars worth of advertising they could not have afforded on their own.

For Pettijohn, the promotion landed dozens of new customers. "At the time, it was really cold here in Detroit," recalls Pettijohn. "Listeners would call in and say, 'I don't mind that I didn't win, I just want to go to Jamaica.' I got dozens of leads. Even employees at the radio station wanted to go. I got that business as well. And because the promotion was so successful, the radio station became a client. I now get all their incentive business."

ners. There are probably businesses in your community with assets that can be put to work for you. The key is to forge complementary relationships based on common interests.

Finally, look at things you already do to promote yourself. Cross-promotional teams pursue joint advertising campaigns, media events, and direct mailings. They offer discounts on each other's products and services, and hang signs or post flyers in one another's places of business. Seek partners who can help you strengthen your existing efforts, share your costs, and expand your customer base.

As with any marketing, understanding your customers is essential in cross-promotions. To spot ideal cross-promotional strategies and partners, you need to know what your customers do when they are not doing business with you. The better you understand your customers, the better you will be at identifying partners who complement your business. Your best allies are organizations and businesses that:

- Serve the same customers, but do not compete with you.
- Serve people you want to attract.
- Have a name that lends prestige, credibility, or other such value to your promotion.
- Have buying cycles that complement yours.
- Are involved in the same kinds of community activities or events.

Don't underestimate your value. If you've been in business for a while, you have probably developed solid relationships with your customers that can be of great value to other businesses. Take stock of everything about your business that can be leveraged to attract and forge cross-promotional partnerships. Also, learn to spot these qualities in potential partners. There are many businesses in your community that have similarly accrued value that can be put to work for you.

Here's a grab bag of cross-promotional possibilities for you and your partners to consider:

- Print joint promotional messages on your cash-register receipts.
- Offer a reduced price, special service, or convenience if customers buy from both you and your partner.
- Hang signs or posters promoting one another on your walls, windows, or products.

- Drop one another's flyers in shopping bags.
- Pool mailing lists and send a joint promotional postcard.
- Promote partners' products during their slow times, and ask them to do the same for you.
- Share inexpensive ads in local shopping papers or a nonprofit event program.
- Give a joint interview to local media.
- Put one another's promotional messages on counter stands or floor stands in waiting areas.
- Train your staff to mention how your partner's products can be used with yours.
- Give a sample of your partner's product to your customers when they buy a large quantity of your product, and have your partner do the same with yours.
- Use door hangers, posters, flyers, or postcards to promote special offers for one another's products.
- Co-produce an in-store or office event—a demonstration, celebrity appearance, free service, or lecture.

Action Groups

One by one, twelve people connect to a conference call led by Terri Levine, founder of Comprehensive Coaching U in Philadelphia, Pennsylvania. Each then takes a turn reading a personal marketing scorecard, ranking progress on goals and acknowledging short-comings. When somebody exceeds a goal such as an income projection, participants applaud and celebrate. If somebody has a problem, everyone offers advice.

What's going on here? It's a small-business marketing action group based on author C.J. Hayden's popular *Get Clients Now!™: A 28-Day Marketing Program for Professionals and Consultants.*

Two national bestselling books, *Your Money or Your Life* and *The Artist's Way*, helped launch goal-oriented groups that combine elements of book circles, support groups, and 12-step programs, but focusing on goals originally presented in these books. Taking a cue from the popularity of book study groups, business marketing action groups endeavor to organize people with common interests for their mutual benefit.

Groups such as these are a natural in the small business arena. Helping participants stay motivated with what could be called "benevolent peer pressure," they provide the motivation to establish and follow through on marketing and sales goals.

"I started my first action group a year and a half ago," says Levine. "But four months into the first program, I ran into *Get Clients Now!*, and saw the value of using a programmatic marketing book as a blueprint for the group. Now, the book is our common ground. Using a book has given the group more structure, and provided everyone the same common denominator."

Levine's action groups are now six months in duration, and meet each month for three 30-minute teleconference sessions. They're geared to service professionals dependent on self-promotion—financial planners, consultants, and freelance writers and designers—and focus on setting goals and achieving results based on specific steps.

"Every participant has their own agenda. Some are concentrating on getting prospects by making more cold calls; others are researching the Internet to develop an e-commerce strategy. When we get together, we review the actions participants committed to at the last meeting, as well as the results or where they got stuck. Participants then commit to new actions based on progress up to that point."

Action groups keep participants focused. "Many psychologists see affiliation as a primary motivational factor for human beings," says Hayden. "Through the act of associating with others on the same path, you can stay motivated to do what it takes to be successful."

Accountability is also at the heart of successful action groups. Members make commitments and share them with the group. At each session, members ask one another about the commitments, what they have accomplished since the last meeting, and what will come next.

"Your fellow team members expect you to follow through on goals you established. If you get stuck, they'll help you. But, if you keep showing up with excuses, they'll call you on it," she says.

Another bonus is support. "Having someone else to complain to or celebrate with delivers psychological and emotional rewards," says Hayden. "It's great to know others care about your progress. When you hit a roadblock, talking about it for a few minutes may be all you need to get back into action. And having people to share your success with makes it so much sweeter."

Annie Hammond, a professional business coach in Santa Cruz, California, says an action group made her feel that she was part of a greater effort. "It was helpful in terms of hearing the challenges people were having and also their breakthroughs," says Hammond. "If somebody else in the group is struggling and suddenly lands a client, it's very encouraging. And when you hear about the successes and failures of others, it helps you stay motivated, focused, and inspired."

Others feel being exposed to different points of view within a group breaks the isolation that often overcomes sole practitioners. "Just hearing your problem restated by another person gives you new insight," says Susan Schwartz, an image consultant in San Mateo, California. "A group lets you share ideas and test your assumptions. Bouncing ideas off others is a great way to brainstorm solutions."

Nancy Albu, a financial advisor in St. Catharine's, Canada, decided to form an action group after her office was directed to develop a sales plan, build prospect lists, design marketing materials, and establish better telephone techniques and a referral-generating process. "Frankly, none of us were marketers," she explains. "We were daunted by the enormity of the challenge and didn't know where to begin."

Based on her previous experiences in networking groups, Albu proposed an intra-office action group. "I said to everyone, 'Let's put our expertise together!' So we created a marketing action group comprising all twelve people in our office. Having this type of structure in place helped us chart our course, stay on track, and achieve our goals without having to reinvent the wheel."

A successful action group is built on the goals and commitments of those involved. Any group of people with similar goals can create a structure for working together. Members don't have to be in the same industry, and sometimes it's better if they aren't. It's amazing how much a freelance technical writer, for example, can contribute to a financial advisor, and vice versa.

A group can have as few as three people, but five to ten is better. Ideally, your group is small enough so that everyone has a chance to report at each meeting, but not so small that the group founders if some members drop out along the way, as often happens.

Some groups benefit from a professional leader. In others, members can take turns leading. In a peer-led group, the meeting leader has to be as strict as a professional would be; he or she has to begin and end sessions on time, and give everyone a chance to report. Leaders must not let members slide on commitments, and must allow time for all members to share successes and failures before focusing on particular issues or challenges chosen by members.

Group meetings can be structured as mini-workshops, focusing, for instance, on a subject as specific as how to market professional services to corporations. Alternatively, a group can spend time brainstorming solutions to challenges facing individual members. The key is that before the meeting ends, members need to commit to something specific they will accomplish before the next meeting.

12 Reach Out and Connect

As a small business owner, you have to be personally involved in your marketing. You need to make human contacts that generate cooperation and referrals, and you must form a network of people who know you, trust you, and respect your business enough to recommend you to prospects when opportunities arise.

Why You Need to Network

Networking is an ongoing strategy, not something to do only when you need business. Networking keeps you visible. It cements your existing relationships with those who know you. Networking ensures that you come immediately to prospects' minds when they, or people they know, need the products or services you offer.

There is no substitute for human contact. The more you network, and the more distinctive you make yourself, the more you will be remembered and recommended. Networking ensures that those who

REAL-WORLD SUCCESS STORY   **Networking Reels In the Big Fish**

R.A. Miller & Company, Inc., a consulting firm that works with food, beverage, chemical, and lubricant packagers, recently landed their first big contract: to modernize the packaging facilities of a multinational company. It was an entrepreneur's dream.

How did Roger Miller, the company president, reel in this big catch? Miller joined a high-profile trade association in his target market, the packaging industry, where he could meet the "movers and shakers" of that industry.

He didn't just join it; he got actively involved in the association. He volunteered to become a member of a high-profile committee, and worked on behalf of association members. This raised his visibility among key association executives, and helped Miller get to know his prospects personally. His involvement also helped him establish trust, while demonstrating his knowledge, expertise, and competence.

When a committee member heard of a large project where Roger's specific talents, industry experience, and knowledge were required, he recommended Roger to the ultimate decision-maker for the large project. This opened the door for Roger to meet with the client, make a presentation, present a quotation, and eventually get the project.

"For small businesses, rubbing shoulders with key decision-makers and developing a stream of high quality leads is one of the most effective ways to grow a business," says Miller.

know you continue to connect with the person behind your *slightly famous* reputation.

Establish a Reputation

Though discussed under different headings, the importance of networking in building a reputation is addressed throughout this book. When you're speaking at a networking venue, discussing your business in a leads-exchange group, or working on a committee in a trade or service organization, you're establishing your reputation.

Jose Mata of Adcom Worldwide, an international freight-forwarding service, built a reputation by giving seminars on international shipping and trade at local Small Business Administration

Susan RoAne on Networking as a Lifestyle

REAL-WORLD SUCCESS STORY

Susan RoAne, author of the bestselling book *How to Work a Room*, defines networking as a reciprocal process where people share ideas, leads, information, and support with each other, enhancing the personal and professional lives of everyone who participates.

"If your goal is to reach the most people who can genuinely make a difference to your business, you need to network," says RoAne. "Networking should be an ongoing strategy, not just something to do when you need the business. It should become a natural part of your life that's rooted in the idea of 'being neighborly' and helping others.

"Because this is a global economy, nobody is truly independent anymore," says RoAne. "If you only stay in your own cubicle, you're missing the opportunity to be part of the great word-of-mouth people can give you because they know you, like you, and trust you."

In researching *The Secrets of Savvy Networking* and *Networking: Beyond the Buzzword*, RoAnne uncovered a number of traits common to great networkers, including:

1. **They treat people as people, not as prospects.** Those who treat people as prospects are usually transparent and have a presence that screams, "I have an agenda!"

2. **They "goodmouth" people.** Great networkers go out of their way to pass on nice things said by a third parties, such as, "Oh, I just talked to Joe Jones who said you are a gifted Web designer."

3. **They help others unconditionally.** Great networkers give and they get, but they do not "give to get," which is manipulative.

4. **They don't view networking as an entitlement program.** Great networkers know they're not entitled to the connections and contacts of others. They know they must earn access to relationships through their deeds.

According to RoAne, the best networkers are so natural in their approach that others don't even realize they're doing it. "Networking is not a numbers game," says RoAne. "It's not a spreadsheet activity you add to your to-do list. Networking is about taking down contrived barriers between business and life, and seeing opportunity everywhere."

offices, banks, and chambers of commerce. Mata's seminars have made him a resource for people thinking about starting import/export companies.

"I always realized that the best way to find new prospects was to approach places where they congregate, and give away my expertise," says Mata. "This way, I position our business as a partner in the minds of seminar attendees. As a result, I enjoy a lot of referrals from businesses that have come to know and trust me."

The more Mata helps prospects understand his industry, the more people seek him out and refer prospects to him. Moreover, he's made many friends among conference organizers who know he has the participants' best interests in mind.

Get More Referrals

The most compelling reason to network is that you'll get more business through referrals. Networking inspires trust, and trust inspires people to refer business to you. The more people who meet you, like you, and trust you, the more relationships you'll develop among people inclined to refer business to you.

Even more important, referred customers come to you ready to do business. In most cases you don't need to educate them about the benefits of your products and services.

Even more important, a referral-based business is a stable business. A steady stream of word-of-mouth referrals means you never have to worry about where your next client or customer will come from. A business built on referrals has tremendous growth potential, as referrals in turn generate further referrals.

Bypass Competition

A loyal network of business contacts can put you in touch with business opportunities and introduce you to decision-makers.

Danna Yuhas, founder and president of the technology marketing

Networking Is Not a Dirty Word

REAL-WORLD SUCCESS STORY

Stephanie West Allen's business, Allen & Nichols Productions, offers humorous keynote addresses and training programs for corporations. Though informal networking has always come easy to her, networking specifically to grow made her uncomfortable. She particularly disliked the idea of being a salesperson.

"I've always been good at networking for non-business activities," says West Allen. "I enjoy meeting people and helping others when I can. But I just couldn't get over the uncomfortable feeling I had when I tried to network at business events."

The problem, she realized, was that she was approaching business networking in the wrong way, and this led to negative connotations. "In the early days, I attended networking events trying to find as many people as possible to drown with information about my company," she recalls. "I did not feel all that comfortable networking, because I felt being pushy was a necessary evil of being in business."

At the same time, she began to notice that most of her business was coming from what she had considered non-business sources, including friends, colleagues, and former co-workers. These were people in her immediate circle who knew and trusted her. These were people with whom she had a relationship first, and from whom referrals followed only as a result.

"One of my friends was the director of the National Kidney Foundation," says West Allen. "Because we were friends and she knew my business, she invited me to speak at her association. Another friend referred me to speak on an educational cruise, and my ex-boss, a lawyer, hired us to come do a program."

Once she realized that networking was about making human contacts, not pushing her business aggressively, she became more comfortable with business networking and found it less of a chore. "This simple realization showed me that networking is not about going into a room full of strangers and pushing yourself on them. Now, I try to learn more about others, looking for ways to help them succeed."

And because she's seen as a genuinely helpful person, referrals come her way. "I initially thought networking meant you had to hard-sell strangers. Now my goal is to connect with others and form mutually supportive relationships, rather than trying to convince everyone I meet that they need me. I've found this to be more comfortable and also more effective."

and communications firm Market Impact, learned that a prospective client was looking for telemarketers. She referred one of her networking contacts, providing a vivid description of this person's eagerness and ability to sell.

Based on her referral, the company called her contact for an interview. "What is so amazing is that, with the exception of her exceptional selling abilities, this telemarketer did not have any of the other qualifications that were specified in the advertisement," recalls Yuhas. "The referral had allowed her to bypass the entire screening process, based on word-of-mouth and trust."

Targeted Networking

Before you try to meet as many people as possible, do your homework: devise a networking strategy likely to advance your business goals by putting you in touch with the best members of your target market.

Scott Testa, chief operating officer of Mindbridge.com, focused his company's networking efforts on profitable industries where they had an established track record. He drew from his experience in the financial services sector, and targeted credit unions through their trade organizations and other centers of influence within the credit union industry.

"We'd spend time at these association meetings; we'd meet prominent people within the industry, introduce ourselves, and demonstrate our track record with credit unions," says Testa. "Once we'd earned their trust, which was easy because we could point to relevant clients and press coverage, we'd ask for names of anyone that might want to learn more about our services."

Testa has successfully networked his way into several industries, including credit unions, financial services, non-profits, payroll companies, and banking. "When you become an industry insider and do a good job, word travels fast, and you become the preferred provider to that industry," says Testa. "We tapped into a sense of camaraderie that exists among members of our target markets."

Like Testa, spend your time networking in groups that will put you in touch with the right people. Here are some different venues to consider:

General Business Organizations General business organizations are as eager to find you as you are to find them. To identify the right organizations, check your library; search the Internet; talk to your peers, clients, and customers; and read the business pages of your newspaper.

Once you've identified a few likely sounding organizations, do some investigative homework before you join. Attend a couple of meetings. Talk to members and read issues of the organization's newsletter. Look for opportunities to get involved that match your goals and expertise, and that will show off your talents and abilities. Only when you're sure the organization will promote your business interests with key contacts in your industry should you become a member.

Associations There are associations for just about every interest, industry, and profession in existence. These groups provide some of your best networking opportunities because they are tightly focused on a specific set of interests or problems, and if your business serves those interests or solves those problems, you've hit paydirt—in fact, the mother lode.

Networking at associations for members of your target market gives you the opportunity to become a preferred vendor among members. For instance, a professional editor might frequent speaking-industry gatherings, and become known within that industry. This strategy works well because you have few or no competitors within the group.

TIPS FROM THE GURU

Bob Burg on the Secrets of Endless Referrals

The larger your network, the more opportunity you have. "There's an old expression about digging a well before you need the water," says Bob Burg, author of *Endless Referrals*. "One of the best ways to build a self-sustaining business is establishing and maintaining a network of people who know you, like you, and trust you. You establish your network before you need it. That's the key."

The problem is that many people don't approach networking the right way. They think networking is an exercise in passing out as many business cards as possible. They talk everyone's ear off. They only think they are networking, and are disappointed when the process doesn't work.

You've Got to Give to Get

The problem with this style of networking is that it does not focus on cultivating mutually beneficial relationships. "Successful networkers get referrals by continually putting other people's needs ahead of their own," says Burg.

Networking with only your own interests in mind will not work. Aggressive networking turns people off because it fails to establish trust. Networking is not just about getting ahead in your own life, but helping others get ahead in their lives as well.

A financial planner who attends networking meetings with the ice-breaking question, "Do you need any help with your investments?" will not get much out of networking, because he seeks only personal gain without bothering to discover what he can do to help the other person.

"Let's say you're an accountant, and you introduce a doctor to a colleague who specializes in working with physicians. It takes nothing to connect these two people, but you'll be seen as a person who goes out of their

---

Chambers of Commerce Your local chamber of commerce can be an excellent networking source. Chambers usually have several types of networking opportunities and leads groups, representing members from different industries.

As with other such groups, membership can be beneficial, but only when you get really involved. Go beyond the popular networking "mixers," where you'll have a hard time targeting your market, and

way to be helpful. People appreciate these types of gestures, which puts you in a position to get their referrals down the road," says Burg.

Listening

Great networkers are great listeners. They invest most of their conversation time getting others to talk about themselves and their businesses. They ask a lot of questions, not aggressive questions, but friendly questions that are fun to answer.

"The 'listen more' principle is ideal for people who don't like a crowd," says Burg. "After all, it's a lot easier to be a good listener than a good talker. Once you've established some sort of genuine rapport, you should then ask for that person's business card."

Burg disputes the notion that networking is primarily about handing out your own business cards. "You should use your business card as a means to get the other person's business card," says Burg. "As far as I'm concerned, this is one of the few truly legitimate benefits of business cards in the networking process."

If you see that person later in an event, make it a point to stop by and call your networking prospect by name. This is impressive, because so few people do it, and because the prospect has by then most likely forgotten your name. This gesture will ensure that he or she remembers you.

Send a Note

Immediately after the event, take a moment to write a brief, handwritten note to each person you met whom you'd like to cultivate. Do this as soon as you've left the event.

"The impression you will make is truly outstanding," says Burg. "Very few people do this. This simple gesture has a lot of class, and shows that you are conscientious. It will impress your prospects to no end, and ensure that you are remembered."

attend special-interest roundtable sessions, or volunteer to lead a committee, or take on important tasks. This not only helps you stand out, but also makes it easier to meet others with common interests.

Leads Groups There are many established business organizations whose sole purpose is to promote networking, such as Le Tip and Women's Business Network. Most leads groups try to reduce industry overlap within the group by limiting the number of members from any one profession. Before joining, visit these groups, and talk to members to evaluate their tone and attitude. Do the members seem supportive of one another? Does the leadership appear competent?

Special Interest Groups There are networking opportunities to be found at any number of special interest groups that are not specifically related to any particular business. These include groups based on hobbies (gardening, cooking, sports), alumni groups at colleges and universities, civic groups like the Lion's Club and Rotary International, and religious organizations.

Volunteer Social Work Another effective networking strategy is to volunteer to help with an organization or cause that lets you meet lots of people. When Eunice Azzani, an executive recruiter, volunteered to serve on the board of the San Francisco AIDS Foundation (SFAF), she did not anticipate that it would put her in touch with executives from Mervyn's, Bank of America, and Wells Fargo Bank, all of whom would eventually hire her to work for their firms.

"People don't hire a piece of paper or a process. They hire people they trust," says Azzani. "Volunteering for a position at a local organization makes you very trustworthy."

Azzani advises business owners to target causes they personally believe in. "It will be much more satisfying for you, and more productive for the group you help," she says. "And you won't come across as a phony. If you're helping with a cause you believe in, people will see that you care. And they'll realize you will probably care as much about your work."

Getting the Most from Memberships

Joining networking organizations can put you in touch with a lot of people, and is an invaluable way to build your professional network. But to get the greatest benefit from any organization you join, you need to work at it consistently. Here are some points to keep in mind:

Show Up!

The degree to which you are successful at networking is determined by the amount of time you invest; it's not enough to pay your membership dues and attend a networking event from time to time. Effective networkers see their efforts as investments that pay tremendous dividends as they expand and maintain their network.

By regularly attending networking events, you maximize your chances of being in the right place at the right time. Since you aren't trying to rush into a business relationship at any one meeting, you will become an accepted part of the scene, and fellow members will feel more comfortable interacting with you when you've become a familiar face.

Get Involved!

The more you assume an active and—even better—a leadership role in an organization, the more likely it is that you'll connect with the people who will bring you business.

"I've been on the board of a professional organization called The Association of Women in Communications (AWC) for five years," says Marika Flatt, National Media Director for Phenix & Phenix Literary Publicists. "The first year I joined the organization I was asked to fill a board position that really opened up networking opportunities. I found that just by being involved in AWC I have people contacting me that I might not have known directly. A lot of times I'm not actively out there trying to network. But because I am so involved in the organization—I've taken a leadership role—I'm very visible."

Follow Up!

Start thinking about follow-up the moment you establish contact with someone. When you discover something unique or interesting about their business, write it down immediately.

REAL-WORLD SUCCESS STORY

Niche Networking Creates a Buzz for Mannequin Madness

When Judi Henderson launched Mannequin Madness, a business that buys, rents, and sells used mannequins, she knew the unique nature of her business meant she'd need to think carefully about targeting prospects. But her first call wasn't to a prospect. Instead, she networked among potential referral sources likely to bring her business.

"I approached major department stores, figuring that people who needed mannequins might begin their search there," says Henderson. "I approached retail managers, letting them know about my business. I kept fanning out to new niche markets of likely prospects, and found a lot of opportunities to establish referral relationships. "

Soon, major department stores were sending her referrals, and even became sources for used mannequins. She approached lawyers (who often need mannequins for display in trials), meeting and convention planners, theater stage designers, and photographers. All became new markets for mannequins.

"All of these groups turned out to be great ongoing referral sources," says Henderson. "Things really kicked in when I joined their trade organizations and started networking at their meetings and trade shows. Word-of-mouth spread fast, because I stood out and everyone in these niches knew one another. Now, people think of me when anyone they know needs a mannequin."

In addition, the unique nature of her business and strong word-of-mouth have created a buzz that not only encourages referrals, but also attracts media attention. "I've been in local newspapers and television, and was interviewed for a special event magazine," says Henderson. "My constant networking and outreach strategies attract a lot of attention, to the point that people now call me 'the mannequin lady.'"

A follow-up can range from a phone call or meeting (when appropriate) to a handwritten note, article, or other information related to your business. Be ready to supply a reminder of who you are and what you do. Make sure to offer something—an idea, information, referral, or resource—of interest to the other person.

A contact-management system—paper-based, computer-based, or a combination of the two—is an essential networking tool that will help you follow up effectively.

Centers of Influence

Centers of influence are easy to spot. They are well established within a networking community. People know and trust them. At networking events, people tend to revolve around them. They stand out as the most sociable people, the "hubs" that link others together within the group. When somebody makes a point, all heads turn to them for a response. When they speak, people pay attention.

If you approach these people, they are usually quite willing to work you into their existing network. The more you connect with centers of influence, the faster you'll become a center of influence yourself.

The most powerful centers of influence are industry pundits, industry Web-site proprietors, writers, speakers, and publication editors. Look for those who interpret and shape your market, and start the trends followed by your industry. If you gain their trust, they can spread the word about you within their network and give you credibility.

Online Networking

Tucked into a space no bigger than a computer monitor is a cyber community of individuals willing to do favors for others—more than

TIPS FROM THE GURU

Ivan Misner on Developing a Networking Contact Sphere

Dr. Ivan Misner, co-author of *Masters of Networking*, and founder of BNI (Business Network International), the largest networking organization in the world, believes that every goal is attainable if you cultivate "human" resources. "Networking is a natural part of life. Each of us relies on a network of people we know and trust," says Misner.

A network starts with any group (formal or informal), organization, institution, company, or individual you associate with for either business or personal reasons. We all have many networks, both formal and informal, to which we belong — groups some call "contact spheres," in which you can develop and benefit from symbiotic relationships.

"My favorite example of a contact sphere is the caterer, the florist, the photographer, and the travel agent. I call this the 'wedding mafia,'" says Misner. "If one gets a referral to a wedding, then they all get a referral to the wedding. These professions, more than most, have truly learned how to work their contact sphere."

Here are a few basic principles Misner recommends for focusing your efforts:

- Identify as many professions as possible that fit within your company's contact sphere. Take a look at the professions your industry tends to work with, so as to get an idea of the natural sources of repeat and reciprocal referrals. Create a list of these professions.

- Identify specific individuals who could fit into your contact sphere. Go to various networking groups, and build your business-card file and database.

- Invite these people to participate in networking groups with you, so that you can formalize your relationship and have a way to stay in regular contact. Maintaining the relationship is key. A good way to do that is to participate in groups that bring you together on a regular basis.

- Evaluate those professionals in your contact sphere to whom you refer clients. If they are not reciprocating, you may have to replace them with others who are willing and able to reciprocate.

11,000 people in all, living in 133 countries. They are members of a group called Friendly Favors, and they are on tap to help out a friend or a friend-of-a-friend—even a friend six times removed—no matter where on the globe they reside.

The creation of Sergio Lub, a master networker and entrepreneur active in over a dozen organizations, Friendly Favors is a Web site that acts as a cyber Rolodex. "The site contains more information than a collection of business cards, and is highly interactive because members are responsible for updating their entries," says Lub. "Friendly Favors harnesses the real value of the Internet, and that's its ability to help people with common interests and concerns to connect with one another."

Cyber- or online networking enables you to escape the limitations of face-to-face interactions. Online communities have been growing at a phenomenal rate, because they allow you to connect with like-minded people all over the world without the expense of attending real-world networking events.

Online networking venues tend to fall into three categories:

E-mail Discussion Groups

E-mail discussion groups, also known as *listservs*, allow participants to join an e-mail network composed of those with a strong interest in the group's topic. Members post messages, which are sent to the group on a daily, weekly, or monthly basis, depending on the group, and participate in ongoing online discussions.

There are e-mail discussion lists devoted to just about every topic imaginable, from knitting to human resources. You can find lists that relate to your target market at Topica (www.topica.com).

Web Forums

Also known as "bulletin boards," Web forums are hosted at specialized Web sites, and are often moderated by a host or site owner. They

TIPS FROM THE GURU

Nancy Roebke on Networking in Online Communities

Nancy Roebke, executive director of Profnet, Inc., a professional business-leads generation corporation, is a champion of online networking, believing that online forums, newsgroups, and e-mail lists provide some of the best ways to "meet" prospects and exchange information. Here are her suggestions for making the most of these opportunities.

Share information. Nancy posts information to such sites regularly to develop name recognition, and also to position herself as an expert in her field. "I currently write for several online and offline publications," says Roebke. "These articles generate a lot of interest in my firm. I get calls on my toll-free line almost every day from people who've read one of my articles."

Connect with like-minded people. "I read posts from other members, and when their opinions or presentations mirror my own," says Nancy, "I send a private response of encouragement, seeking to build a circle of like-minded individuals." Because she had gone out of her way to connect with certain people, Nancy was invited to join the board of a significant project being undertaken by members of this list. "This was a direct result of the responses I made to the like-minded members of the group."

Be helpful. As with all networking, the philosophy of giving before receiving works best. Read the interactions and contribute positive, helpful information. You will be amazed at the people who contact you saying, "I saw your post on the list. How can your services help my firm?" And your post wasn't even about your firm. It was just a helping hand to someone.

allow participants to post messages in common areas that members can read and reply to at any time. Web forums are like ongoing group conversations. One of the largest directories of forums can be found at Delphi Forums (www.delphiforums.com).

Newsgroups

These are similar to Web forums, but usually not moderated. There are tens of thousands of newsgroups around the world, on as many subjects. To read newsgroup messages, you need a newsreader (avail-

Applaud the efforts of others. Nancy sends private messages to members in response to useful posts. "The community is stronger when people feel comfortable and develop personal relationships," she says. "Accolades are always appreciated, and can be great marketing tools if used properly."

Nancy sends virtual postcards to everyone who introduces himself or herself, welcoming them to the group and offering a friendly ear. "In these postcards, I also asked for info about their businesses. This was one of the best relationship-building tools I used."

Use your signature file. The right signature, or "sig," can generate more leads than you can handle. "My current sig offers a free report on how to stop cold calling," she says. "This report is set up on an autoresponder that is available 24 hours a day, 7 days a week. When someone requests the report, I am notified of that request." Her current "sig" reads:

Nancy Roebke
mailto:execdirector@profnet.org
Executive Director, ProfNet
http://www.profnet.org
How To Stop Cold Calling . . . And Get MORE Business!
Free report tells you 10 secrets of getting referrals.
Get your copy by e-mailing mailto:secrets@profnet.org today!

Expect it to take time. There is no way to shorten the relationship-building process, but the time you have to spend to build mutually beneficial relationships online is well worth it. "Online networking has a lot of appeal because of the volume of people you can reach," says Roebke. "But the chances of building relationships with all those people at one time are slim to none. The best online networkers build relationships one person at a time."

able in most e-mail programs). DejaNews (www.dejanews.com) provides an easy gateway to just about any newsgroup in existence.

Most of the rules of successful face-to-face networking also carry over to online networking. Don't approach online networking with the intent of aggressively pitching your products and services. In online as in other kinds of networks, that approach will do more harm than good. Online networking is about creating visibility and familiarity, and helping others in a way that results in trust and relationships.

Cultivating Referrals

When prospects come to you by referral, they are predisposed to doing business with you. And most people are happy to refer business to those who deserve it. Why? It makes them look and feel good.

"Do you ever remember sitting around a table with some friends and someone says they're looking for, say, a good house cleaner?" says Robert Middleton of Action Plan Marketing. "All of a sudden everyone at the table starts to vie for who can give the best referral. We want our friend to use our reference because we get an ego boost. We win. Someone noticed us and paid attention to us. That feels good."

Referral expert Joanne Black teaches small business owners and corporations the art of "referral selling," something that she has designed to help businesses attract the type of customers they want. "In over thirty years of working in selling professions, I appreciate that the best way to build any business is through referrals," says Black. "Referral prospects are pre-qualified. And because someone they trust has recommended you, you have immediate credibility and don't have to sell them as much. Best of all, referral business comes to you!"

Although referrals are the best way to get new business, most businesses do not employ a strategy that encourages and rewards referrals. The trick is seeing your *slightly famous* universe as a breeding ground for referrals. Where do referrals come from? From satisfied clients (both active and inactive); business associates who know you personally; and anyone who trusts your firm and the quality of your work enough to recommend you to others.

Black suggests the following strategy for easily increasing your referrals:

Cultivate trust. People will only refer business to those they trust. Attending networking functions to see how many business cards you can get, or pass out, will not amount to much. That's why implementing a long-term referral strategy takes time, patience, and personal integrity.

Businesses that get the most referrals are those that go out of their way to connect with people. They don't meet someone for three minutes at a networking event, and immediately ask for a referral. Instead, they establish a relationship, gain trust, and ask for referrals only once the "human connection" has been established.

Ask. Getting referrals from your clients, customers, vendors, or anyone else with a relationship to your business can be as easy as letting them know you want them. Often, people in the best position to refer business to you don't realize they are sources for business leads. Or, like many of us, they may be just too busy to think about referring customers to your business, so they need a boost or reminder.

"Before asking for referrals, be absolutely clear on what you are asking for," says Black. "Do not be overly broad. The more specific you are about what you are looking for, the easier it is for someone to think of someone to refer."

Asking clients and customers for referrals can be awkward. A way around this is sending clients a form letter upon the completion of some work you've done for them. Tell them that you would appreciate being allowed to use them as a reference, and that you appreciate referrals, if they know of people who might need your services.

Educate. Your potential referral sources may not recognize the referral opportunities that are right for you. If you make use of the advice in previous chapters on how to clearly identify your market niche through positioning and branding strategies, this will be less of a problem.

Reward referrals. Always acknowledge referrals. Eva Patel, a *slightly famous* skin care specialist in San Francisco, developed a "referral club" to reward current clients who refer others to her Skin

Rejuvenation Clinic. She offers free skin treatments, T-shirts, and caps, as well as items from her own line of skin care products, as rewards for referrals. She rewards "referral superstars" with gourmet lunches and jewelry.

"We've built our business on client relationships and the referrals that result from them," says Patel. "We go out of our way to thank clients who believe in us enough to recommend us to their friends. It makes them feel special, and it shows our genuine appreciation for the part they play helping us grow our business."

The biggest mistake regarding referrals is that too many people take others' generosity for granted, forgetting to acknowledge the favor someone has done them in referring business—and reciprocating, if possible. For small referrals, a thank-you note or phone call will suffice. But if a colleague refers a major piece of business to you, send a gift that is appropriate to the size and scope of the referral.

CHAPTER 13 Keeping in Touch with Newsletters

lise Benun began publishing her newsletter, *The Art of Self Promotion,* several years ago as a promotional vehicle for her business. A well-known marketing consultant, she filled her newsletter with information drawn from her experience. She used her newsletter to provide solutions to her prospects' most pressing marketing challenges, and chose topics that demonstrated her abilities and credentials.

"I used my newsletter as a brochure when someone wanted to know more about my work. It gave me tremendous credibility, and helped me keep in touch without being seen as a pest," says Benun. "The best keep-in-touch methods provide useful information while reminding people that you have something valuable to offer."

Building long-term business relationships isn't a hit-and-run proposition. If clients, customers, or prospects haven't heard from you lately, it's unlikely your name will come to mind when they need your products and services. To make the most of your business relationships, you need to keep in touch regularly with everyone who's part of your business world—your clients, customers, vendors, associates, and prospects.

Newsletters provide one of the best ways to keep in touch with all of them, and maintain their awareness of your brand. A newsletter can help you increase customer loyalty, and make those who've never met you feel like they've known you for years. The best newsletters provide useful information that positions you as a source of information. This not only builds your credibility, but also establishes top-of-mind awareness that results in sales and referrals. If your newsletter is done correctly, people will not only come to expect it, they'll eagerly look forward to receiving it.

Print Newsletters

A simple newsletter can be created using a single $8\frac{1}{2}" \times 11"$ sheet that is printed and folded to become a self-mailer. More elaborate presentations usually involve larger sheets that are folded to become envelope inserts. Printing costs will naturally vary widely, depending on the format, quantity, complexity, and use of color. In addition, you will have expenses for graphic design, editorial help, mailing list management, and postage.

Whatever your budget, you need to make some basic decisions about your newsletter's layout, and put some thought into creating a design that supports your brand identity. Because most people do not have the necessary design skills to produce a quality newsletter themselves, a smart strategy is to concentrate on developing the copy in-house, and hire a designer for layout and production. Consider hiring a good designer to develop a template for your newsletter. This involves an initial investment, but saves money in the long run, because you can use the template for all future issues.

A money-saving shortcut is to use newsletter templates that come

Jeff Rubin Shows Off His Skills in a Newsletter for Newsletter Clients

TIPS FROM THE GURU

Jeff Rubin has become known for his expertise in writing, designing, and producing company newsletters through his company, Put-It-In-Writing. Jeff advises clients to use newsletters to build the person-to-person connections that are, ultimately, the foundation of any successful business.

"The best businesses provide their clients and customers with exceptional service and value," says Rubin. "A newsletter is a way to connect with people while giving them information they can use. A regularly distributed newsletter can help you spend less time chasing work, and more time building relationships that attract new business."

Jeff's own newsletter, *The Write Stuff*, helps him regularly connect with prospects, vendors, and colleagues. He also uses his newsletter as a cross-promotional tool by profiling his vendors, who also promote his newsletter at their businesses. Jeff sends his newsletter to professional speakers — one of his target markets — and also features articles written by colleagues in the National Speakers Association.

The newsletter brings him most of his new clients; it "is an extension of my overall relationship-building strategy because of its reader-valued articles and dependable presence," says Rubin. "It's been the best way for me to stay visible and maintain a competitive edge. By maintaining personal relationships with customers and referral sources, they see me as a person always looking for ways to help them succeed and prosper. And because I mail my newsletter once a quarter to everyone in my network, people remember me."

with popular word-processing programs like Microsoft Word, and print your newsletters on a laser printer. Although these templates are somewhat bland, they can be personalized with company photos and graphics to present a distinctive appearance.

E-Mail Newsletters

Due in large part to their cost-effectiveness, e-mail newsletters are becoming the keep-in-touch tools of choice for businesses small and large. Whether you mail daily, weekly, or monthly, e-mail newsletters avoid the high cost of producing and distributing print messages, and the savings grow as your list of subscribers grows. E-mail newsletters can be used to:

- distribute articles, tip sheets, and anything else you've written.
- express your opinion about topics related to your business.
- direct recipients to your Web site, helping you sell more products and services.
- help the media and other centers of influence stay attuned to your business.
- increase income by selling products and services through affiliate arrangements.
- encourage feedback from clients and customers.

If you create a really valuable newsletter, it will be passed along to friends and colleagues, creating virtual word-of-mouth and attracting new subscribers.

Janine Giorgenti, a New York-based image consultant and custom clothing designer, saw her daily e-mail newsletter, *Dressing Tips*, increase sales by 20 percent in the first six weeks after she started it. In separate daily e-mails to men and women, Giorgenti answers one simple fashion question a day. For instance, "Can what I wear make me look taller?" (Yes, wear vertical stripes in your suits. This will add an inch to your apparent height.) Or, "Can I wear a button-down-collar shirt with a suit?" (No! A button down collar is sporty, and should be worn with a sport coat and slacks.)

As a testament to the success of the newsletter strategy, Giorgenti has attracted more than 6,000 subscribers since her campaign began. New customers generated by *Dressing Tips* have driven as far as 200 miles to meet with Giorgenti, and one new customer gave her a $6,000 order at their first meeting.

International Living Uses Its E-mail Newsletter to Reach a Global Audience

REAL-WORLD SUCCESS STORY

International Living, a resource for people planning to buy foreign real estate or live abroad, was launched 22 years ago as a print newsletter. Today, the company still mails its monthly print newsletter to 30,000 subscribers, but has established an even greater global presence with its e-mail newsletter, which reaches 175,000 subscribers.

"Our newsletters are at the heart of International Living, the seed from which everything else grows," says publisher Kathleen Peddicord, who credits their e-mail newsletter with taking the business to another level. "Our e-mail newsletter now provides an opportunity to communicate more often with our readers without the associated expenses of printing and mailing, and has helped us develop deeper, more personal relationships with them."

Even though the newsletters do not directly turn a profit, she explains, "they fuel other aspects of the business. Without our newsletters, we wouldn't have a business at all. They drive our consulting business, real estate business, and everything else we do."

Peddicord pays special attention to the writing that goes into each newsletter. Their e-mail newsletter is based on the personal narratives of several writers who live abroad. "We write in a very personal style, telling stories and evoking images of places around the world; our readers feel like we're part of their lives and develop an emotional attachment to us," says Peddicord. "We see this at our conferences where we meet 100 to 150 readers at a time, and they speak with us as though we're long-lost friends."

The strongest testament to their newsletters' success is their fiercely loyal following, and a long history of reader success stories. "Many of our readers have bought dream homes and started new lives overseas because they've been inspired by our newsletters," says Peddicord. "Many of them now live on beaches in Mexico, or country homes in the south of France, or own hotels in small coastal towns in places like Nicaragua. Our newsletters help readers achieve dreams of living abroad, and inspire them to take action."

Provide Useful Information

People subscribe to newsletters because they believe they will receive something valuable that's not readily available elsewhere. The more relevant the information, the more readers will look forward to receiving your e-mail newsletter.

Even though your newsletter may be built around your products or services, your message must be that you are an impartial source of useful information. You can do this by offering material drawn from a variety of sources. Scan publications in your field for topics that relate to your business, and use them as starting points for your own articles. This not only supports your expertise, but also demonstrates that you have a broad understanding of your industry.

Jim Davis, a financial adviser in San Francisco, sends out regular e-mail stock market and investment reports that interpret current market conditions. His articles are filled with data, calculations, and information drawn from the financial press.

Support Your Brand

Your newsletter is an extension of your brand. Make your newsletter personal. Because people build relationships with people, not faceless corporations, inject your personality into your newsletter, and write in a conversational style. Your voice and manner should become more familiar to your customers with each issue. Avoid jargon and don't be overly formal. Consider your newsletter as an ongoing conversation between friends meant to provide solutions, solve problems, and build trust.

Make It Consistent

Sending your newsletter out on a regular basis not only looks professional, it exploits the power of repetition. Remember, subscribers who haven't bought from you will form their impression of you by the quality of your newsletter and how dependably it arrives.

How frequently should you send your e-mail newsletter? Start conservatively; base your schedule on the level of effort you're sure you can maintain, increasing frequency only when you know that you can pick up the pace, and that people are interested in receiving it more often. Most businesses start with a monthly newsletter, since this is well within their power to produce, and it's frequent enough to keep them in front of their prospects. Some newsletters go out more often, sometimes on a weekly or even daily basis. But before you assume that your recipients want to hear from you that often, poll your readers about their wants and needs.

Get Permission

Before you add someone to your e-mail newsletter list, get his or her express permission. With the onslaught of unsolicited bulk commercial e-mail, commonly called "spam," most people have a low tolerance for e-mail messages that arrive uninvited. As discussed in chapter eight, you want to try to get subscribers to "opt in" to your e-mail newsletter from your Web site. Most important, whenever promoting your e-mail newsletter, let people know that you will never sell or rent e-mail addresses and that they can easily "unsubscribe" at any time.

A survey commissioned by DoubleClick, an Internet advertising company, found that permission-based e-mail produces a tremendous response rate. The survey, based on a sample of 1,000 users, and with a 94 percent accuracy rate, reports that 69 percent of American e-mail users have made online purchases from companies sending them permission-based e-mails.

Coming Up with Content

While every newsletter lives or dies by the quality of its content, they are relatively doable for any small businessperson. The bottom line is to provide "news you can use" in bite-sized pieces of information related to your business. When thinking about what kind of content to offer, you can begin with real-life examples and client case studies that allow you to share insights and show readers how they can apply your solutions to their situation.

TIPS FROM THE GURU

MarketingSherpa on the Elements of Great Newsletter Content

The following newsletter content tips are excerpted from *Best Practices in Marketing with E-mail Newsletters*, a report authored by MarketingSherpa, a media company that publishes case studies and best-practices data about Internet marketing.

News. News is easy to find online. If you plan on featuring industry, topical, or specialty news in your newsletter, then you must have one or more of the following:

- A truly valuable perspective on the news
- News that's so up-to-the-minute or so highly specialized that the mainstream press either hasn't covered it yet, or never will
- News that has a significant impact on the lives of your readers

The more you provide content, whether news or a news digest, that's not available elsewhere, the more value for your subscribers.

Articles or columns. You can run articles or columns written by your newsletter editor, staff members of your organization, volunteer contributors, paid writers or reporters, or syndicated columnists. Such articles can be practical, or incisive, or opinionated, or entertaining, or — best of all — have some combination of these qualities.

Fun features. Quizzes, cartoons, gossip, advice to the lovelorn, horoscopes, crossword puzzles, contests, topical jokes all have obvious appeal for consumer readers, and in many cases can benefit a newsletter as well.

Humor. The former BizTravel.com tested a less serious and nonverbal approach to drawing more of its half million subscribers to its Web site by incorporating cartoons into its newsletter. In fact, the first two times a cartoon ran in the newsletter, it outperformed all the articles except one in getting people to visit the Web site.

Facts or data. Often you can obtain these at no cost, or compile them with a bit of in-house research. For instance, a pharmacy could pass along consumer safety alerts about medications. A corporate travel agency could advise its clients about both the issuing and the lifting of travel advisories and travel warnings by the U.S. State Department.

Instruction or advice. How-to advice draws tremendously on the Internet, and if well done, it gets people reading their e-mail with attention. How to disguise bags under one's eyes would work for a cosmetics company, while steps for finding and plugging e-commerce security holes would enhance the reputation and promote the services of a firm of security experts.

Reader-contributed content. Not counting columnists who are also readers, reader-generated content consists of four main varieties:

- **Polls.** These usually involve one brief question, along with a set of short answers. Readers tell you which answer they prefer, and you soon have a fun factoid of results for the next issue.
- **Surveys.** These generally involve more than a single question. Surveys let you know how to tailor your editorial content better to your audience.
- **Questions.** Q&A provides very powerful content, because readers get a feeling of interactivity, see their peers actively participating in the newsletter, and see the newsletter editor demonstrating expertise.
- **Letters to the Editor.** Letters are equally powerful because they show readers that other people read the newsletter too, establishing credibility and community.

Resources. Truly useful or highly entertaining links that are relevant to the needs of your target audience can become either the main dish or the dessert of your newsletter. If you're working with a time lag between your compiling of the links and their inclusion in your newsletter, always verify the links just before finalizing that issue for distribution. Sending out dead links is a recipe for loss of customer confidence.

Year-end best-of revelations. Instead of choosing his personal top 10 favorites for his year-end issue, Brian Livingston, editor of InfoWorld's E-Business Secrets newsletter, asked his Webmaster for a report showing the issues and the individual stories that got the greatest response from readers in the past year.

Reviews. Both consumer and business audiences can find a lot of value in your guidance on which software programs, books, restaurants, telecom vendors, and so on to patronize, and which to avoid. Reviews have the greatest value for readers when your opinions are grounded in experience and expertise, and when you offer even adverse criticism when it's due.

Case studies. If you sell complex, customized services, narrative case studies can be a good way to edify and entertain your clientele and prospects in issue after issue of your newsletter. A good plan for presenting such material is to begin with the problem or challenge faced by the individual or company, proceed to the strategy you used to address the problem, and end with the results achieved by that solution.

Other Content Considerations

The top of your newsletter should include, close to its title, a benefit-oriented tagline that clearly states its purpose and target audience. For example, "Feline Facts: Keeping Your Cat Healthy" or "End Clutter: Weekly Tips to Keep Your Home Organized." Also include the issue date and a link to your Web site, near the top of the newsletter.

When planning the content of your newsletter, pay close attention to the e-mail "from" and "subject" lines. Studies have shown that as many as 40 percent of e-mail recipients look at the "from" name first when deciding what to delete and what to read. Your best choices are to use your business name or your personal name, whichever has the greater brand recognition, or whichever you want to become recognized.

A standardized "subject" line brands your newsletter among recipients, and helps to ensure that it gets opened. With the rise of unsolicited e-mail, it's important that your subject line brands your newsletter, issue after issue, until recipients remember it, feel safe with it, and don't even think of deleting it as spam. If you've chosen your newsletter name well, this is all you'll need. You can use your e-mail name, with slight variations as appropriate, to become a regular, welcome visitor in recipients' inboxes.

Write for easy reading. Post a table of contents or a concise summary at the beginning of each newsletter so readers can decide quickly whether the content is of interest to them.

Reading large blocks of text on a computer screen is difficult—more difficult than on paper. Aim for an overall word count that's 50 percent less than you would write for a print medium. Write for easy scanning, highlighting important words and phrases, and keeping paragraphs short. Set line length at 70 characters or less to avoid awkward line wrapping. Divide longer segments into smaller parts. Use caps, asterisks, dashes, and white space to set items apart.

If you have something you want to advertise, surround it with useful content, and put it somewhere in the middle. Never put an ad at the top.

Provide a "spam" disclaimer by reminding recipients how they got onto your list. Also provide clear instructions for unsubscribing: "You've received this newsletter because you subscribed to it. If you wish to unsubscribe, please follow the instructions at the end of this newsletter."

Don't forget to include full contact information, including your name, the name of your business, a phone number, an e-mail address, and your Web site address. It's also a good idea to add a copyright notice at the very end.

Getting Subscribers

Now that you've got content, start attracting subscribers. Take every opportunity to invite people to subscribe. You can do this in a variety of ways; here are some.

Announce your newsletter. A quick and easy way to get people to subscribe to your newsletter is to send a simple mailing to your existing mailing list, including current and past customers and contacts. People you know are much, much more likely to respond to your mailings than strangers. Keep it cheap and simple; a postcard mailing works fine.

Talk it up! If you give talks, ask people at the end if they'd like to be on your e-mail list. If you write articles, mention at the end that you have a newsletter. Talk about your newsletter in networking situations.

Make it easy to opt in from your Web site. Many subscribers from your e-mail newsletter will come from your Web site. Make sure you place sign-up fields on every page of your site. The easier it is to sign up, the more opt-ins you'll get. Also be sure to archive several back issues for those who will want a taste of your newsletter before subscribing.

Offer an enrollment premium. Why not give people a reward for opting onto your list? Consider premiums based on timely content, such as special reports or white papers. The trick is to offer rewards that have perceived value, but cost you little or nothing to deliver.

Joint ventures. Contact the owners of similar lists, and propose that you swap sponsorships. This can take the form of contributing articles to one another's newsletters, or swapping promotional "plugs" for each other's newsletters on your Web sites and e-mail newsletters, or both.

Online groups and discussion boards. Look for ones that fit your niche. The idea is not to sell something, but to give something away. Although groups are quick to crack down on sales messages, you'll be fine as long as you're giving away genuinely valuable information.

Encourage referrals. Viral, or referral, marketing is the best way to build your list. We all tell our friends about good service experiences, great stores and restaurants, something nice someone has done for you, an offer that is too good to pass up—this is what it's about. An e-mail newsletter facilitates this process by providing clients with e-mail text that can be passed along to friends and colleagues. Include an easy way for readers to forward your message to friends. And provide a "printer-friendly" alternative format, so that they can print out your message without extra screen images.

Be bold about asking subscribers to help you spread the word. Ask for referrals in the body of the newsletter. Also consider creating a campaign that rewards people who actually bring new subscribers to your list.

Distribution

There are two ways you can distribute your e-mail newsletter: do it yourself, or use an e-mail distribution service or "listserver."

If your list is relatively small, you can send your e-mail newsletter from your own computer, using popular programs like Microsoft Outlook or Eudora. Note that you must send your newsletter to recipients using the "blind carbon copy" feature, which means that no subscriber will see the e-mail addresses of any other—the ultimate Internet faux pas. The downside is that you'll have to manually add and remove subscribers, and deal with any bounce-backs should people change e-mail addresses. You'll also find it helpful to break your list into groups of 50 names or less, so they won't be kicked out by Internet service providers as spam.

If you want to eliminate much of the administrative hassle, you can use a "listserver," an outside service that automates the process. Options include free services such as Topica (www.topica.com) and professional list hosts such as SparkList.com or BigList Inc. (www.biglist.com). Using one of these services, you send all your e-mail addresses to the company that manages it, and they handle all additions, deletions, unsubscribes, and bounce-backs. You can link your newsletter sign-up form to the listserver to automate the subscription process.

When choosing a mailing service or listserver, look for one that includes bounce management (to keep your list continually updated and free of invalid or obsolete e-mail addresses), basic management reports, a security system, and easy access to your list at all times.

A Solid Investment

Keeping in touch by means of newsletters requires a commitment. The best keep-in-touch strategies run like clockwork, put out with perfect regularity by marketers who view their newsletter as a necessary cost of doing business, like paying taxes.

A keep-in-touch newsletter program should do more than remind clients that you're still in business. It should raise your stature and enhance your credibility by sharing information and ideas that make recipients better appreciate the expertise you bring to your market niche. Don't just educate, make compelling offers to subscribers that motivate them to do business with you again and again.

While it's understandable to want visible results fairly soon after a marketing initiative, several issues of your newsletter may have to arrive before a prospect is moved to place an order or hire you. Just remember that the more you keep in touch, the greater your rewards in goodwill, an enhanced reputation, repeat business, and word-of-mouth referrals—all the benefits of becoming *slightly famous*.

RESOURCES

Stephanie West Allen
Allen & Nichols Productions
P.O. Box 9311
Denver, Colorado 80209-0311
Phone: 303-935-8866
Web site: www.allen-nichols.com
E-mail: Stephanie@allen-nichols.
 com

Alpha Books
Marie Butler-Knight
Publisher
201 West 103rd Street
Indianapolis, Indiana 46290
Phone: 317-581-3665

American Society of Association
 Executives
1575 I Street, N.W.
Washington, DC 20005
Phone: 202-626-2723
Web site: www.asaenet.org
E-mail: service@asaenet.org

Kare Anderson
"Say It Better!"
Author of *Walk Your Talk*
15 Sausalito Boulevard
Sausalito, California 94965
Phone: 415-331-6336
Web site: www.sayitbetter.com/
E-mail: kare@sayitbetter.com

Tom Antion
Antion & Associates
Author of *Wake 'Em Up! Business
 Presentations*
Box 2630
Landover Hills, Maryland 20784
Phone: 800-448-6280
Web site: www.antion.com/
E-mail: tom@Antion.com

Eunice Azzani
Korn/Ferry International
One Embarcadero Center
Suite 2101
San Francisco, California 94111
Phone: 415-956-1834
Web site: www.kornferry.com
E-mail: azzanie@kornferry.com

Bacon's Information, Inc.
332 South Michigan Avenue
Chicago, Illinois 60604
Phone: 312-922-2400
Web site: www.bacons.com
E-mail: directories@bacons.com

Bart Baggett
Handwriting University.com
Author of *Success Secrets of the Rich &*
Happy
2633 Commerce Street
Dallas, Texas 75226
Phone: 310-614-6593
Web site: www.myhandwriting.com/
E-mail: bart@myhandwriting.com

Robert E. Balon
The Benchmark Company
907 South Congress Avenue, Suite 7
Austin, Texas 78704
Phone: 512-707-7500
Web site: www.thebenchmark
company.net
E-mail: bmark@flash.net

Mark Beckloff and Dan Dye
Three Dog Bakery
1627 Main Street, Suite 700
Kansas City, Missouri 64108
Phone: 800-487-3287
Web site: www.threedog.com/
E-mail: threedog@threedog.com

Ilise Benun
The Art of Self Promotion
Author of *Self Promotion Online*
P.O. Box 23
Hoboken, New Jersey 07030
Phone: 800-737-0783
Web site: www.artofselfpromotion
.com
E-mail: ilise@artofselfpromotion
.com

Joanne S. Black
No More Cold Calling™
Phone: 415-461-8763
Web site: www.NoMoreColdCalling
.com
E-mail: joanne@nomorecoldcalling
.com

Bob Blumer
The Surreal Gourmet
Author of *Off the Eaten Path*
P.O. Box 2961
Hollywood, California 90078
Phone: 800-FAUX-PAS
Web site: www.surrealgourmet.com
E-mail: bbakasg@aol.com

Robert W. Bly
Author of *Become a Recognized*
Authority
22 East Quackenbush Avenue, 3rd
Floor
Dumont, New Jersey 07628
Phone: 201-385-1220
Web site: www.bly.com
E-mail: rwbly@bly.com

Book Marketing Update
Bradley Communications Corp.
135 East Plumstead Avenue
Lansdowne, Pennsylvania 19050
Phone 610-259-0707
Web site: www.bookmarketingup
  date.com
Bill Harrison, Publisher
E-mail: billh@rtir.com
John Kremer, Editor-In-Chief
E-mail: JohnKremer@bookmarket
  .com

Books In Print
R.R. Bowker
121 Chanlon Road
New Providence, New Jersey 07974
Phone: 800-323-3288
Web site: www.booksinprint.com
E-mail: bip.feedback@bowker.com

Carol Watson-Brand
Carol's Challenge
Silver City, New Mexico
Phone: 505-535-4005
Web site: www.carolschallenge.com
E-mail: carol@carolschallenge.com

Bill Brooks
The Brooks Group
Author of *High Impact Selling*
1903 Ashwood Court, Suite C
Greensboro, North Carolina 27455
Phone: 800-633-7762
Web site: www.brooksgroup.com
E-mail: bill@thebrooksgroup.com

Bob Burg
Burg Communications, Inc.
Author of *Endless Referrals*
P.O. Box 7002
Jupiter, Florida 33468
Phone: 800-726-3667
Web site: www.burg.com/
E-mail: bob@burg.com

Gordon Burgett
SOPS.com
Author of *Publishing to Niche Markets*
P.O. Box 6405
Santa Maria, California 93456
Phone: 800-563-1454
Web site: www.sops.com/
E-mail sops@sops.com

Michelle M. Burke
Executive Counterparts
Author of *The Valuable Office
  Professional*
2459 152nd Avenue, NE
Redmond, Washington 98052
Phone: 425-867-5521
Web site: www.executivecounter
  parts.com
E-mail: info@executivecounterparts
  .com

Burrelle's Information Services
75 E. Northfield Road
Livingston, New Jersey 07039
Phone: 800-631-1160
Web site: www.burrelles.com

Alex Carroll
Radio Publicity
Author of *Beat the Cops*
924 Chapala Street, Suite D
Santa Barbara, California 93101
Phone: 805-564-6868
Web site: www.radiopublicity.com/
E-mail: Alex@RadioPublicity.com

Chambers of Commerce and
 Industry Directory
Web site: www.worldchambers.com/
 CCII/index1.htm
E-mail: secretariat@worldchambers
 .com

Larry Chase
Co-author of *Essential Business
 Tactics for the Net*
29 John Street, #102
New York, New York 10038
Phone: 212-619-4780
Web site: www.larrychase.com
E-mail: me@larrychase.com

Carol Cherkis
Gene Networks Inc.
560 South Winchester Boulevard,
 Suite 500
San Jose, California 95128
Phone: 408-572-5562
Web site: www.gene-networks.com
E-mail: carol@gene-networks.com

David Cole
Gemini Marketing &
 Communications
Author of *The Complete Guide to Book
 Marketing*
721 Creston Road
Berkeley, California 94708
Phone: 510-525-6902
Web site: www.geminicole.com/
E-mail: dcole@geminicole.com

Guy Davis
Davis Family Vineyards
2555 Laguna Road
Santa Rosa, California 95401
Phone: 866-338-9463
Web site: www.davisfamilyvineyards
 .com
E-mail: dfv@sonic.net

Jim Davis
299 Arguello Boulevard, Suite 306
San Francisco, California 94118
Phone: 415-752-6222
Web site: www.moneyjungle.com
E-mail: jdavis@moneyjungle.com

Jeff Dobkin
The Danielle Adams Publishing
 Company
Author of *How to Market a Product for
 Under $500!*
P.O. Box 100
Merion Station, Pennsylvania 19066
Phone: 610-642-1000
Web site: www.dobkin.com/
E-mail: jdobkin@bellatlantic.net

Steve Dubin
PR Works
167 Washington Street
Norwell, Massachusetts 02061
Phone: 781-878-9533
Web site: www.prworkzone.com/
Email: sdubin@prworkzone.com

Earthworks Press
Publisher of *50 Simple Things You Can
Do to Save the Earth*
1400 Shattuck Avenue #25
Berkeley, California 94709
Phone: 510-841-5866

Jim Edwards
E Book Fire
Author of e-book *Selling Your Home
Alone*
P.O. Box 878
Lightfoot, Virginia 23090
Phone: 757-715-2157
Web site: www.ebookfire.com/
E-mail: jim@ebookfire.com

Paulette Ensign
Tips Products International
Author of home study course *How to
Promote Your Business with Booklets*
12675 Camino Mira Del Mar #179
San Diego, California 92130
Phone: 858-481-0890
Web site: www.tipsbooklets.com/
E-mail: Paulette@tipsbooklets.com

Entrepreneur Media Inc.
2445 McCabe Way
Irvine, California 92614
Phone: 949-261-2325
Web site: www.entrepreneur.com

Josiane Feigon
TeleSmart Communications
2340 Irving Street, Suite 104
San Francisco, California 94122
Phone: 415-759-6537
Web site: www.tele-smart.com
E-mail: josiane@tele-smart.com

Alex Fisenko
Espresso Business Success
Author of *Espresso Success Business
Program*
Phone: 503-590-9423
Web site: www.espressobusiness.com
E-mail: alex@espressobusiness.com

Marika Flatt
Phenix & Phenix Literary Publicists
2525 West Anderson Lane, Suite 540
Austin, Texas 78757
Phone: 512-478-2028
Web site: www.bookpros.com/
E-mail: marika@bookpros.com

Rob Frankel
Author of *The Revenge of Brand X*
Phone: 888-ROBFRANKEL
Web site: www.robfrankel.com/
E-mail: rob@robfrankel.com

Patricia Fripp
Author of *Make It, So You Don't Have
to Fake It!*
527 Hugo Street
San Francisco, California 94122
Phone: 800-634-3035
Web site: www.fripp.com/
E-mail: pfripp@fripp.com

David Garfinkel
Overnight Marketing
Author of *Money-Making Copywriting
Course*
236 West Portal Avenue
PMB 255
San Francisco, California 94127
Phone: 415-564-4475
Web site: www.davidgarfinkel.com/
E-mail: Garfinkel@aol.com

Janine Giorgenti
Phone: 516-428-7466
Web site: www.clothesforsuccess
.com
E-mail: janine@giorgenti.com

Amit Gilboa
Author of *Off the Rails in Phnom Penh*
Phone: 435-417-2860
Web site: www.offtherails.com/
index.html
E-mail: amitgilboa@offtherails.com

Seth Godin
Author of *Unleashing the Idea Virus*
145 Palisade Street
Dobbs Ferry, New York 10522
Web site: www.sethgodin.com
E-mail: sethgodin@yahoo.com

Caron Goode
Inspired Parenting
Author of *Nurture Your Child's Gift*
5921 Miramar Drive
Tucson, Arizona 85715
Phone: 520-886-0538
Web site: www.inspiredparenting.net
E-mail: caron@inspiredparenting
.net

Mari Gottdiener
Outsource Solutions
25 Kensington Avenue
Northhampton, Massachusetts
01060
Phone: 800-810-2739
Web site: www.outsolve.com
E-mail: info@outsolve.com

Susan Grant
Winguth Grant & Company
505 Montgomery Street
11th Floor
San Francisco, California 94111
Phone: 415-283-1970
Web site: www.winguthgrant.com/
E-mail: sgrant@wgdsearch.com

T. Scott Gross
T. Scott Gross & Co., Inc.
Author of *MicroBranding*
P. O. Drawer 1515
Center Point, Texas 78010
Phone: 800-635-7524
Web site: www.tscottgross.com/
E-mail: tscott@hctc.net

Alexis D. Gutzman
MarketingSherpa
P.O. Box 963
Clayton, North Carolina 27520
Phone: 919-975-1705
Web site: www.marketingsherpa
.com
E-mail: alexisg@marketingsherpa
.com

Haddon Group
Lynne Wardell
360 Grand Avenue #346
Oakland, California 94610
Phone: 510-832-2877
Web site: www.haddongroup.com
E-mail: lynne@haddongroup.com

Kimberly Hathaway
Hathaway Public Relations
760 Market Street, Suite 925
San Francisco, California 94102
Phone: 415-989-0230
Web site: www.hathawaypr.com
E-mail: kimberly@hathawaypr.com

C.J. Hayden
Wings Business Coaching, LLC
Author of *Get Clients Now!*™
P.O. Box 225008
San Francisco, California 94122
Phone: 877-946-4722
Web site: www.getclientsnow.com
E-mail: coachcj@getclientsnow.com

Barbara Hemphill
Hemphill Productivity Institute
Author of *Taming the Paper Tiger*
1464 Garner Station Boulevard #330
Raleigh, North Carolina 27603
Phone: 800-427-0237
Web site: www.productiveenviron
  ment.com
E-mail: barbara@productiveenviron
  ment.com

Judi Henderson
Mannequin Madness
430 Orange Street, Suite B
Oakland, California 94610
Phone: 510-444-0650
Web site: www.mannequinmadness.
  com
E-mail: sales@mannequinmadness.
  com

Elliott Hester
Author of *Plane Insanity*
Phone: 786-553-5642
Web site: www.planeinsanity.com
E-mail: uzapme@aol.com

Dave Hirschkop
Dave's Gourmet Inc.
2000 McKinnon Avenue, Bldg. 428, #5
San Francisco, California 94124
Phone: 800-758-0372
Web site: www.davesgourmet.com/
E-mail: insanity@davesgourmet.com

Jeff Holper
Animal & Insect Solutions Inc.
9223 Gravois
St. Louis, Missouri 63123
Phone: 314-544-7378
Web site: www.molehunter.com/
E-mail: holperin@brick.net

Bill Hodges
Hodges Seminars International, Inc.
Author of *Within Your Reach*
P.O. Box 89033
Tampa, Florida 33689
Phone: 866-641-0816
Web site: www.billhodges.com/
E-mail: bill@billhodges.com

Shel Horowitz
Accurate Writing & More
Author of *Grassroots Marketing*
P.O. Box 1164
Northampton, Massachusetts 01061
Phone: 800-683-WORD
Web site: www.frugalfun.com
E-mail: shel@frugalfun.com

Glen & Steve Ikeda
Ikeda's Country Market
P.O. Box 3306
Auburn, California 95604
Phone: 530-885-4243
Web site: www.ikedas.com/
E-mail: customercare@ikedas.com

International Living
Kathleen Peddicord
5 Catherine Street
Waterford, Ireland
Phone: 353-51-304-557
Web site: www.internationalliving
   .com

Mark Joyner
Aesop.com
Author of *MindControl Marketing.com*
6741 Hollywood Boulevard
Los Angeles, California 90028
Phone: 323-769-3620
Web site: www.aesop.com
Web site: www.mindcontrolmarket
   ing.com/

Izzy Kalman
Author of the audiotape "How to
   Stop Being Teased and Bullied
   Without Really Trying"
Phone: 718-983-1333
Web site: www.bullies2buddies.com
E-mail: izzy@bullies2buddies.com

Dan Kennedy
Million Dollar Strategies
5818 N. 7th Street #103
Phoenix, Arizona 85014
Phone: 602-997-7707
Web site: www.dankennedy.com

King, Brown & Partners
Hal King
2320 Marinship Way, Suite 150
Sausalito, California 94965
Phone: 415-339-7100
Web site: www.kingbrown.com
E-mail: info@kingbrown.com

Larry Klein
NF Communications
Author of *Marketing Financial
   Services to Seniors*
1700 N. Broadway, Suite 405
Walnut Creek, California 94596
Phone: 800-980-0192
Web site: www.nfcom.com
E-mail: help@nfcom.com

Paul Krupin
Direct Contact
Author of e-book *Trash Proof News Releases*
P. O. Box 6726
Kennewick, Washington 99336
Phone: 800-457-8746
Web site: www.imediafax.com
E-mail: dircon@owt.com

Alfred J. Lautenslager
Market For Profits
3931 Broadmoor Circle, Suite 210
Naperville, Illinois 60564
Phone: 630-871-0085
Web site: www.market-for-profits.com/
E-mail: al@market-for-profits.com

Anthony Lemme
Source Intermarketing Corp.
E-mail: Epicurean333@aol.com

Terri Levine
Comprehensive Coaching U
727 Mallard Place
North Wales, Pennsylvania 19454
Phone: 877-401-6165
Web site: www.comprehensivecoachingu.com
E-mail: terri@comprehensivecoaching.com

Jay Conrad Levinson
Guerrilla Marketing International
Author of *Guerrilla Marketing* series
P.O. Box 1336
Mill Valley, California 94942
Phone: 800-748-6444
Web site: www.jayconradlevinson.com
E-mail: JAYVIEW@aol.com

Terri Lonier
Working Solo, Inc.
Author of *Working Solo*
126 Climbing Ridge Road
New Paltz, New York 12561
Phone: 845-255-7171
Web site: www.workingsolo.com/
E-mail: wsoffice@workingsolo.com

Michael Losier
Law of Attraction
110-777 Fort Street
Victoria BC Canada
V8W 1G9
Phone: 877-550-9282
Web site: www.michaellosier.com/
E-mail: michael@michaelosier.com

Sergio Lub
Friendly Favors
Web site: www.favors.org/FF/
E-mail: Sergio@sergiolub.com

Jill Lublin
Promising Promotion
Co-author of *Guerilla Publicity*
P.O. Box 5428
Novato, California 94948
Phone: 415-883-5455
Web site: www.jilllublin.com

Janet Luhr
Simple Living Oasis
Author of *The Simple Living Guide*
4509 Interlake Avenue N. PMB 149
Seattle, Washington 98103
Phone: 206-464-4800
Web site: www.simpleliving.com
E-mail: janet@simpleliving.com

Ed Lyon
Tax Tuneup
3432 Edwards Road, Suite 201
Cincinnati, Ohio 45208
Phone: 800-474-1801
Web site: www.taxtuneup.com
E-mail: elyon@taxtuneup.com

Homer McDonald
Co-author of e-book *Stop Your
    Divorce!*
Phone: 863-318-0464
Web site: www.stopyourdivorce.com
E-mail: help@stopyourdivorce.com

Gerry McGovern
Co-author of *The Web Content Style
    Guide*
Phone: 353-87-238-6136
Web site: www.gerrymcgovern.com
E-mail:
    contact@gerrymcgovern.com

Mark McMahon
581 N. Tanque Verde Loop Road
Tucson, Arizona 85748
Phone: 520-290-6916
Web site: www.filmtrips.com
E-mail: mark@filmtrips.com

Terry McVey
McVey Associates Inc.
150 Ford Way
Novato, California 94945
Phone: 800-227-7888
Web site: www.mcveyseminars.com

Steve Mariotti
The National Foundation for
    Teaching Entrepreneurship
Author of *The Young Entrepreneur's
    Guide to Starting and Running a
    Business*
120 Wall Street, 29th Floor
New York, New York 10005
Phone: 800-367-6383
Web site: www.nfte.com
E-mail: nfte@nfte.com

Douglas Markham
Total Health
Author of *Total Health*
3835-R East Thousand Oaks
    Boulevard, Suite 130
Westlake Village, California 91362
Phone: 800-891-5165
Web site: www.totalhealthdoc.com
E-mail: zonedok@aol.com

Jeffrey Marshall
Editor-in-Chief
Financial Executive Magazine
200 Campus Drive
Box 674
Florham Park, New Jersey 07932
Phone: 973-765-1024
Web site: www.fei.org/mag/
E-mail: jmarshall@fei.org

Jose Mata
Adcom Worldwide
377 Oyster Point Boulevard, Unit 18
South San Francisco, California
94080
Phone: 800-814-8732
Web site: www.adcomworldwide
.com
E-mail: jamata@adcomworldwide
.com

Johnny "Love" Metheny
Phone: 415-939-9040
E-mail: johnnymetheny@yahoo
.com

Robert Middleton
Action Plan Marketing
Author of *InfoGuru Marketing
Manual*
210 Riverside Drive
Boulder Creek, California 95006
Phone: 831-338-7790
Web site: www.actionplan.com/
E-mail: robmid@actionplan.com

Roger A. Miller
R.A. Miller & Company, Inc.
5 Glendale Road, Thornhill,
Ontario
L3T 6X4 Canada
Phone: 888-847-9213
Web site: www.ramiller.on.ca
E-mail: customersupport@ramiller
.on.ca

Ivan Misner
Business Network International
Co-author of *Masters of Networking*
199 S. Monte Vista, Suite 6
San Dimas, California 91773
Phone: 800-825-8286
Web site: www.bni.com/
E-mail: misner@bni.com

Donald Moine
Co-author of *Ultimate Selling Power*
Sales & Marketing Psychologist
President of the Association for
Human Achievement, Inc.
Phone: 310-378-2666
E-mail: drmoine@aol.com

Peter Montoya
Peter Montoya Inc.
Author of *The Personal Branding
Phenomenon*
1540 South Lyon Street
Santa Ana, California 92705
Phone: 866-288-9300
Web site: www.petermontoya.com/
E-mail: peter@milladv.com

Anthony Mora
Anthony Mora Communications
Author of *Spin to Win*
12304 Santa Monica Boulevard, 3rd
Floor
Los Angeles, California 90025
Phone: 310-207-6615
Web site: www.anthonymora.com/
E-mail: anthonym@anthonymora
.com

Nancy Mueller
International Adaptations
Author of *Work Worldwide*
6531 Palatine Avenue N
Seattle, Washington 98103
Phone: 206-784-8277
Web site: www.AboutWorkWorld
  wide.com
E-mail: NTMueller@aol.com

National Speakers Association
1500 S. Priest Drive
Tempe, Arizona 85281
Phone: 480-968-2552
Web site: www.nsaspeaker.org/

New World Library
14 Pamaron Way
Novato, California 94949
Phone: 800-972-6657
Web site: www.newworldlibrary.com

North American Industry
  Classification System (NAICS)
U.S. Census Bureau
Washington DC 20233
Web site: www.census.gov/epcd/
  www/naics.html
E-mail: webmaster@census.gov

B.L. Ochman
What's Next Online.com, Inc.
Author of *Reality PR*
345 East 94th Street
New York, New York 10128
Phone: 212-369-8312
Web site: www.whatsnextonline.com
E-mail: BLOchman@whatsnexton
  line.com

Tom Peters
Tom Peters Company!
101 Commerce Boulevard
Loveland, Ohio 45140
Phone: 888-221-8685
Web site: www.tompeters.com/
E-mail: info@tompeters.com

Fanny Pettijohn
Malachi Travel Group
West 12 Mile Road, Suite 12
Southfield, Michigan 48076
Phone: 877-625-2244
Web site: www.travelbrokers.com/

PinkMonkey.com
Web site: www.pinkmonkey.com
E-mail: support@pinkmonkey.com

Fred Phillips
Restquip Food Service
2642 Van Ness Avenue #201
San Francisco, California 94109
Phone: 415-716-0688
E-mail: uncfred1@aol.com

Dan Poynter
Para Publishing
Author of *The Self-Publishing Manual*
P.O. Box 8206-240
Santa Barbara, California 93118
Phone: 800-PARAPUB
Web site: www.parapublishing.com/
E-mail: info@parapublishing.com

QuickBooks
Phone: 888-246-8848
Web site: www.quickbooks.com

Caterina Rando
Author of *Learn to Power Think*
Phone: 800-966-3603
Web site: www.caterinar.com/
E-mail: cpr@caterinar.com

Anne-Marie Rennick
Learningbyphone.com
173 Birch Avenue, RR#2
Carleton Place, Ontario K7C 3P2
Canada
Phone: 866-207-7857
Web site: www.learningbyphone
.com/
E-mail: amr@learningbyphone.com

Ed Rigsbee, CSP
Rigsbee Enterprises, Inc.
Author of *Partner Shift*
3595 Old Conejo Road
Thousand Oaks, California 91320
Phone: 800-839-1520
Web site: www.rigsbee.com/
E-mail: EdRigsbee@aol.com

Susan RoAne
The RoAne Group
Author of *How to Work a Room*
320 Via Casitas, Suite 310
Greenbrae, California 94904
Phone: 415-461-3915
Web site: www.susanroane.com/
E-mail: Susan@susanroane.com

Darryl M. Roberts
Wine X Magazine
880 Second Street
Santa Rosa, California 95404
Phone: 866-545-0992
Web site: www.winexwired.com/
E-mail: darryl@winexmagazine
.com

Nancy Roebke
Profnet, Inc.
702 E. 25th Street
Erie, Pennsylvania 16503
Phone: 800-214-1999
Web site: www.profnet.org
E-mail: nancy@profnet.org

Tony Roeder
Redwagons.com
30 Chicago Avenue
Oak Park, Illinois 60302
Phone: 877-739-2466
Web site: www.redwagons.com
E-mail: custserv@redwagons.com

Jeff Rubin
Put It In Writing Newsletter
1517 Buckeye Court
Pinole, California 94564
Phone: 877-588-1212
Web site: www.put-it-in-writing
.com
E-mail: jeff@put-it-in-writing.com

Harriet Schechter
The Miracle Worker
Author of *Let Go of Clutter*
1324 State Street, Suite J-168
Santa Barbara, California 93101
Phone: 858-581-1241
Web site: www.miracleorganizing
   .com/
E-mail: miracle@cts.com

Harry Shepherd
836 2nd Street West
Sonoma, California 95476
Phone: 707-938-0938

Karl Speak
Beyond Marketing Thought
Co-author of *Be Your Own Brand*
510 First Avenue North, Suite 605
Minneapolis, Minnesota 55403
Phone: 612-338-5009
Web site: www.brandnetwork.com
E-mail: speakk@brandnetwork.com

Sonoma County Woodworkers
   Association (SCWA)
Burt Hutt
P.O. Box 4124
Santa Rosa, California 95402
Phone: 707-579-1505
Web site: www.sonomawoodworkers
   .com
E-mail: metallease@earthlink.net

Bill Stoller
Publicity Insider
Stoller and Bard Communications
6 Horizon Road, Suite 1705
Fort Lee, New Jersey 07024
Phone: 201-224-3737
Web site: www.publicityinsider
   .com/
E-mail: bill@publicityinsider.com

Pat Sullivan
Visionary Resources
Author of *Work with Meaning; Work
   with Joy*
4200 Park Blvd., #119
Oakland, California 94602
Phone: 510-530-0284
Web site: www.visionary-resources
   .com/
E-mail: visionpat@aol.com

Roseann Sullivan
Sullivan Communications
2 Embarcadero Center, Suite 200
San Francisco, California 94111
Phone: 888-773-2528
Web site: www.sullivancommunica
   tions.com
E-mail: info@sullivancommunica
   tions.com

Bruce Smith
Veiled Voyage
3245 E. Joyce Drive
Salt Lake City, Utah 84109
Phone: 801-487-9320
Web site: www.veiledvoyage.com
E-mail: VVoyage@aol.com

Kimberly Stanséll
Author of *Bootstrapper's Success Secrets*
P.O. Box 881495
Los Angeles, California 90009
Phone: 310-568-9861
Web site: www.kimberlystansell.com
E-mail: kimberly@kimberlystansell
.com

Scott Testa
Mindbridge
1305 Catfish Lane, Suite 202
Norristown, Pennsylvania 19403
Phone: 610-666-5262
Web site: www.mindbridge.com
E-mail: stesta@mindbridge.com

Frederick M. Tibbitts, Jr.
Fred Tibbitts & Associates, Inc.
Dutch Village 13-AR
Menands, New York 12204
Phone: 518-426-0262
Web site: www.fredtibbitts.com/
E-mail: fredbev@fredtibbitts.com

Toastmasters International
P.O. Box 9052
Mission Viejo, California 92690
Phone: 949-858-8255
Web site: www.toastmasters.org
E-mail: tminfo@toastmasters.org

Topica
620 Folsom Street, Suite 300
San Francisco, California 94107
Web site: www.topica.com
E-mail: support@get.topica.com

Lisa Tomaszewski
Assistant Editor
Physician's Money Digest
Phone: 732-656-1140, ext. 195
Web site: www.pmdnet.com
E-mail: ltomaszewski@mwc.com

Debra Valle
Marketing U
11278 Los Alamitos Boulvard, #139
Los Alamitos, California 90720
Phone: 800-517-3450
Web site: www.marketingu.net/
E-mail: debravalle@marketingu.net

Lillian Vernon
Lillian Vernon Corporation
100 Lillian Vernon Drive
Virginia Beach, Virginia 23479
Phone: 800-545-5426
Web site: www.lillianvernon.com/

Joe Vitale
Hypnotic Marketing, Inc.
Author of *Spiritual Marketing*
121 Canyon Cap Road
Wimberley, Texas 78676
Phone: 512-847-3414
Web site: www.mrfire.com/
E-mail: ceo@mrfire.com

Dottie Walters
Co-author of *Speak and Grow Rich*
Walters Speaker Services
P.O. Box 398
Glendora, California 91740
Phone: 626-335-8069
Web site: www.walters-intl.com
E-mail: Dottie@walters-intl.com

Tom Williams
WestMark Realtors
4105 84th Street
Lubbock, Texas 79423
Phone: 800-753-3889
Web site: www.westmarkrealtors
  .com
E-mail: twilliams@westmark
  realtors.com

Ralph F. Wilson
Wilson Internet Services
Author of *Planning Your Internet
  Marketing Strategy*
P.O. Box 308
Rocklin, California 95677
Phone: 916-652-4659
Web site: www.wilsonweb.com/
E-mail: rfwilson@wilsonweb.com

Writer's Digest
4700 E. Galbraith Road
Cincinnati, Ohio 45236
Phone: 513-531-2222
Web site: www.writersdigest.com/
E-mail: writersdig@fwpubs.com

Steven V. Yoder
Get The Word Out
  Communications
Author of *Get Slightly Famous*
537 Jones Street, #2436
San Francisco, California 94102
Phone: 415-931-3195
Web site: www.getthewordout.net
E-mail: svy@getthewordout.net

Danna Yuhas
Market Impact
44-646 Village Parkway
Markham, Ontario
Canada L3R2S7
Phone: 416-410-5608
Web site: www.market-impact.com
E-mail: results@market-impact.com

INDEX

Steven Van Yoder has been self-employed all of his adult life. As the owner of Get The Word Out Communications, he helps businesses embrace the media to become recognized leaders in their industries. A seasoned journalist, his writing has appeared in over 200 publications, including *The Washington Post, Financial Executive, Home Office Computing, Costco Connection, Industry Week, Brand Marketing,* and dozens of trade, business, and consumer publications. Steven Van Yoder lives in San Francisco and can be reached at steven@get slightlyfamous.com.